INTRODUCTION TO REHABILITATION

THE SYMBOL OF ACCESS

The international Symbol of Access (white on dark blue) is used "to identify, mark or show the way to buildings and facilities that are accessible to and useable by all persons whose mobility is restricted, including wheelchair users" (Rehabilitation International Assembly, Baguio, Philippines, January 22, 1978).

INTRODUCTION TO
REHABILITATION

JAMES A. BITTER

University of Northern Colorado
Greeley, Colorado

Illustrated

THE C. V. MOSBY COMPANY

ST. LOUIS • TORONTO • LONDON   1979

Printed in the United States of America

The C. V. Mosby Company
11830 Westline Industrial Drive, St. Louis, Missouri 63141

Library of Congress Cataloging in Publication Data

Bitter, James A
    Introduction to rehabilitation.

    Bibliography: p.
    Includes index.
    1. Vocational rehabilitation—United States.
I. Title.
HD7256.U5B57   362.8'5   78-24530
ISBN 0-8016-0693-4

GW/CB/B 9 8 7 6 5 4 3 2   01/D/052

To my wife
SANDY
and our daughters
MARIA, MAUREEN, and ELLEN
and the many others who have influenced
my life and career

FOREWORD

Rehabilitation in recent years has taken on a less exclusive attitude. After some sixty years of emphasis upon persons whose prospects for gainful occupation were good, attention is being given to those who may not have vocational goals.

This can be viewed as partly an accident of history. As Dr. Bitter's volume points out clearly, there was a legislative base which stressed services that made individuals employable. Whatever services, however comprehensive, were provided, they had to have a vocational employment goal in mind. This met the needs of the time.

Gradually the perspective is changing. The first inroad has been the emphasis upon the severely handicapped. By definition these were persons who required concerted services of great variety to enable them, over an extended time frame, to engage in some type of gainful occupation. The vocational goal in many cases was blurred, necessitating the benefit of extended evaluation. More and more persons provided such services turned out as not rehabilitated, i.e., not able to become employable. Rather than look upon these people as "failures," one began to consciously reckon that any service-delivery program must meet individual needs. If goals less than vocational were the true reflection of those needs, then the service program should be ready to modify its goals.

This would appear to be the situation today. Such programs go by a variety of names, the most common of which is independent living. That the group in need is sizable has been established by the Comprehensive Needs Study (authorized by the Rehabilitation Act of 1973). Some 10,000,000 such individuals would seem to be the best estimate, and some $22.5 billion is being expended on their behalf—but little of it for rehabilitation programs. What is interesting about this is the fact that the Study suggests we have most of the technological know-how to rehabilitate these persons. We are just not deploying our resources in such a manner as to meet the needs. The human as well as the economic costs become staggering.

Introduction to Rehabilitation is geared to present what is known about the rehabilitation process. The book is an overview of rehabilitation with a vocational emphasis written in a systematic fashion. What is important to keep in mind is that the rehabilitation process is applicable regardless of the goal—employability or not. The process deals with adequate assessment, setting of goals, an individual plan for goal achievement, constant reassessment, a program of services, and follow-up and follow-along together with program evaluation. It is oriented toward vocational goal setting because that is our societal emphasis. But anything less than that is acceptable if part of the client's rehabilitation plan. The advantage of this approach is the emphasis on regular and constant reappraisal. One can start with a vocational goal and settle on another goal (e.g., independent living) if indicated. Or one can start with an independent living goal and settle on a vocational goal. Maximum emphasis is on flexibility, reasessment, and individual needs. Both Congress and the Administration are ready to accept this redirection. The severely disabled have expressed their needs, and affirmative action seems to be the result.

Dr. Bitter's book summarizes our state of knowledge which is pertinent to meeting the needs of the disabled. It provides background information and describes rehabilitation clients and methods. The book should be a useful text not only for those in rehabilitation counseling courses but also for those already in the field working with disabled clients.

James F. Garrett, Ph.D.

Vice-President
World Rehabilitation Fund

PREFACE

Introduction to Rehabilitation is intended to serve as an overview of rehabilitation as practiced in the United States. Its emphasis is vocational, to reflect the past and present state of the art in this country's public-private rehabilitation program.

There is, however, a trend in rehabilitation toward greater emphasis on independent living services for the disabled. Consequently the term "vocational rehabilitation" is gradually being replaced by "rehabilitation" in legislation, agency names, and the literature.

This text emphasizes a comprehensive approach to rehabilitation, involving many professions and professionals, for serving the needs of the total individual; but directed toward a vocational outcome. The book is descriptive rather than evaluative and intended primarily for use in undergraduate and graduate-level introductory courses in rehabilitation counseling. It should also be useful as a basic resource document in many rehabilitation-related professions, including physical medicine and rehabilitation, occupational therapy, physical therapy, rehabilitation nursing, prosthetics and orthotics, psychology, speech-language pathology and audiology, therapeutic recreation, social work, and special education. In addition, I hope that the text will also be useful to continuing education and in-service training programs with a rehabilitation emphasis.

There are three sections in the book. Section One provides background information. Included is the purpose, philosophy, and organization of the public-private rehabilitation program, its history, and a description of the rehabilitation process.

Section Two describes rehabilitation clients. In addition to a brief orientation to medical terminology, 15 types of disability are described in terms of the etiology of each disability, classification system(s) used to categorize the disability, the vocational problems it presents, and rehabilitation service considerations. A separate chapter is related to the psychological and vocational adjustment of the disabled.

Section Three describes rehabilitation methods. It includes chapters on case-work methods, vocational evaluation techniques, counseling approaches, job placement techniques, and community resources.

The appendices briefly describe special rehabilitation centers in the United States, a list of federally supported rehabilitation education programs, and a glossary of acronyms.

Each of the 10 chapters is similarly organized. Each begins with a chapter overview and objectives and concludes with a summary, self-evaluation questions which are intended to serve as a review for the reader, references cited in the text, additional reading related to the subject of the chapter, and media resources. The visual and audio resources can be a helpful supplement to the basic content of each chapter.

I have made every attempt to be nonsexist in my writing; however, when it was difficult, to avoid awkwardness I chose the indefinite pronoun "he." Hopefully this will not offend any of my readers.

I am very grateful to the many people who helped me in various ways in the development of this book. Some offered material, some suggestions, and many encouragement. I am particularly grateful to my colleagues who graciously reviewed selected chapters for appropriateness of content, technical accuracy, and readability. These include Dr. James W. McDaniel, Associate Professor of Physical Medicine and Rehabilitation and Psychiatry and Associate Director of the University of Colorado Rehabilitation Research and Training Center; Dr. Craig Mills, formerly the Director of the Florida state rehabilitation agency and now privately engaged in public service; Richard W. Nelson, President, National Rehabilitation Consultants, Inc., St. Paul, Minnesota; Dr. Elia Nickoloff, Associate Professor in the rehabilitation program at Eastern Montana College in Billings; Dr. Mel W. Weishahn, Professor of Special Education at the University of Northern Colorado, and my rehabilitation colleagues at the University of Northern Colorado: Dr. Jack A. Bowen, Associate Professor, Dr. John H. Cronin, Professor, Dr. Garth M. Eldredge, Professor, Dr. Dennis A. Gay, Professor and Assistant Dean of the Graduate School, and Dr. Richard R. Wolfe, Professor and Chairperson, Department of Social and Rehabilitation Service. I would also like to thank Dr. Sid Levy, Assistant Professor of Special Education, George Peabody College for Teachers, for his review of eight chapters of manuscript. My sincere appreciation goes to Dr. Ekkehard J. Petring, Associate Professor and Chairperson of the Rehabilitation Department at Seattle University, and William E. Martin, Jr., doctoral candidate in rehabilitation counseling at the University of Northern Colorado, for reviewing the final draft of the entire manuscript. Dr. Petring and Mr. Martin offered many constructive comments and editorial suggestions which, I feel, greatly enhanced the book. Finally, my deepest appreciation is to my wife, Sandy, who typed all drafts of the manuscript, offered many suggestions, and generously gave her support.

James A. Bitter

CONTENTS

BACKGROUND

The purpose of Section One is to provide the reader with an orientation to the public-private rehabilitation program and to serve as a basis for relating to the content of Sections Two and Three, which discuss rehabilitation clients and rehabilitation methods. Chapter 1 presents a purpose and philosophy for rehabilitation and emphasizes rehabilitation as an individualized sequential process oriented toward a vocational goal. Chapter 2 traces the historical development of rehabilitation — including legislation, public agencies, and private resources. Chapter 3 concentrates on the sequential rehabilitation process. In addition to describing the range of rehabilitation services, the third chapter focuses on the individualized and flexible nature of rehabilitation client planning.

1

Rehabilitation: an introduction

OVERVIEW AND OBJECTIVES

This chapter is intended to orient the reader to the general field of rehabilitation. It is organized into four major sections: (1) characteristics of the rehabilitation program, (2) organization of the rehabilitation program, (3) basic concepts in rehabilitation, and (4) definitions common to the rehabilitation process.

Objectives of this chapter are to acquaint the reader with the general purpose, philosophy, process, and value of rehabilitation as practiced in the United States; to provide an organizational overview of the United States public-private program; to describe two basic program concepts, including (1) the distinction between a disability and a handicap and (2) eligibility for rehabilitation services through the public program; and finally to furnish definitions for frequently used terms in rehabilitation.

CHARACTERISTICS OF THE REHABILITATION PROGRAM
Purpose of rehabilitation

The National Council on Rehabilitation in August, 1943, defined rehabilitation as "the restoration of the handicapped to the fullest physical, mental, social, vocational and economic usefulness of which they are capable" (Townsend, 1966).

Whitehouse (1953) makes a distinction between rehabilitation and habilitation. According to him rehabilitation is concerned with reeducation, and habilitation with education, of the handicapped. Rehabilitation clients need services that will restore them to self-sufficient or nearly self-sufficient living. Most habilitation clients, however, have never lived independent lives; they need to be educated in basic vocational adjustment and to develop fundamental capabilities, knowledge, experiences, and attitudes.

Thus rehabilitation refers to a readaptation process following injury or a disorder, and habilitation refers to a learning process for persons born with a disability or having one very early in life (Jaques, 1970). In this text the term *rehabilitation* will be used in the generic sense to reflect all activities and services of rehabilitation programming, including those which could be referred to as habilitation services.

Rehabilitation philosophy in the United States program

Basic to rehabilitation in the United States is the value of the human being. Every human being is deserving of respect (DiMichael, 1969) and is entitled to an inherent right to earn a living in a democratic society (McGowan & Porter, 1967).

There are three principles which form a philosophical foundation for the practice of rehabilitation in America:

1. Equality of opportunity must be present for all United States citizens. This principle obligates the American people to provide specialized services to disabled persons so the handicapped are just as prepared for employment and participation in the privileges and responsibilities of citizenship as are nonhandicapped people (Garrett, 1969).

2. A person is holistic; that is, he cannot be divided into parts such as physical, mental, social, vocational, and economic. Each person is a complete individual; and in each, these dimensions interact with the others to form the whole (Jaques, 1970).

3. Every person is unique. The psychological and personal reactions to disability vary from individual to individual. No two people have exactly the same needs or potential; each has unique assets, ways of coping, and goals.

Because rehabilitation deals with the whole person and because professions are specialized and composed of categories, it is necessary for rehabilitation to be interdisciplinary in nature. The complexity of humans necessitates specialization to achieve depth in both understanding and service delivery.

To make rehabilitation an individualized process requires integrating a myriad of specialties and resources into a comprehensive approach for serving the whole individual. This is generally accomplished in two ways: One way is the *team approach* among professionals which, depending on a client's needs, coordinates the specialized skills of the physician, nurse, physical therapist, occupational therapist, speech-language pathologist, audiologist, psychologist, social worker, educator, vocational counselor, etc. (Whitehouse, 1960; Jaques, 1970; Rusk, 1977). The second way is by using a *generalist,* known as a *rehabilitation counselor,* who not only provides services but also coordinates multidisciplinary services on behalf of the individual. This generalist must be aware of everything going on and must direct the rehabilitation process into a master plan (Talbot, 1971).

Thus rehabilitation in the United States is a continuous process of treatment involving the whole person which varies to meet the special needs of each individual; it emphasizes the assets of the person and is interdisciplinary in the delivery of services (DiMichael, 1969).

The rehabilitation process

The rehabilitation process is a goal-oriented and individualized sequence of services designed to assist handicapped people achieve vocational adjustment.

It begins with case finding or referral and it culminates, if successful, in gainful activity which renders the handicapped person a productive wage-earning and tax-paying member of society. The process of rehabilitation may, depending on a client's need, include medical, psychological, social, and vocational services, and may last just a few months or require several years.

Goal orientation. The primary objective of vocational rehabilitation services is employment. Employment can include work in the competitive labor market, the practice of a profession, self-employment, homemaking, farm or family work, sheltered employment, home employment, or any other gainful activity.

Individualization. In the rehabilitation process the potential of each disabled person is determined by a rehabilitation professional, and an individualized written rehabilitation program of services is planned through which the individual can develop his potential.

Sequential service delivery. The rehabilitation process emphasizes the delivery of services at the proper time and in the most appropriate sequence for each person. This sequence usually includes evaluation, treatment, training, job placement, and postemployment services.

Social and economic implications of rehabilitation

The value and dignity of the individual human being for participation in the privileges and responsibilities of United States citizenship offer immeasureable justification for a public rehabilitation program. Rehabilitation can lead to self-respect, to improved personal, family, and social adjustment, and to the elimination of despair, frustration, bitterness, and grief. It can provide meaning for one's life in addition to relief from financial stresses or the humiliation of being unable to carry on an acceptable social role (Conley, 1965).

Though somewhat less important, the economic benefits of rehabilitation offer an additional rationale for the conduct of a public program in the United States. In a study of the economics of vocational rehabilitation conducted by Conley (1965), it was indicated that for each dollar spent on rehabilitation services by state and federal rehabilitation agencies a stream of future earnings worth between $9 and $17 is set in motion and a return in tax dollars of somewhere between one and a half and five times the cost is realized. In 1969, Conley elaborated on his 1965 work and computed a benefit-cost ratio of 8 to 1 for disabled persons rehabilitated in the 1967 fiscal year—i.e., $8 in increased lifetime earnings for every dollar spent for services (Conley, 1969).

Other studies have demonstrated a more dramatic economic impact resulting from rehabilitation programming. A 1966 study conducted by the Department of Health, Education, and Welfare (HEW) indicated a benefit-cost ratio estimated at 30 to 1. A study by the Michigan Division of Vocational Rehabilitation in 1970 found a benefit-cost ratio of nearly 33 to 1, and a Wisconsin study calculated ratios of 25 to 1 and 27 to 1 for the rehabilitation of the medically handicapped (Reagles & Wright, 1971).

Even though the public rehabilitation program has high social and economic returns, appropriations from the United States Congress for rehabilitation services ($760,472,000 in fiscal year 1978) are sufficient to serve only a small fraction of the disabled in need of such service.

ORGANIZATION OF THE REHABILITATION PROGRAM
The federal-state program

The public program of rehabilitation in the United States is composed of a central federal office in Washington, D.C., and ten regional offices throughout the United States. In addition to providing most of the funding for rehabilitation services, the federal agency offers guidance in program implementation to states by interpreting legislation and monitoring state-operated programs. There are 56 state rehabilitation agencies including agencies in the District of Columbia, Guam, Puerto Rico, American Samoa, Trust Territory, and the Virgin Islands. There are also 28 separate state rehabilitation agencies for the blind.

Rehabilitation Services Administration. The Rehabilitation Services Administration (RSA) is the central rehabilitation agency of the U.S. Department of Health, Education, and Welfare (HEW). Operating under authority of the Rehabilitation Act, it administers the federal program of rehabilitation services. It also supports special grants and programs for (1) evaluation and work adjustment services, (2) service delivery innovation, program expansion, activities with employers, career development in the field of rehabilitation, career development of handicapped persons in public service, research, and demonstrations, (3) training to increase the supply of rehabilitation personnel, and (4) construction of rehabilitation facilities and improvement of facility services. The federal program operates under the leadership of a Commissioner. In addition, a director of an Office of Rehabilitation Services in each of the ten HEW regions supervises rehabilitation programs and activities of the federal agency in his region (Rehabilitation Services Administration, 1971).

State rehabilitation agencies. In about half the states there are two rehabilitation agencies—one for persons who are blind, the other for persons with any other disability. In the remaining states a single rehabilitation agency serves persons with any disability, including blindness. Funds are allocated by the federal agency to each state agency by a formula involving the state's population and its fiscal capacity as measured by per capita income. The federal funds augment state appropriations for these services as provided by federal rehabilitation legislation. The Vocational Rehabilitation Act Amendments of 1968 authorized an 80% federal to 20% state matching ratio for appropriations, i.e., 4 federal dollars for each state dollar appropriated for rehabilitation to a maximum as determined by the aforementioned formula. The 1978 Rehabilitation Act Amendments, however, established $3 million as the minimum state allotment of federal funds for basic rehabilitation services.

Under the federal-state program of rehabilitation, a wide range of services is provided to individual disabled persons. Eligibility is based on the presence in the individual of a physical or mental disability which constitutes a substantial handicap to employment but for which there is a reasonable expectation that vocational rehabilitation services will enable the individual to engage in a gainful occupation. As determined by a particular client's needs—the services may include (1) comprehensive evaluation, including medical studies and diagnosis and psychological, social, educational, and vocational studies, (2) medical, surgical, and hospital care and related therapy to remove or reduce a disability, (3) prosthetic and orthotic devices, (4) counseling and guidance, (5) training, (6) services in rehabilitation facilities, (7) maintenance and transportation during rehabilitation, (8) tools, equipment, and occupational licenses, (9) initial stock and supplies in managing a small business, (10) readers for blind persons and interpreters for the deaf, (11) recruitment and training to provide new careers for handicapped people in the field of rehabilitation and other areas, (12) services which contribute to a group of handicapped people though perhaps unrelated directly to the rehabilitation of any one person, (13) services to the families of handicapped persons that will contribute substantially to the rehabilitation of the handicapped client, (14) job placement assistance including follow-up to aid handicapped individuals in maintaining their employment, and (15) any other goods or services which may be necessary to render a handicapped person employable.

Generally services must be made available by state agencies on a state-wide basis. A state agency may obtain a waiver from this requirement, however, to take advantage of an opportunity to increase a service in a geographic area where local funds are available to supplement the state appropriation. Besides this waiver provision, a state rehabilitation agency can, in order to expand its services, enter into financial arrangements with other public agencies whose services relate to the needs of handicapped persons. Such arrangements are known as third-party agreements. Third-party agreements enable rehabilitation services to be offered simultaneously with the services of another agency or to expand services beyond those which are normally the responsibility of another agency (Rehabilitation Services Administration, 1971).

State plans for rehabilitation services. State plans for rehabilitation services are required by federal rehabilitation legislation. The annual state plan must identify a state agency to administer the program. The state agency must be concerned with just the rehabilitation of handicapped individuals or it must be concerned with education, vocational education, or one or more of the major public education, health, welfare, or labor programs of the state. The rehabilitation program must have a full-time director and be located at an organizational level within the state that is comparable to other major organizational units. Sufficient staff with appropriate qualifications to carry out the requirements of the legislation must also be employed.

The state plan must contain the plans, policies, and methods to be followed in implementing the state rehabilitation program. For example, the agency must conduct continuing statewide studies of the needs of handicapped individuals within the state and must describe its methods for expanding and improving services to handicapped individuals with the most severe handicaps. If all the eligible disabled persons cannot be served by the rehabilitation program, the state plan will identify an order to be followed in selecting individuals to whom services will be provided. In this regard, the Rehabilitation Act of 1973 requires that the first priority be given to persons with the most severe handicaps. No state residency requirements may be imposed upon individuals as a condition of eligibility for services.

The state plans must also provide for the development of an Individualized Written Rehabilitation Program (IWRP) for each handicapped individual accepted for services. Maximum utilization of community resources must be made. In addition, the state plan should provide for maximum coordination among programs relating to the rehabilitation of disabled veterans.

Each state agency must provide for an annual comprehensive evaluation of the effectiveness of its rehabilitation program. As determined by such evaluation and the required continuing statewide studies of rehabilitation needs, agencies may appropriately amend their state plan (United States Senate and House of Representatives, 1973; Department of Health, Education, and Welfare, 1974).

In general, there are three written sources of guidance for the administration of the public rehabilitation program: (1) legislation enacted by the Congress of the United States, (2) rules and regulations which interpret the legislation, and (3) guidelines for implementing the rules and regulations. The rules and regulations represent an interpretation of the legislation by the federal agency authorized by Congress to administer the public program. They are published in the *Federal Register* of the Department of Health, Education, and Welfare; and an opportunity for suggestions and comments is provided to the general public before they are finalized. The guidelines for implementing these rules and regulations are also developed by staff of the federal agency.

Private rehabilitation resources. Though state rehabilitation counselors are generalists who coordinate the rehabilitation process and multidisciplinary services for the individual, the most frequent direct treatment service provided by the public agency counselor is counseling and guidance. Usually the majority of rehabilitation services are provided through private resources purchased by the state agency counselor. Examples of such resources are physicians, hospitals, clinics, rehabilitation centers, workshops, and educational programs. Some state rehabilitation agencies, however, do operate their own centers for the delivery of rehabilitation services.

The rehabilitation legislation makes federal funds available for the construction and initial staffing of private rehabilitation facilities. Funds are also available for the improvement of facilities—including the cost of planning, developing, and increasing business operations which will enable better efficiency. In addition, technical assistance by expert consultants is available to facilities. Thus the public program of rehabilitation represents a partnership with private rehabilitation agencies in the delivery of services to eligible disabled individuals.

BASIC CONCEPTS IN REHABILITATION
Disability and handicapping conditions

A disability is either a physical or a mental condition which limits a person's activities or functioning (Department of Health, Education, and Welfare, 1974). Handicapping conditions, on the other hand, represent obstacles to maximum functioning. In vocational rehabilitation a handicapped individual is one who has a physical or mental disability that constitutes or results in a handicap to employment. Rehabilitation service delivery addresses the handicapping conditions resulting from disability rather than the disability itself (McGowan & Porter, 1967).

Eligibility for rehabilitation services

An individual is eligible for rehabilitation services through the federal-state program if two criteria are met (Department of Health, Education, and Welfare, 1974):

1. The individual has a physical or mental disability which constitutes or results in a substantial handicap to employment.
2. The services may reasonably be expected to benefit the individual in terms of employability.

It is important to note that the handicap must relate to employment and must be linked to the disability. Thus an unemployed right-handed elementary classroom teacher with an amputated left hand may not be eligible for service through the public program. Though the determination of a disability is usually made by a physician, the determination of eligibility is made by the state agency rehabilitation counselor. Two professional judgments of the counselor are necessary: that the handicap to employment results from the disability and that services will help the individual become employable.

DEFINITIONS

The following represent definitions of terms common to the rehabilitation process:

client One who has applied for rehabilitation services and has been determined eligible on the basis of a physical or mental disability which results in a substantial handicap to employment and for whom there is a reasonable expectation of employability if rehabilitation services are provided

comprehensive rehabilitation center A center that offers medical, psychological, social, and vocational services to clients principally under one roof

developmental disability (legislative definition, Rehabilitation Act Amendments, 1978) A severe chronic disability of a person which (1) is attributable to a mental or physical impairment or combination of mental or physical impairments, (2) is manifested before the person obtains age 22, (3) is likely to continue indefinitely, (4) results in substantial limitations in three or more of the following areas of major life activity: (a) self-care, (b) receptive and expressive language, (c) learning, (d) mobility, (e) self-direction, (f) capacity for independent living, (g) economic self-sufficiency, and (5) reflects the person's need for a combination and sequence of special interdisciplinary or generic care, treatment or other services which are of life-long or extended duration and are individually planned and coordinated

employment Work in the competitive labor market, the practice of a profession, self-employment, homemaking, farm or family work, sheltered employment, home-bound employment, or other gainful activity

evaluation (1) A preliminary diagnostic study to determine applicant eligibility for rehabilitation services and (2) a thorough diagnostic study relative to an individual's handicap and rehabilitation potential

job placement The finding of employment; the goal of matching a given pattern of job knowledge and skills which a client has with the requirements of identifiable occupations (Ninth Institute on Rehabilitation Services, 1971)

physical and mental restoration Services necessary to either correct or improve a physical or mental condition which is stable or slowly progressive

rehabilitated Achievement of the fullest physical, mental, social, vocational, and economic usefulness of which the handicapped individual is capable

rehabilitation counseling A process involving a counselor and a client to help the client understand his problems and potential, and to help the client make effective use of personal and environmental resources for the best possible vocational, personal, and social adjustment (Jaques, 1970)

rehabilitation facility An organization with a program which is operated for the primary purpose of providing rehabilitation services to handicapped individuals

rehabilitation services Medical, psychological, social, and vocational services including any goods or services which are necessary for rendering a handicapped person fit to engage in gainful activity

severe disability A physical or mental condition which so limits the *functional* capabilities of an individual that he cannot perform some key life functions and which is expected to last indefinitely; the 1973 Rehabilitation Act defines severe handicap as a "disability which requires multiple services over an extended period of time and results from amputation, blindness, cancer, cerebral palsy, cystic fibrosis, deafness, heart disease, hemiplegia, mental retardation, mental illness, multiple sclerosis, muscular dystrophy, neurological disorders (including stroke and epilepsy), paraplegia, quadriplegia and other spinal cord conditions, renal failure, respiratory or pulmonary dysfunction, and any other disability specified by the Secretary in regulations he shall prescribe"

sheltered workshop A rehabilitation facility, or part of one, which utilizes production and work experience in a controlled environment for assisting the handicapped person to progress to the competitive labor market or engage in extended employment until such time as competitive employment opportunities become available

state rehabilitation agency The only agency designated to administer the state plan for rehabilitation services (also the state agency for the blind if separate from the general state rehabilitation agency)

training Activities by which physical, mental, and/or vocational skills are developed by the client

work adjustment A training process which involves individuals and groups in work-related activities to help them understand the meaning, value, and demands of work in general and to modify or develop their attitudes, personal characteristics, work behaviors, and functional capacities as required for achieving their optimal level of vocational development (Tenth Institute on Rehabilitation Services, 1972)

SUMMARY

To rehabilitate means to restore. The public-private program of rehabilitation in the United States is based on principles of human value, equality of opportunity, individual uniqueness, and the holistic nature of humans. The rehabilitation process is a goal-oriented, individualized, sequence of services designed to help handicapped persons achieve vocational adjustment. The process requires a team approach involving many human service specialties and a professional service coordinator and counselor. In the United States rehabilitation program this person is called a rehabilitation counselor. Vocational rehabilitation offers economic benefits which are worth at least eight times the cost, and perhaps as much as thirty-three times the cost.

The federal-state program is composed of a central federal office in Washington, D.C., 10 regional federal offices, 56 general state agencies, and 28 separate state agencies for the blind. Through the public program a wide range of rehabilitation services is available to render a handicapped person employable. Eligibility for service by individuals is based upon two criteria: (1) the presence of a physical or mental disability that constitutes or results in a substantial handicap to employment for the individual, and (2) a reasonable expectation that rehabilitation services may benefit the individual in terms of employability.

To receive federal funding assistance, each state is required to have a state plan for rehabilitation services. Recent legislation emphasizes that state plans provide for continuing statewide studies of the needs of handicapped persons, priority service to the most severely handicapped persons, structured individualized written rehabilitation programs for clients, and an annual comprehensive evaluation of program effectiveness.

Private rehabilitation agencies and resources are the primary service deliverers in rehabilitation. These services are generally purchased by the public agency rehabilitation counselor, who provides the rehabilitation process with guidance and coordination.

SELF-EVALUATION QUESTIONS

1. What is the definition for rehabilitation?
2. What is the distinction between rehabilitation and habilitation?
3. What are three basic principles which form a philosophical foundation for the practice of rehabilitation?

4. What are two approaches for integrating multidisciplinary practice and resources into an individualized rehabilitation process?
5. What are the important features of the rehabilitation process?
6. What has been the lowest benefit-cost ratio determined for vocational rehabilitation (earnings-cost)?
7. What are the primary functions of the federal rehabilitation agency?
8. What are some special programs supported by the Rehabilitation Services Administration?
9. How are rehabilitation funds allocated to state agencies?
10. What is the federal-state matching ratio for appropriations authorized by the Vocational Rehabilitation Amendments of 1968?
11. What is the minimum federal funding level for any state?
12. What are the two criteria for determining eligibility for rehabilitation services through the public program?
13. What services are offered by the public rehabilitation program?
14. What are third-party agreements?
15. What are some of the requirements for inclusion in the annual state plans for rehabilitation services?
16. To which group of disabled does the Rehabilitation Act of 1973 give first priority for service?
17. Are residency requirements as a condition of service eligibility an option for states?
18. What written sources are available for guidance in the implementation of the public rehabilitation program?
19. What are some examples of private rehabilitation resources?
20. What are three purposes for which federal funds are available to private rehabilitation facilities?
21. How is a disability different from a handicap?
22. Who determines eligibility for rehabilitation services through the public program?
23. What is the definition for employment?
24. What is rehabilitation counseling?
25. What are four types of rehabilitation services?

REFERENCES

Conley, R. W. *The economics of vocational rehabilitation.* Baltimore: Johns Hopkins Press, 1965.
Conley, R. W. A benefit-cost analysis of the vocational rehabilitation program. *Journal of Human Resources,* 1969, 4(2), 226-252.
Department of Health, Education, and Welfare. Vocational rehabilitation program: implementation provisions, rules and regulations. *Federal Register,* 1974, 39(235), 42470-42507.
DiMichael, S. G. The current scene. In D. Malikin & H. Rusalem (Eds.), *Vocational rehabilitation of the disabled: an overview.* New York: New York University Press, 1969.
Garrett, J. F. Historical background. In D. Malikin & H. Rusalem (Eds.), *Vocational rehabilitation of the disabled: an overview.* New York: New York University Press, 1969.
Jaques, M. E. *Rehabilitation counseling: scope and services.* Boston: Houghton Mifflin Co., 1970.
McGowan, J. F., & Porter, T. L. *An introduction to the vocational rehabilitation process.* Washington, D.C.: Government Printing Office, 1967.
Ninth Institute on Rehabilitation Services. *Placement and follow-up in the vocational rehabilitation process.* Washington, D.C.: Rehabilitation Services Administration, Department of Health, Education, and Welfare, 1971.
Reagles, K. W., & Wright, G. N. *A benefit-cost analysis of the Wood County project: an illustrated lecture.* Madison, Wis.: Regional Rehabilitation Research Institute, University of Wisconsin, 1971.
Rehabilitation Services Administration. *Programs.* Washington, D.C.: RSA, Department of Health, Education, and Welfare, 1971. (SRS Publication No. 152)

Rusk, H. A. *Rehabilitation medicine*. St. Louis: The C. V. Mosby Co., 1977.
Talbot, H. S. A concept of rehabilitation. In H. A. Moses & C. H. Patterson (Eds.), *Readings in rehabilitation counseling* (2nd ed.). Champaign, Ill.: Stipes Publishing Co., 1971.
Tenth Institute of Rehabilitation Services. *Vocational evaluation and work adjustment services in vocational rehabilitation*. Washington, D.C.: Rehabilitation Services Administration, Department of Health, Education, and Welfare, 1972.
Townsend, M. R. *Sheltered workshops—a handbook* (2nd ed.). Washington, D.C.: National Association of Sheltered Workshops and Homebound Programs, 1966.
United States Senate and House of Representatives. *Rehabilitation Act of 1973*, Public Law 112, 93rd Congress, 1973.
Whitehouse, F. A. Habilitation—concept and process. *Journal of Rehabilitation*, 1953, *19*(2), 3-7.
Whitehouse, F. A. Humanitation: a philosophy for human resources. In C. H. Patterson (Ed.), *Readings in rehabilitation counseling*. Champaign, Ill.: Stipes Publishing Co., 1960.

ADDITIONAL READINGS

Angell, D. L., DeSau, G. T., & Havrilla, A. A. Rehabilitation counselor versus coordinator . . . one of rehabilitation's great straw men. In H. A. Moses & C. H. Patterson (Eds.), *Readings in rehabilitation counseling* (2nd ed.). Champaign, Ill.: Stipes Publishing Co., 1971.
Burk, R. D. The nature of disability. *Journal of Rehabilitation*, 1967, *33*(6), 10-14, 34-35.
McCauley, W. A. The professional status of the rehabilitation counselor. In J. G. Cull & R. E. Hardy (Eds.), *Vocational rehabilitation: profession and process*. Springfield, Ill.: Charles C Thomas, Publisher, 1972.
National Rehabilitation Counseling Association Professional Standards Committee. The rehabilitation counselor: what he is and does. *Journal of Rehabilitation*, 1962, *28*(3), 17.
Patterson, C. H. Counselor or coordinator? *Journal of Rehabilitation*, 1957, *23*(3), 13-15.
Reedy, C. Developing trends in rehabilitation. In J. G. Cull & R. E. Hardy (Eds.), *Vocational rehabilitation: profession and process*. Springfield, Ill.: Charles C Thomas, Publisher, 1972.
Switzer, M. E. Role of the federal government in vocational rehabilitation. *Archives of Physical Medicine and Rehabilitation*, 1956, *37*, 542-546.
Wright, G. N., & Reagles, K. W. *The economic impact of an expanded program of vocational rehabilitation*, Monograph XV, Series 2, Madison, Wis.: Regional Rehabilitation Research Institute, University of Wisconsin, 1971.

MEDIA RESOURCES

Visual
  1. "Bridge to Disability" (16 mm film, 11 minutes). Developed by the University of Minnesota Medical Rehabilitation Research and Training Center, 860 Mayo Building, Minneapolis, Minn. 55455.
     Depicts accident, rescue, and emergency room scenes from a spinal cord injured patient's viewpoint. The patient's relationships with the physician, nurse, orderly, and wife are illustrated.
  2. "Handicapped Workers: 'Making it'" (five filmstrips with phonodiscs and scripts). Developed by the Western Electric Company, Community Relations Organization, 222 Broadway, New York, N.Y. 10038.
     Presentations by five disabled employees of Western Electric Company describing their stories as an aid to public understanding about the handicapped.
  3. "The Job" (16 mm film, 12 minutes). Available from ICD Rehabilitation and Research Center, 340 East 24th St., New York, N.Y. 10010.
     Describes the vocational evaluation, training, counseling, and placement process in vocational rehabilitation.
  4. "You and Rehab" (16 mm film, 20 minutes). Available from Alabama Rehabilitation Media Services, 216 Petrie Hall, Auburn University, Auburn, Ala. 36830.
     Provides an overview of the vocational rehabilitation process to new clients including eligibility, services, personnel, and outcomes.
  5. "Count Us In" (16 mm film, 26 minutes). Available from Canadian Film Institute, 1762 Carling Ave., Ottawa, Ontario, Canada.
     Filmed in Sweden at the Swedish State Vocational Rehabilitation Center to describe how the disabled can be vocationally rehabilitated.

6. "Rehabilitation: the Science and the Art" (16 mm film, 13 minutes). Available from ICD Rehabilitation and Research Center, 340 East 24th St., New York, N.Y. 10010.

    Describes how professions work together in rehabilitation.

7. "Team Conference: Assessment of Aphasia" (1″ videotape, 24 minutes). Developed by the University of Minnesota Medical Rehabilitation Research and Training Center, 860 Mayo Building, Minneapolis, Minn. 55455.

    Presents a brief patient history followed by a team discussion of the patient's status and prognosis, an evaluation of the patient's home, and a plan of action.

8. "The Interdisciplinary Team and the Spinal Cord Injured Individual" (½″ videotape, 180 minutes). Developed by the Arkansas Rehabilitation Research and Training Center, Hot Springs Rehabilitation Center, P. O. Box 1358, Hot Springs, Ark. 71901.

    Presents a panel discussion on the integration of social services, counseling, physical therapy, occupational therapy, nursing services, and vocational training for spinal cord injured persons.

9. "An Overview of the Rehabilitation Center" (100 slides). Developed by the University of Minnesota Medical Rehabilitation Research and Training Center, 860 Mayo Building, Minneapolis, Minn. 55455.

    Presents a rehabilitation team approach with clients involving physicians, nurses, physical therapy, occupational therapy, speech-language pathology, social service, work evaluation, and psychological testing.

10. "Three to Make Ready" (16 mm film, 45 minutes). Available from International Society for Rehabilitation of the Disabled, Film Library, 219 East 44th St., New York, N.Y. 10017.

    Three client stories which illustrate a client-centered and team approach to rehabilitation involving physicians, therapists, teachers, social workers, psychologists, and others.

11. "The Climb-Out" (filmstrip with cassette tape). Developed by the Utah Division of Rehabilitation Services, 250 East 5th South St., Salt Lake City, Utah 84111.

    Intended to inform state legislators and the general public about the services and organization of the Utah Division of Rehabilitation Services.

12. "Yes We Can" (filmstrip with cassette tape). Developed by the Utah Division of Rehabilitation Services, 250 East 5th South St., Salt Lake City, Utah 84111.

    Describes the functions and services of the Utah Division of Rehabilitation Services from the client's point of view.

13. "Federal and State Administration of the VR Program" (85 slides, 20 minutes). Developed by the Vocational Rehabilitation Division Training Center, Department of Human Resources, 505 Edgewater, N.W., Salem, Ore. 97304.

    Describes the roles of Congress and federal and state offices of vocational rehabilitation. An emphasis is given to the Oregon State rehabilitation agency administrative structure.

14. "Island of Understanding" (16 mm film, 29 minutes). Available from National Audiovisual Center, Washington, D.C. 20409.

    Presents a broad range of rehabilitation projects conducted in facilities in Israel, Yugoslavia, and India.

Audio

1. "Philosophical Concepts of Rehabilitation" (audiotape, 136 minutes). Available from National Medical Audiovisual Center Annex, Station K, Atlanta, Ga. 30324.

    Describes rehabilitation in the past, present, and (perhaps) future.

2. "The Federal-State Program of Vocational Rehabilitation in the United States" (audiotape, 98 minutes). Produced by the New York University Medical Center, Institute of Rehabilitation Medicine, Learning Resources Facility, 550 First Ave., New York, N.Y. 10016.

    Traces the growth of the federal rehabilitation agency and its cooperation with the states in establishing vocational rehabilitation programs.

2

History of the rehabilitation program

OVERVIEW AND OBJECTIVES

This chapter offers the reader a general overview of the history and development of the rehabilitation program in the United States. It is divided into three major sections: (1) significant legislation since 1916, (2) development of the public program in the United States, and (3) development of significant private rehabilitation resources, including national rehabilitation programs, rehabilitation centers, and professional organizations with rehabilitation objectives.

Objectives of this chapter are to familiarize the reader with the major components of significant rehabilitation-related legislation in the United States between 1916 and 1978, to furnish an overview of public federal and state rehabilitation-related program developments beginning with Worker's Compensation provisions in 1908 through the establishment of a separate federal rehabilitation agency by Congress in 1975, and to describe some private rehabilitation resources with a history in the rehabilitation movement.

REHABILITATION LEGISLATION
National Defense Act, 1916

The National Defense Act of 1916 placed importance on the provision of vocational training for soldiers while in active military service. The Act provided an opportunity for soldiers to receive instruction and study to increase their military efficiency and enable them to return to civilian life better equipped for competitive occupations. In many ways this Act was the beginning of a congressional attitude toward rehabilitation which would result in the large national program of today.

Smith-Hughes Act, 1917

The 64th Congress passed Public Law 347 on February 23, 1917. Known as the Smith-Hughes Act, it established a federal-state program in vocational education. It also created a Federal Board for Vocational Education which had the authority and responsibility for the vocational rehabilitation of veterans. In addition, it provided federal assistance grants in support of vocational education to the states on a matching basis.

15

The Smith-Hughes legislation and the Federal Board of Vocational Education provided a basis for a system of vocational rehabilitation. Funds were provided for vocational education services to the states which met certain requirements. To receive these funds, each state had to pass "enabling" legislation and was required to establish a state board. Money was then provided to the states according to a federal plan (Obermann, 1965; McGowan & Porter, 1967; Dean, 1972; Lassiter, 1972).

Soldier Rehabilitation Act, 1918

Public Law 178, the Soldier Rehabilitation Act, was passed on June 27, 1918, by the 65th Congress. Under this act the role of the Federal Board for Vocational Education was expanded to include authorization to provide programs of vocational rehabilitation for disabled veterans. To be eligible, the disabled veteran had to be unable to engage successfully in a gainful occupation. The legislation became known as the Smith-Sears Veterans Rehabilitation Act and, later, was to provide a basis for the vocational rehabilitation of civilians (Obermann, 1965; Lassiter, 1972).

Vocational Rehabilitation Act, 1920

June 2, 1920, was to mark the beginning of the public rehabilitation program in the United States. On this date the Smith-Fess Act was passed to become Public Law 236 of the 66th Congress.

The Smith-Fess Act not only established the federal-state program in rehabilitation but also provided for an equal expenditure of funds by state and federal governments. It required (1) development of a state plan to be submitted and approved by the federal agency, (2) an annual report to the Federal Board for Vocational Education, (3) establishment of the state program under the state's Vocational Education Board, and (4) prohibition of fund expenditures for buildings or equipment (Lassiter, 1972).

The Vocational Rehabilitation Act of 1920, as interpreted by the Federal Board of Vocational Education, provided funds only for vocational guidance, training, occupational adjustment, prostheses, and placement services. Rehabilitation services were to be for the physically disabled and were to be vocational in nature. They could not include physical restoration or socially oriented rehabilitation (Obermann, 1965). The new Act did not specify a minimum age, but the Federal Board considered the minimum age of legal employability within the state to be the service eligibility policy. Homemaking was considered to be a legitimate occupation.

Within 18 months of the passage of the 1920 Vocational Rehabilitation Act, 34 states passed enabling legislation to organize a program of services that could accept the federal funds available to them on a 50-50 matching basis (Lassiter, 1972).

A 1921 bulletin issued by the Federal Board for Vocational Education identified specific case procedures and techniques to be used by rehabilitation agents (counselors) in managing the rehabilitation service process. A determination of client eligibility had to be made by the agent in terms of the applicant's age, physical disability, and feasibility for rehabilitation success. A job objective was then identified based on an intensive study of the case. After study a tentative rehabilitation plan had to be formulated in accordance with the client's job objective. Follow-up by the rehabilitation agent was to be provided during training and after job placement until the disabled person was producing at his maximum efficiency (Lassiter, 1972). The Federal Board for Vocational Education emphasized that its role was only in promoting vocational rehabilitation of persons. It clearly stated that the primary responsibility for vocational rehabilitation programming was with the state (Obermann, 1965).

The new rehabilitation program encountered a fiscal crisis in 1924. The 1920 Act was due to expire in June. Unfortunately Congress adjourned without providing appropriations for the program. An appeal by the Federal Board for Vocational Education to President Coolidge, however, resulted in permission to spend the administrative funds necessary to maintain the federal program under a deficit arrangement. This funding was only for federal administration and did not include funding grants to states. Nevertheless, all but one of the 39 states cooperating in the federal-state rehabilitation program at the time were able to keep their activities going by utilizing their own resources. Congress then gave authority to continue the program for an additional six years, to 1930. The necessary appropriations were to follow.

In 1930 the Vocational Rehabilitation Act was again renewed for an additional three years. By this time 44 states were participating in the federal-state program, and in 1932 a further extension of four years was granted to the program by Congress.

Social Security Act, 1935

Prior to 1935 the rehabilitation program was the result of a series of short-term congressional extensions. The Social Security Act of 1935 was the first permanent base for the federal vocational rehabilitation program. It provided for continuous authorization, increased grants, and increased support for the federal administration. It also allowed partial reimbursement by the federal government to the states for assistance given to the needy blind. Thus the vocational rehabilitation program was both continued and strengthened by the 1935 Social Security Act.

Randolph-Sheppard Act, 1936

The Randolph-Sheppard Act of 1936 authorized states to license qualified blind persons to operate vending stands in federal buildings. It also set a precedent for many states to make similar arrangements in state-owned buildings with assistance and supervision from a public agency.

Vocational Rehabilitation Act Amendments, 1943

These Amendments, enacted on June 6, 1943, as Public Law 113, 78th Congress, made changes in the federal-state program of rehabilitation. For example:

1. Vocational rehabilitation was defined to include any services necessary for a disabled person to become employed (Obermann, 1965). This meant that physical restoration services were to be made available to the disabled. The range of available rehabilitation services included corrective surgery, therapeutic treatment, hospitalization, transportation, occupational licenses, occupational tools and equipment, maintenance during training, placement in employment, prosthesis training, medical examinations, and guidance.

2. Vocational rehabilitation was extended for the first time to the mentally handicapped and the mentally ill.

3. Federal administration of grants was transferred from the Commissioner of Education to the Federal Security Administrator, who established an Office of Vocational Rehabilitation on September 8, 1943.

4. Each state was required to submit a state plan for vocational rehabilitation to be approved by the Federal Security Administrator. States were also required to designate the State Board of Vocational Education as the sole agency for the administration of the state rehabilitation plan. An exception was programs for the blind, which could continue under their own administration and still be eligible for federal rehabilitation funds. Thus separate state agencies for the blind were included in the federal-state program.

5. State agency administration, guidance, and placement costs (including staff salaries) would be paid by the federal government. In addition, the 1943 Amendments provided authorization for the federal agency to pay the entire expense of rehabilitating disabled veterans and half the expense for other disabled persons. The federal government also paid the entire cost of administering state programs. Previously program costs were shared equally between the states and the federal government.

Thus the Vocational Rehabilitation Act Amendments of 1943 broadened the program's financial provisions, offered a comprehensive definition for vocational rehabilitation, expanded service provisions to include physical restoration, required state plans for approval by the federal agency, expanded service provision to include the mentally handicapped and mentally ill, and fostered separate agencies for general rehabilitation and rehabilitation of the blind to be monitored by one federal agency (Kratz, 1960; Obermann, 1965; Dean, 1972; Lassiter, 1972).

Vocational Rehabilitation Act Amendments, 1954

Public Law 565 of the 83rd Congress, signed by President Eisenhower on August 3, 1954, was a milestone in the development of the rehabilitation program. It reshaped the role of the federal government in the rehabilitation program and established the basis for a working relationship between public and private rehabilitation organizations.

The 1954 Amendments provided more funds and additional program options for state agencies. They established a federally funded research program and provided training for staff of both public and private programs. They also authorized grants to expand or improve facilities (Dean, 1972). Significant features of the 1954 Amendments were as follows:

1. A new and variable funding formula meant that the most any state would be required to contribute to public program financing was 40% of the total spent in the general rehabilitation program. The federal share varied from state to state, with greater financial support going to states with large populations and small per capita income.

2. For the first time state agencies were permitted to use funds to expand or remodel buildings to make the buildings suitable for rehabilitation of the disabled (Lassiter, 1972).

3. Special grants were authorized to permit states to develop new aspects of their program or extend services to needy disability groups or geographic areas (McGowan & Porter, 1967).

4. Research and demonstration project grants were authorized to support studies for improving rehabilitation services and demonstrations of new knowledge application. Though the required matching funds of grantees was determined on an individual project basis, congressional appropriations limited the federal share to no more than two thirds of project costs (Obermann, 1965).

5. Training for physicians, nurses, rehabilitation counselors, physical therapists, occupational therapists, social workers, psychologists, and other specialists was authorized to meet the needs of a rapidly expanding rehabilitation program. Grants were given to colleges and universities to develop or expand curricula and to provide financial assistance and incentives in the form of traineeships to graduate students. The Act also provided authority for short-term training grants for seminars and workshops, for in-service training programs in state vocational rehabilitation agencies, and for rehabilitation research fellowships to individuals (Obermann, 1965; McGowan & Porter, 1967; Lassiter, 1972).

Vocational Rehabilitation Act Amendments, 1965

Public Law 333 of the 89th Congress provided for increased federal spending. The Vocational Rehabilitation Act Amendments of 1965 enlarged the federal cost share of rehabilitation to 75%. It provided innovative project grant monies to states for the development of new methods of providing services and for serving the severely disabled. Federal funds were authorized to cover 90% of the project cost in three-year projects and 75% of the cost for the remaining two years in five-year grants (McGowan & Porter, 1967). A program of construction assistance was also authorized for building rehabilitation centers and workshops, expanding present ones, and helping with the initial staffing costs of new or expanded centers and workshops (Dean, 1972).

The 1965 Amendments created a broader base of services to handicapped persons, including persons with socially handicapping conditions. Economic need was eliminated as a requisite for rehabilitation service. The states were permitted, however, to use an economic need test for services other than diagnostic related services, counseling, and placement.

The 1965 Amendments also allowed extended client evaluation to determine whether there was reasonable expectation that rehabilitation services would help the handicapped person to become employable. This extended evaluation feature permitted services to be provided up to a maximum of 6 months, and 18 months for the severely disabled, in determining employability. The Amendments also authorized special grants for statewide planning of vocational rehabilitation. The purpose of these special grants was to develop a comprehensive vocational rehabilitation plan and program within each state to make services available to all eligible handicapped persons by July 1, 1975 (Lamborn, 1970).

Besides enabling expansion of rehabilitation facilities, the 1965 Amendments created a National Policy and Performance Council to guide the HEW Secretary in the development of policies for improving and expanding rehabilitation facilities. A National Commission on Architectural Barriers was also authorized for the development of proposals for making buildings accessible to the handicapped.

Educational benefits were extended to a maximum of four years under the legislation, as opposed to two years provided under previous law for professional training in the field of vocational rehabilitation. A national data system was established, and intramural research within the vocational rehabilitation agency authorized (Obermann, 1965; McGowan & Porter, 1967; Dean, 1972).

The Vocational Rehabilitation Act was again amended in 1967 to separately provide (1) rehabilitation services for migratory workers, (2) elimination of state residency requirements for serving the disabled in need of rehabilitation services, and (3) construction and operation of a National Center for Deaf-Blind Youths and Adults (Dean, 1972).

Vocational Rehabilitation Act Amendments, 1968

The Amendments to the Vocational Rehabilitation Act of 1968 included (1) a change in the federal-state matching ratio for appropriations from 75-25 to 80-20, (2) approval to expend funds for new construction of rehabilitation facilities, (3) approval to provide follow-up services for maintaining an individual in employment and to provide services for family members of handicapped individuals, (4) permission to amend state plans so one state agency could share funding and administration responsibility with another in carrying out a joint project, and (5) authorization to provide vocational evaluation and work adjustment services to disadvantaged persons by reason of age, educational attainment, or ethnic or other factors (Lassiter, 1972).

Rehabilitation Act, 1973

Public Law 112 of the 93rd Congress was signed by President Nixon on September 26, 1973. This Act replaced the Vocational Rehabilitation Act as amended in 1968 but did retain the major provisions of the 1968 Amendments. There were, however, some important changes.

1. The Act established, by statute, the Rehabilitation Services Administration.

2. The Act emphasized priority service for persons with the most severe handicaps and mandated state agencies to establish an order of selection that would place the most severely handicapped person first for service as part of the state plan.

3. States were required by the Act to conduct continuing statewide studies relative to the needs of handicapped persons and how these needs might be effectively met. The intent of this requirement was to explore the expansion of services for the most severely handicapped. In addition, states were required to conduct periodic reviews of persons in sheltered workshops to determine their suitability for employment or employment-related training.

4. Under the 1973 legislation every client accepted for services had to be provided an Individualized Written Rehabilitation Program (IWRP). It also required joint counselor-client consultation and development of the IWRP and outlined the program in terms of a vocational goal, intermediate objectives, identification of anticipated dates of initiation and completion of services, and evaluation procedures and schedules. It further indicated that the opportunity for the client to achieve a vocational goal must remain available to the client at least until such time as the counselor could, beyond a reasonable doubt, support a change in the goal.

5. The 1973 Rehabilitation Act also required that several special studies be conducted to (a) determine methods of providing comprehensive services to persons for whom a vocational goal might not be feasible and to determine how services could help these individuals live more independently, (b) identify the role of the sheltered workshop in the rehabilitation process and explore the wage payment structure in sheltered workshops, and (c) determine how the basic state grant allocation formula could be improved.

In addition, the 1973 Act provided several other changes from earlier Acts (LaVor & Duncan, 1974):

A new federal mortgage insurance program to assist in the construction of rehabilitation facilities

An Architectural and Transportation Barriers Compliance Board to enforce federal statutory requirements concerning access to public buildings and transportation for the handicapped

The requirement that state rehabilitation agencies would have to seek funds from other existing federal assistance programs before using rehabilitation funds for higher education case service

An annual report on the national program to be submitted to the President and Congress

A clearing house to be established for information concerning programs for handicapped individuals

A federal interagency committee to facilitate employment and advancement of the handicapped in federal government jobs

Prohibition against discrimination solely by reason of a handicap in any program receiving federal financial assistance

Client assistance demonstration projects to inform clients of available benefits under the Act

As indicated in the Preface to this text, there is a trend toward a greater emphasis on independent living services for the disabled. The term "vocational rehabilitation" is gradually being replaced by "rehabilitation" in legislation, in agency names, and in the literature. Some of this change began with the reorganization of the Department of Health, Education, and Welfare in 1967 which created the Social and Rehabilitation Service. However, most of this change in emphasis started with the Rehabilitation Act of 1973—when considerable discussion occurred in Congress regarding the provision of comprehensive services to individuals for whom a vocational goal might not be feasible.

Rehabilitation Act Amendments, 1974

Public Law 516 of the 93rd Congress amended the Rehabilitation Act of 1973 by (1) extending the authorization of appropriations for one year, to June 30, 1976, (2) transferring the Rehabilitation Services Administration to the HEW Secretary (from the Social and Rehabilitation Service) and requiring that the RSA Commissioner be appointed by the President with the consent of the Senate, (3) strengthening the programs for the blind authorized by the Randolph-Sheppard Act of 1936, and (4) providing for a White House Conference on Handicapped Individuals within two years to develop recommendations for solutions to problems facing handicapped persons.

The Rehabilitation Act of 1973 was again extended in 1975 from June 30, 1976, to September 30, 1978.

Rehabilitation Act Amendments, 1978

The Rehabilitation Act of 1973 was again amended on November 6, 1978 (Public Law 602, 95th Congress). Major features are (1) authorization of an annual increase in appropriations for the basic state grant program based on increases in the cost of living, (2) an increase in the minimum state allotment of funds to $3 million, (3) authorization of a comprehensive program of independent living services for severely handicapped persons, (4) authorization of community service employment programs for handicapped individuals, (5) authorization of a National Institute of Handicapped Research, and (6) a change in the definition for developmental disabilities from a categorical one to a functional one for any disability occurring before age 22. These Amendments are also referred to as "the Rehabilitation, Comprehensive Services, and Developmental Disabilities Amendments of 1978."

DEVELOPMENT OF THE PUBLIC PROGRAM
Worker's compensation

During the first ten years of the twentieth century, a number of states passed laws protecting the employee from disabilities resulting from work. In 1908 the federal government enacted a law referred to as Workmen's Compensation (now as Worker's Compensation) which covered federal employees. These initial worker's compensation laws did not include vocational rehabilitation services. Their purpose was to provide some sort of financial compensation for a disability or physical loss resulting from employment. Most employers carried insurance for protection. Worker's compensation laws following the federal law of 1908 were quickly enacted within the states. By 1921, 45 of the states and territories had some form of worker's compensation legislation concerned with medical services and compensation for lost income. Worker's compensation laws were a first step in seeking to return injured workers to employment (Obermann, 1965).

Federal Board for Vocational Education, 1917

The Smith-Hughes Act of 1917 created a Federal Board for Vocational Education. The Board was organized on July 21, 1917, and was composed of the Secretary of Commerce, the United States Commissioner of Education, and three civilians representing labor, commerce and manufacturing, and agriculture (Obermann, 1965). It later administered the vocational rehabilitation program for World War I veterans and the federal-state program in rehabilitation (Lassiter, 1972).

Since the Federal Board for Vocational Education was a civilian agency, it could not accept a veteran into the rehabilitation program until after the veteran's eligibility under the War Risk Insurance Act of 1914 had been determined. This determination was made by an agency independent of the Board because the Board was unable to keep up with the many claims for compensation. Thus thousands of disabled veterans who were eligible for rehabilitation had to wait. In 1919, however, Congress passed an amendment to the Soldier Rehabilitation Act of 1918 giving the Board authority to make eligibility determinations in addition to its responsibility for administering the program for the rehabilitation of disabled veterans. In 1933 the Federal Board for Vocational Education was transferred to the Department of the Interior.

Federal-state vocational rehabilitation

In the 18 months following the passage of the Vocational Rehabilitation Act of 1920, 34 states passed enabling legislation to organize a program of services to accommodate federal funds on a 50-50 matching ratio through the Federal Board for Vocational Education (Lassiter, 1972). By 1940 all the United States and its territories had entered into a partnership with the federal government (Kratz, 1960).

The administration of the vocational rehabilitation program by the Federal Board for Vocational Education was democratic. The Board did not intend to direct rehabilitation within the states; rather, it considered itself to be promotive (Lamborn, 1970). The federal government served as both a funding agency and a stimulus for the development of programs. States had the responsibility for organizing and operating rehabilitation programs. They also were required to develop a plan for approval by the federal agency, submit an annual report to the Federal Board, and administer the rehabilitation program under a state vocational education board. A cooperative agreement between the rehabilitation program and the states' worker's compensation agency, where one existed, was also required.

The federal-state relationship remained rather stable until 1933, when the Federal Board for Vocational Education was transferred to the Department of the Interior. The Secretary of the Interior assigned the rehabilitation program to the Office of Education (Lassiter, 1972). In 1939 the executive branch of the government was reorganized and a Federal Security Agency was established. The Office of Education was transferred from the Department of the Interior to this new Federal Security Agency, and with it went the rehabilitation program (Obermann, 1965).

Office of Vocational Rehabilitation, 1943

In 1943 the Office of Vocational Rehabilitation was established within the Federal Security Agency. It was separate from the Office of Education. Federal rehabilitation representatives were stationed in each of the regional offices throughout the country. A National Rehabilitation Advisory Council was formed to advise the federal office on policies and programs. An increased emphasis on physical restoration services resulted in the formation of a professional advisory committee consisting of representatives from various medical specialties to help with the planning of these new physical restoration activities (Obermann, 1965). State rehabilitation directors were given additional status by the requirement that they be full-time program directors (Obermann, 1965).

The rehabilitation program continued to grow in the 1940s, and in 1945 Congress passed a resolution which established a Committee on Employment of the Handicapped. The primary objective of this committee was to publish information that would promote the employment of handicapped persons.

In 1951 Mary E. Switzer was named Director of the Office of Vocational Rehabilitation in the Federal Security Agency. Miss Switzer was to serve as the chief of vocational rehabilitation for the following twenty years and have a marked impact on the development of the rehabilitation program.

The Department of Health, Education, and Welfare was organized in 1953, replacing the Federal Security Agency. The scope of rehabilitation services was broadened with the enactment of the 1954 Vocational Rehabilitation Amendments. These Amendments provided greater autonomy for state agencies and greater administrative flexibility in the organizational location of the agencies within the states (Lamborn, 1970).

In 1960 the federal vocational rehabilitation program established the first international plan. The purpose was to share experience and ideas through mutual exchange of rehabilitation experts among nations.

Vocational Rehabilitation Administration, 1963

In 1963 the Office of Vocational Rehabilitation became the Vocational Rehabilitation Administration. Two years later the 1965 Amendments provided states with even greater organizational and administrative flexibilities. States had three options to the organizational location of a general rehabilitation program: (1) a state agency concerned primarily with rehabilitation, (2) a state agency that administered education or vocational education in the state, or (3) a state agency that included at least two other major organizational units each of which administered one or more of the major education, health, welfare, or labor programs of the state (Lamborn, 1970).

Most general rehabilitation agencies were located with educational agencies. Almost two thirds of the remainder were either independent agencies or organizationally affiliated with another state agency. Thirty-four states also had separate agencies for rehabilitation of the blind. The 1965 Amendments required, furthermore, that the agency be concerned primarily with rehabilitation and have a full-time director with full-time staff for the rehabilitation work (Lamborn, 1970).

Rehabilitation Services Administration, 1967 and 1975

The Department of Health, Education, and Welfare was reorganized in 1967, and a Social and Rehabilitation Service was established within it. The Social and Rehabilitation Service was composed of five major divisions: a Rehabilitation Services Administration (previously called the Vocational Rehabilitation Administration), a Children's Bureau, an Administration on Aging, a Medical Services Administration, and an Assistance Payments Administration (Lassiter, 1972). The reorganization was to more effectively coordinate related social service agencies and to emphasize the rehabilitation model. For example, the rehabilitation program was asked to assume responsibility for determination of disability required in the Social Security Act. This model for reorganization of social services into one umbrella agency hopefully would be followed in the states.

Rather than coordinating and using rehabilitation as a model for human service programming, the reorganization resulted in a dilution of the rehabilitation program. Congressional intent and financial resources were diverted to other programs. Thus, in 1975, on the basis of the 1974 Amendments to the Rehabilitation Act, the Rehabilitation Services Administration was removed administratively from the Social and Rehabilitation Service agency and placed in the Office of Human Development as a unit of the Department of Health, Education, and Welfare.

Veterans Administration

The War Risk Insurance Act of 1914 (Public Law 90, 65th Congress) was one of the first efforts in the twentieth century for providing rehabilitation and vocational training to veterans injured in military service. The Veterans Bureau was created in 1921 through Public Law 47, 67th Congress, in an effort to bring together a number of veterans services and benefits administered by separate organizations. The new agency consolidated veteran-related functions of the Bureau of War Risk Insurance, the Veterans and Rehabilitation Divisions of the Federal Board for Vocational Education, the Pension Bureau, the Public Health Service, and the National Home for Volunteer Soldiers (Obermann, 1965). The Veterans Bureau was reorganized and designated the Veterans Administration in 1933 under Public Law 2, 73rd Congress.

During World War II, efforts were made to pass a bill in Congress that would meet the needs of both disabled civilians and veterans. The bills were a result of many meetings between representatives of the Federal Security Administration and the Veterans Administration and were an attempt to develop a unified rehabilitation program for civilians and veterans and to eliminate unnecessary duplication of services, personnel, and facilities. Representatives of various veterans organizations, however, insisted on separate legislation for disabled veterans. The result was Public Law 16, 78th Congress, which made provisions for serving the disabled veteran by the Veterans Administration as a separate program (Obermann, 1965).

The Servicemens Readjustment Act of 1944 (Public Law 346, 78th Congress) was a comprehensive Act to give veterans a variety of services. Public Law 346 provided training, tuition and subsistence, direct loans, unemployment allowances, and a variety of readjustment benefits (e.g., hospitalization, disability compensation, mustering-out pay, preferential employment and referral services) (Obermann, 1965).

Many disabled veterans were discharged from military service and sent directly to veterans hospitals. Others were hospitalized after a period in civilian life. Counseling was recognized as an important part of the rehabilitation process. With the passing of the Public Law 346, the Veterans Administration formed a Vocational Rehabilitation and Education Service. By 1953 this Service was well organized and, in cooperation with universities, could offer graduate training in psychology and counseling as well as a doctorate level service delivery program (Obermann, 1965).

After the Korean conflict, the Veterans Readjustment Assistance Act of 1952 (Public Law 550, 82nd Congress) was passed. Basically this Act was similar to previous legislation for returning veterans.

DEVELOPMENT OF PRIVATE REHABILITATION RESOURCES
Perkins Institute

The first sheltered workshop for the disabled in the United States was the Perkins Institute, founded by Samuel Gridley Howe. The workshop was established in connection with the Perkins Institution for the Blind, a school near Boston. Its name was changed to Perkins School for the Blind in 1955. It was incorporated in 1829 (Cruickshank & Johnson, 1958), and the workshop was established in 1837 (Nelson, 1971).

The Perkins Institute workshop was intended to train the blind so they could work in the community. They manufactured mattresses, cushions, pillows, brushes, brooms, floor mats, and similar articles. Placing the visually handicapped in employment was difficult. Thus later workshops for the blind were generally not associated with schools for the blind because of the difficulty in financing and managing workshops (Nelson, 1971).

Facilities sponsored by religious organizations

Society of St. Vincent de Paul. The Society of St. Vincent de Paul was organized to provide both spiritual and material subsistence to the needy, particularly the poor. It began a system of collecting and cleaning discarded clothes to give to poor people. It was founded in Paris in 1833, and in 1945 the first United States outlet was started in St. Louis (Nelson, 1971).

Salvation Army. The Salvation Army came to America from England in 1879 (Lassiter, 1972). It engaged in the renovation of various discarded goods. The work provided in the salvage operation was intended to be a means of helping troubled people find salvation. The Salvation Army only provided room, board, and work (without pay) until individuals were able to face their problems and become independent.

Goodwill Industries of America. The first Goodwill Industries operation was established in Boston by a young Methodist minister named Edgar J. Helms in 1902. The program was nondenominational and, like the Society of St. Vincent de Paul and the Salvation Army, collected and renovated used clothing and other materials for distribution to the needy poor.

Goodwill Industries would hire and pay unemployed persons to do the renovation work and would then sell the goods at a price that would be enough to pay the workers. Many of the unemployed who came to work at Dr. Helms' Morgan Memorial Chapel in Boston were skilled workmen who were temporarily unemployed. As these workers left, Dr. Helms sought disabled persons or others who had difficulty in finding jobs (Obermann, 1965). The Goodwill Industries were adopted as a function of the Methodist Church in 1918 by a Board of Missions of the Methodist Church. As the program served more and more handicapped persons, state rehabilitation agencies began using the Goodwill Industries as a training resource (Nelson, 1971).

Rehabilitation centers

Vocational Guidance and Rehabilitation Services, Cleveland. The Vocational Guidance and Rehabilitation Services originated just prior to 1900, when a group of volunteer women in Cleveland known as the Sunbeam Circle made handiwork to sell for the benefit of crippled children. In 1901 the women started a kindergarten for crippled children, and in 1910 special education classes.

The Sunbeam Circle expanded into sewing classes and then a sewing shop. In 1918 it became an association for the crippled and disabled, and by 1922 it had a workshop program, an orthopedic center, and a social service department. Its name was changed in 1939 to the Cleveland Rehabilitation Center, and in 1956 it merged with the Vocational Guidance Bureau of Cleveland to form a new agency, the Vocational Guidance and Rehabilitation Services (Nelson, 1971; Dean, 1972).

ICD Rehabilitation and Research Center, New York. The ICD Rehabilitation and Research Center began as the Red Cross Institution for Crippled and Disabled Men. In 1917 Jeremiah Milbank, a New York philanthropist, proposed a plan to the American Red Cross for providing a program of services for disabled veterans. Mr. Milbank offered a building on the northeast corner of 23rd Street and 4th Avenue in New York City and a cash contribution for the establishment of a rehabilitation facility. The proposal was accepted. The Institute provided medical and surgical services through New York clinics and hospitals. It also provided social services and job placement.

After the War, in 1919, the Institute became a private organization, and in 1930 Jeremiah Milbank made a large contribution to building a new Institute for the Crippled and Disabled to serve as a comprehensive rehabilitation center. During the middle 1930's a medical service component was added to eliminate the need for relying on city hospitals and clinics for medical service to disabled clients.

The Institute for the Crippled and Disabled continued to grow and, through the years, made significant contributions in service and to knowledge about rehabilitating the disabled. In 1972 it became the ICD Rehabilitation and Research Center offering comprehensive medically and vocationally oriented services, in addition to a strong research component through its Milbank Research Laboratories (Dean, 1972).

Curative Workshop of Milwaukee. The Curative Workshop of Milwaukee was started soon after World War I (1919) through the Milwaukee Junior League to provide a program of occupational and physical therapy for handicapped children. In 1931 the Curative Workshop became incorporated and, shortly thereafter, offered a wide variety of services to the handicapped including a nursery school for cerebral palsy children, a medical-social service program, psychological services, vocationally oriented services, and research and training. A vocational program was started in 1945 which consisted primarily of occupational therapy with simulated work activity. Ten years later a vocational evaluation unit was established, and soon after sheltered work, work adjustment, and vocational training on the job were added to the program. Other curative workshops, patterned after the Curative Workshop of Milwaukee, were to be established throughout the United States (Nelson, 1971).

Jewish Vocational Service Agencies. Jewish Vocational Service agencies were established in the United States primarily to provide vocational guidance and placement to Jewish young people, the aged, and the handicapped. Particular emphasis was given in these programs to serving immigrants to help them adjust to the United States. Most Jewish Vocational Service agencies emphasized vocational adjustment; others provided employment in workshops. Generally the emphasis was, and continues to be, on transitional services to community employment. There is a National Association of Jewish Vocational Services (formerly known as the Jewish Occupational Council and founded in 1939) located in New York City. The Jewish Vocational Service agencies in the United States have done much to provide leadership and direction in rehabilitation for the development of work adjustment programs for the handicapped and disadvantaged (Nelson, 1971).

Community mental health centers. The Mental Health Study Act of 1955 (Public Law 182, 84th Congress) authorized a Joint Commission on Mental Illness and Health to evaluate the needs and resources of the mentally ill in the United States and make recommendations for a national mental health program (Joint Commission on Mental Illness and Health, 1961). As a result the Community Mental Health Centers Act (Public Law 164, 88th Congress) was passed in 1964 which established treatment centers in local communities throughout the country. The primary purposes of the centers are to provide inpatient, outpatient, emergency, day care, and indirect services to disturbed and mentally ill persons, to prevent recurrence of mental illness, and to reduce the need for long-term institutionalization in mental hospitals. Community mental health centers are supported jointly by federal, state, and local funds.

Organizations

National Rehabilitation Association. The National Rehabilitation Association (NRA) began as the National Civilian Rehabilitation Conference in 1924 and 1925. It was founded by a group of state rehabilitation program workers in an effort to protect and advance their interest in the public rehabilitation program (Dean, 1972). Initially the organization limited membership to employees of the public program. Other professional rehabilitation workers were eligible to become associate members. The organization became known as the National Rehabilitation Association in 1927. Membership statuses were reviewed in 1930 and four types became available: individual, organization, contributing, and life. All types of members could vote (Obermann, 1965). By 1932 the Association was formulating standing committees and making plans for a journal, professional membership designation, and the formation of local chapters restricted to physically disabled persons (Obermann, 1965). The idea of local chapters for disabled persons was discontinued in 1934. Publications of the National Rehabilitation Association began with a NRA yearbook in 1932, followed by a news bulletin, and a journal which in 1945, as the *Journal of Rehabilitation,* was designated to be the official publication of the NRA (Obermann, 1965). The Association's first executive secretary, E. B. Whitten, was hired in 1948. He retired in 1974.

The National Rehabilitation Association has expanded considerably in recent years and includes many divisions representing various rehabilitation workers. These are the National Rehabilitation Counseling Association, the Vocational Evaluation and Work Adjustment Association, the Job Placement Division, the National Association of Disability Examiners, the National Association of Rehabilitation Instructors, the National Association of Rehabilitation Secretaries, the National Congress on the Rehabilitation of Homebound and Institutionalized Persons, and the National Rehabilitation Administration Association. The National Rehabilitation Association is open for membership to professional workers in all phases of rehabilitation including physicians, nurses, psychologists, occupational, physical and speech therapists, social workers, hospital and rehabilitation facility personnel, and others who are interested in the problems of the handicapped.

Council of State Administrators of Vocational Rehabilitation. The Council of State Administrators of Vocational Rehabilitation (CSAVR) was founded in 1940 to serve as a forum for the directors of state rehabilitation agencies to study, discuss and communicate with others on issues of concern in rehabilitation. The council is a principal resource for the formulation of a collective opinion on issues from state rehabilitation agency administrators and also serves as an advisory body to the Rehabilitation Services Administration.

National Council on Rehabilitation Education. The National Council on Rehabilitation Education (NCRE) began as the Council of Rehabilitation Counselor Educators in 1970. Its purpose is similar to that of the CSAVR just described—by providing a forum for rehabilitation educators but also to discuss and influence the direction of rehabilitation education/training.

In 1976 the organization broadened its membership, from persons employed primarily in graduate programs in rehabilitation counseling to persons employed in all rehabilitation education settings—including undergraduate programs in rehabilitation services education, rehabilitation facility education, rehabilitation administration, rehabilitation continuing education, and any others engaged in rehabilitation-related education and training.

National Society for Crippled Children and Adults. The National Society for Crippled Children and Adults began in 1919 when a small group of people in Ohio who were interested in crippled children formed an organization. As state organizations emerged, a federation of state societies were formed in 1921 and became the National Society for Crippled Children. Donations for Easter Seals to raise money was inaugurated in 1934 as a national effort. Consequently the National Society for Crippled Children and Adults is also known as the Easter Seal Society.

The Society has its headquarters in Chicago. The organization has been instrumental in establishing many rehabilitation programs, centers, and workshops for handicapped persons and has been active in the support of both service and research programs by others. It produces a major journal, entitled *Rehabilitation Literature,* which synthesizes and abstracts publications from many rehabilitation-related journals in addition to publishing full-length articles.

United Cerebral Palsy Association. The United Cerebral Palsy Association, Inc., was formed as a national organization in 1948 to bring together local associations of parents of cerebral palsy children. These local groups of parents developed sheltered workshop units and rehabilitation programs for their children during the early 1940s (Nelson, 1971). The primary purposes of the national organization are to promote research in cerebral palsy, to further professional and public education concerning the problems of cerebral palsy, to promote diagnosis and treatment techniques and facilities for the cerebral palsied, and to promote employment of persons with cerebral palsy (UCPA, Inc., 1972).

Though each local cerebral palsy association differs somewhat from one community to another, most offer education and rehabilitation services for the cerebral palsied.

National Association for Retarded Citizens. The National Association for Retarded Citizens was founded in 1950 as a voluntary nationwide organization interested in the welfare of mentally retarded persons. It is predominantly a parent member organization with state and local units. The Association fosters public awareness of mental retardation, progressive legislation, improved residential facilities, employment opportunities and the advancement of research and services on behalf of mentally retarded persons.

President's Committee on Employment of the Handicapped. A joint resolution by Congress in 1945 established the President's Committee on Employment of the Handicapped. It also designated the first week of October as National Employ the Handicapped Week. The primary purpose of the President's Committee is to promote the employment of the handicapped by business and industry (Lassiter, 1972). The first National Employ the Handicapped Week was in 1947 (Obermann, 1965).

Originally the committee was called the President's Committee on National Employ the Physically Handicapped Week. It was changed in 1952 by President Truman to the President's Committee on Employment of the Physically Handicapped. In 1962 President Kennedy changed its name to the President's Committee on Employment of the Handicapped. The President's Committee works with counterpart governors' committees in all the states to promote employment of the disabled. Many cities also have mayor's committees. In addition, the committee publishes materials and promotes related special events (Obermann, 1965).

Association of Rehabilitation Facilities. The Association of Rehabilitation Facilities (ARF) resulted from a 1969 merger between the Association of Rehabilitation Centers established in 1952 and the National Association of Sheltered Workshops and Homebound Programs established in 1949. The two organizations formulated a Commission on Accreditation of Rehabilitation Facilities (CARF) and developed accreditation standards (Nelson, 1971). Created in 1966, CARF serves as the accrediting organization for rehabilitation centers and workshops. CARF has as its purpose the development and improvement of facility services to the disabled.

American Rehabilitation Counseling Association. The American Rehabilitation Counseling Association (ARCA) was established in 1957 as the Division of Rehabilitation Counseling in the American Personnel and Guidance Association (APGA). The parent organization (APGA) was established in 1952 to advance the educational aspects of guidance, counseling, and student personnel work. The purpose of the American Rehabilitation Counseling Association division is to foster professional development of rehabilitation counseling and the promotion of research, training and professional standards related to rehabilitation. The ARCA organization publishes a professional journal, *Rehabilitation Counseling Bulletin,* four times a year and makes an annual rehabilitation research award.

American Foundation for the Blind. The American Foundation for the Blind is a private nonprofit agency established in 1921 to conduct research, disseminate information, and provide counsel relative to blind persons. The Foundation offers services pertaining to aids and appliances for use by the blind, talking books, field consultation to local agencies, a special library on the subject of blindness, legislative consultation, professional and public education, and research on blindness. The Foundation maintains six regional offices with regional consultants to extend and strengthen services at the local level.

SUMMARY

The history of the rehabilitation program in the United States has been characterized by steady growth. The public program officially began with the Vocational Rehabilitation Act of 1920 which provided vocational training and guidance services for the physically disabled. The 1943 Amendments made many changes in the program, the most significant of which were to (1) offer any rehabilitation services necessary to assist the disabled to employment and (2) extend services to the mentally handicapped and mentally ill. The 1954 Amendments also significantly strengthened the public-private rehabilitation program by authorizing a research and demonstration program, professional training, special project grants, and an increased federal share for funding state programs. Other changes were made through the 1965 and 1968 Amendments and the public program received a new rehabilitation Act in 1973 which emphasized services to the most severely handicapped, more structured Individualized Written Rehabilitation Programs for clients, and program evaluation.

The federal agency with the responsibility for administering the legislation also changed significantly since 1920. Beginning with assignment to a Federal Board for Vocational Education in an education office, the federal agency became in 1975, by congressional mandate, a separate agency placed in the Office of Human Development as a unit of the Department of Health, Education, and Welfare.

The private sector of the rehabilitation program in the United States has always been a primary deliverer of services to the disabled. Many early efforts were sponsored by religious organizations. With the development of rehabilitation methods and techniques by rehabilitation centers and workshops, the private agencies became a more integral part of the public-private rehabilitation effort.

Voluntary associations of professionals, parents, and interest groups also emerged. One of the most encompassing organizations in the rehabilitation field is the National Rehabilitation Association, started in 1925.

From a very modest beginning in 1920, the public-private program of rehabilitation has become perhaps the most successful human service program in the United States.

SELF-EVALUATION QUESTIONS

1. Why was the National Defense Act of 1916 important in the history of the public rehabilitation program in the United States?
2. What legislative act established the Federal Board for Vocational Education, which directly administered the public rehabilitation program between 1920 and 1933?
3. What were the significant features of the 1920 Vocational Rehabilitation Act?
4. Why is the Social Security Act of 1935 important to the rehabilitation movement?
5. What was the purpose of the Randolph-Sheppard Act of 1936?
6. What were the significant program changes made by the 1943 Amendments to the Vocational Rehabilitation Act?
7. What were the significant features of the 1954 Amendments to the Vocational Rehabilitation Act?
8. What were the federal-state funding ratios created by the Vocational Rehabilitation Act Amendments of 1965 and 1968?
9. What were the significant changes in the public rehabilitation program created by the legislative Amendments of 1965 and 1968?
10. What are the major features of the 1973 Rehabilitation Act?

11. In what way did the 1974 Amendments extend the 1973 Rehabilitation Act?
12. What was the significance of Worker's Compensation laws to the rehabilitation program?
13. What was the composition of the Federal Board for Vocational Education, which administered the federal rehabilitation program in the early years?
14. In what year and for what purpose was a National Rehabilitation Advisory Council first formed?
15. What were the three options to states for the organizational location of a general vocational rehabilitation program resulting from the 1965 Amendments to the Vocational Rehabilitation Act?
16. In what state agency were most state rehabilitation programs organizationally located?
17. What were the purposes for organization of an umbrella agency, the Social and Rehabilitation Service, which included the federal rehabilitation program in 1967?
18. Organizationally, where was the Rehabilitation Services Administration assigned in 1975?
19. Why has the Veterans Administration always administered a rehabilitation program separate from the federal-state program?
20. What was the name of the first sheltered workshop in the United States, and when was it established?
21. What were the primary purposes of rehabilitation-related facilities sponsored by religious organizations?
22. The Sunbeam Circle, a volunteer group of women, was the origin of which major rehabilitation center?
23. Who was the founder of the ICD Rehabilitation and Research Center in New York?
24. What kind of services were, and are, offered by the Curative Workshop of Milwaukee?
25. Why were community mental health centers established?
26. When, why, and by whom was the National Rehabilitation Association organized?
27. What are some primarily parent organizations with interest in rehabilitation?
28. What are the purposes and some activities of the President's Committee on Employment of the Handicapped?
29. The Association of Rehabilitation Facilities is the result of a merger in 1969 between what two organizations?
30. The American Rehabilitation Counseling Association is a division of which major professional Association?

REFERENCES

Cruickshank, W. M., & Johnson, G. O. *Education of exceptional children and youth.* Englewood Cliffs, N.J.: Prentice-Hall, Inc., 1958.

Dean, R. J. N. *New life for millions: rehabilitation for America's disabled.* New York: Hastings House, Publishers, 1972.

Joint Commission on Mental Illness and Health. *Action for mental health: final report of the Joint Commission on Mental Illness and Health.* New York: John Wiley & Sons, Inc., 1961.

Kratz, J. A. Vocational rehabilitation, past, present, and future in the United States. In C. H. Patterson (Ed.), *Readings in rehabilitation counseling.* Champaign, Ill.: Stipes Publishing Co., 1960.

Lamborn, E. The state-federal partnership. *Journal of Rehabilitation,* 1970, *36*(5), 10-15.

Lassiter, R. A. History of the rehabilitation movement in America. In J. G. Cull & R. E. Hardy (Eds.), *Vocational rehabilitation: profession and process.* Springfield, Ill.: Charles C Thomas, Publisher, 1972.

LaVor, M. L., & Duncan, J. C. Rehabilitation Act of 1973, P. L. 93-112. *Exceptional Children,* 1974, *40*(6), 443-449.

McGowan, J. F., & Porter, T. L. *An introduction to the vocational rehabilitation process.* Washington, D.C.: Superintendent of Documents, Government Printing Office, 1967.

Nelson, N. *Workshops for the handicapped in the United States: an historical and developmental perspective.* Springfield, Ill.: Charles C Thomas, Publisher, 1971.

Obermann, C. E. *A history of vocational rehabilitation in America.* Minneapolis: T. S. Denison & Co., Inc., 1965.

United Cerebral Palsy Association, Inc. *By-laws of United Cerebral Palsy Association, Inc.* New York: UCPA, 1972.

ADDITIONAL READINGS

Department of Health, Education, and Welfare. Vocational rehabilitation programs.: implementation provisions, rules and regulation. *Federal Register,* 1974, *39*(235), 42470-42507.

Garrett, J. F. Historical background. In D. Malikin & H. Rusalem (Eds.), *Vocational rehabilitation of the disabled: an overview.* New York: New York University Press, 1969.

Jaques, M. Rehabilitation: historical origins. In C. H. Patterson (Ed.), *Readings in rehabilitation counseling.* Champaign, Ill.: Stipes Publishing Co., 1960.

Jaques, M. Treatment of the disabled in primitive cultures. In C. H. Patterson (Ed.), *Readings in rehabilitation counseling.* Champaign, Ill.: Stipes Publishing Co., 1960.

Risley, B. L., & Hoehne, C. W. The Vocational Rehabilitation Act related to the blind: the hope, the promise—and the reality. *Journal of Rehabilitation,* 1970, *36*(5), 26-31.

Switzer, M. Legislative contribution. In D. Malikin & H. Rusalem (Eds.), *Vocational rehabilitation of the disabled: an overview.* New York: New York University Press, 1969.

Thompson, R. C. Hotel continental. *Journal of Rehabilitation,* 1951, *17*(5), 15-18.

United States Senate and House of Representatives. *Rehabilitation Act of 1973,* Public Law 112, 93rd Congress, 1973.

United States Senate and House of Representatives, *Rehabilitation Act Amendments of 1974,* Public Law 516, 93rd Congress, 1974.

Whitten, E. B. The Rehabilitation Act of 1973 and the severely disabled. *Journal of Rehabilitation,* 1974, *40*(4), 2 & 39-40.

MEDIA RESOURCES

Visual

1. "History and Philosophy of the Vocational Rehabilitation Program in the United States" (140 slides with audiotape narration, 20 minutes). Developed by the Vocational Rehabilitation Division Training Center, Department of Human Resources, 505 Edgewater, N.W., Salem, Ore. 97304.

   Depicts the beginning of the rehabilitation movement and program in the United States including legislation through the proposed Rehabilitation Act in 1972.

2. "Federal and State Administration of the Vocational Rehabilitation Program" (85 slides with audiotape narration, 20 minutes). Developed by the Vocational Rehabilitation Division Training Center, Department of Human Resources, 505 Edgewater, N.W., Salem, Ore. 97304.

   Describes the roles of Congress and federal and state offices of vocational rehabilitation. An emphasis is given to the Oregon State rehabilitation agency administrative structure.

3. "The Rehabilitation Act of 1973" (16 mm film, 27 minutes). Developed by the West Virginia Research and Training Center, University of West Virginia, Institute, W. Va. 25112.

   An overview film of the 1973 Rehabilitation Act which highlights important changes from previous legislation and the implications for operation of vocational rehabilitation agencies.

4. "Understanding the Guidelines on the Rehabilitation Act of 1973 on Order of Selection, Priorities, Outcomes and Service Goals" (four-part slide-tape, study guide series, 60 minutes). Developed by the West Virginia Research and Training Center, University of West Virginia, Institute, W. Va. 25112.

   An interpretation of the 1973 Rehabilitation Act program guidelines, Section 2001.

5. "Understanding the Guidelines on the Rehabilitation Act of 1973 on the Individualized Written Rehabilitation Program" (slide-tape, study guide, 20 minutes). Developed by the West Virginia Research and Training Center, University of West Virginia, Institute, W. Va. 25112.

6. "Understanding the Guidelines on the Rehabilitation Act of 1973 on Post-Employment Services" (slide-tape, study guide, 20 minutes). Developed by the West Virginia Research and Training Center, University of West Virginia, Institute, W. Va. 25112.
7. "Expanding and Improving Service to the Severely Handicapped as Covered in the Rehabilitation Act of 1973" (four-part slide-tape, study guide series, 60 minutes). Developed by the West Virginia Research and Training Center, University of West Virginia, Institute, W. Va. 25112.
8. "Randolph-Sheppard Act" (slide-tape, audio cassette, or braille format). Available from The Center for Continuing Education in Rehabilitation, Box 1358, Hot Springs, Ark. 71901.

   A comprehensive introduction to the Randolph-Sheppard Act. Covers the origin of the Act, original provisions, weaknesses, and amendments and their effects.

Audio

1. "The Early Days of Vocational Rehabilitation" By H. B. Cummings (an interview with Frank H. Echols on audiotape, 48 minutes). Available from National Clearinghouse of Rehabilitation Materials, Oklahoma State University, Stillwater, Okla. 74074.
2. "The Early Days of Vocational Rehabilitation" By O. F. Wise (an interview with Frank H. Echols on audiotape, 48 minutes). Available from National Clearinghouse of Rehabilitation Materials, Oklahoma State University, Stillwater, Okla. 74074.
3. "The Federal-State Program of Vocational Rehabilitation in the United States" (tape, 98 minutes). Available from National Medical Audiovisual Center Annex, Station K, Atlanta, Ga. 30324.

   A 1966 audiotape which traces the growth of the federal-state program.

3

Rehabilitation process

OVERVIEW AND OBJECTIVES

This chapter provides the reader with an overview of the rehabilitation process that is utilized in the implementation of the public-private rehabilitation program in the United States. It is divided into two major sections (1) the sequence of rehabilitation services and (2) rehabilitation client programming.

Objectives of this chapter are to acquaint the reader with the public program status codes used to identify client progress through the rehabilitation process, to describe the services utilized during the rehabilitation process and the bases for client selection and program priorities, outcome, and service goals, and to detail the Individualized Written Rehabilitation Program for clients.

SEQUENCE OF REHABILITATION SERVICES

As indicated in Chapter 1, the rehabilitation process is a goal-oriented individualized sequence of services designed to assist handicapped persons in achieving vocational adjustment. The delivery of services is based on the development of a rehabilitation program, or plan, for the individual client. This program is the culmination of preliminary and thorough diagnostic studies.

A strength of the rehabilitation program in the United States is that it is goal oriented. Successful delivery of rehabilitation services will enable the disabled person to engage in employment or other gainful activity.

Status codes

To facilitate the implementation of the public program, the rehabilitation process is categorized in terms of status codes. These codes are intended to reflect the service delivery status and progress of clients through the rehabilitation process. There are sixteen two-digit and even-numbered status codes which range from 00 to 32. There is no status 04. Prior to the Rehabilitation Act of 1973, status 04 reflected a 6-month extended evaluation of applicant rehabilitation potential for those with disabilities which were not severe. However, all applicants may now receive up to 18 months of extended evaluation (status 06) for determination of service eligibility. Status codes can be divided into four major types—including referral processing (statuses 00 to 08), preservice (statuses 10 to 12), in-service (statuses 14 to 24; 32), and closure of active cases (statuses 26 to 30).

A flow diagram of the rehabilitation process as represented by the status codes is presented in Fig. 3-1.

Status 00 represents *referral* to the rehabilitation program. The referral may be from another agency or individual or a self-referral to the state rehabilitation agency. Whether by personal contact, telephone, or letter, the referral information should include: name and address of the disabled individual, the nature of the disability, age and sex of the individual, the date of referral, and the source of referral.

Status 02 represents *application* for rehabilitation services. This application can be made on an agency form or merely be a letter signed by the individual. While the individual is in this status, information is acquired by the rehabilitation counselor to make a determination of eligibility or ineligibility for rehabilitation services. The rehabilitation counselor may decide to provide an extended evaluation period to make such a determination (status 06).

Status 06 represents an *extended evaluation* period. In the event the rehabilitation counselor is unable to determine whether a client will vocationally benefit if provided rehabilitation services, he may authorize an extended period, not to exceed 18 months, in which to evaluate the person's rehabilitation potential and to determine eligibility or ineligibility for services.

Status 08 is an *ineligible closure* status for all persons processed through referral application and/or extended evaluation and not accepted into the active caseload for rehabilitation services.

Status 10 designates a person as eligible for rehabilitation services and permits *Individualized Written Rehabilitation Program development.* At this point the client becomes an active case. During this stage of the rehabilitation process, the counselor utilizes information from the thorough diagnostic study and, with the client's involvement, prepares an Individualized Written Rehabilitation Program of rehabilitation services for the client.

Status 12 is an administrative code representing *completion of the written program* of service for the client. The client remains in this status until the necessary arrangements are made with service delivery agencies for implementing the Individualized Written Rehabilitation Program.

Status 14 is intended as an in-service classification for cases which require *counseling and guidance only,* and possibly placement services, for preparing the client for employment. It should be noted, however, that counseling and guidance occur throughout the rehabilitation process and support other services. If other services are unnecessary for achieving the rehabilitation objectives and goal, status 14 is an appropriate categorization.

Status 16 represents *physical and mental restoration* services, including medical, surgical, psychiatric or therapeutic treatment, and/or the fitting of a prosthetic appliance.

Status 18 represents *training.* This status may be used to reflect almost any sort of learning situation, including school training, on-the-job training, tutoring, and training by correspondence. Many times physical or mental restoration services are also needed. In such cases the client is generally identified with the status which will represent the longest period of time.

Status 20, like status 12, is an administrative code indicating that the individual is *ready for employment*. The client has completed the preparation stages for employment and is either ready to accept a job or has been placed and has not yet begun employment.

Status 22 signifies that the client is *in employment*. Federal legislation requires that the client remain in this status a minimum of 60 days before being closed as successfully rehabilitated (status 26).

Status 24 is also an administrative classification which indicates *service interruption* in the rehabilitation process (statuses 14 to 22). The client remains in this status until he returns to one of the in-service statuses or his case is closed.

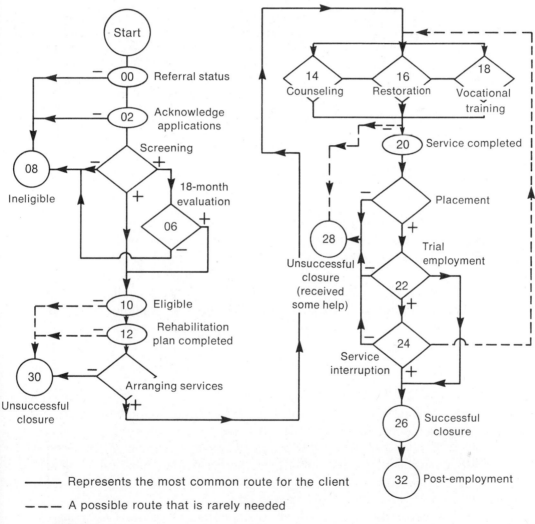

—— Represents the most common route for the client

——— A possible route that is rarely needed

FIG. 3-1

Flow diagram of the rehabilitation process. (Modified from Leary, P.A., & Tseng, M. S. The vocational rehabilitation process—explained. *Journal of Rehabilitation*, 1974, 40[1], 9, 34.)

Status 26 represents *closed, rehabilitated.* This status is the end result of the successful rehabilitation process. To be closed as successfully rehabilitated, the client must have been declared eligible for rehabilitation services, must have received appropriate diagnostic and related services, must have had an Individualized Written Rehabilitation Program, must have completed the program of services, and finally must have been determined to be suitably employed for a minimum of 60 days.

Status 28 indicates that the client's case is *closed for other reasons after the Individualized Written Rehabilitation Program* was initiated. Cases closed in this status have met the eligibility criteria for services and have been provided at least one of the services of the rehabilitation program but the client has not become successfully employed.

Status 30 represents cases *closed for other reasons before the Individualized Written Rehabilitation Program* was initiated. Such clients have been accepted for rehabilitation services but have not progressed to the point where any services were actually implemented under the Individualized Written Rehabilitation Program.

Status 32 is a *postemployment service* phase for assisting rehabilitated clients in maintaining employment. Any rehabilitation service that relates to the client's original goal and does not entail a new comprehensive effort may be provided.

Preliminary diagnostic study

A preliminary diagnostic study is conducted in the public program during the application stage of the rehabilitation process in order to determine whether the individual is eligible for rehabilitation services. This preliminary diagnostic study is for the purpose of determining whether the individual has a physical or mental disability which constitutes a substantial handicap to employment and whether services may be expected to help him achieve employment.

If the benefits of service cannot be anticipated on the bases of the preliminary diagnostic study, an extended evaluation of rehabilitation potential can be conducted to make such a determination. In all cases this preliminary diagnostic study includes a general health examination. If the client has a mental or emotional disorder, an examination must be provided by a psychiatrist or a licensed psychologist (Department of Health, Education, and Welfare, 1974).

Thorough diagnostic study

For each client in the public rehabilitation program, a thorough diagnostic study must be conducted to determine which services are needed. This comprehensive evaluation can include medical, psychological, vocational, educational, and other considerations that might relate to the person's handicap to employment. The findings of the study are then included in considering the Individualized Written Rehabilitation Program with the client.

Medical evaluation. The medical evaluation is one of the most important aspects of the evaluation process. In addition to identifying major and secondary disabilities, the medical evaluation helps identify any functional limitations or disabilities, particularly as they apply to occupations. The medical evaluation, it is hoped, will contribute to the decision to alleviate or remove the disabling condition; to appraise the capacity and limitations of the client in terms of rehabilitation potential and goals, and for determining how services might best be provided (McGowan & Porter, 1967).

Fundamental to the medical evaluation is obtaining a medical history of the patient/client. The medical history can provide valuable information as to diagnoses and rehabilitation procedures as well as insight to social and vocational problems. As a minimum, the medical history should include identifying information about the patient/client, his chief complaint, a history of present and past illnesses, a family history, the person's habits, a vocational history, a psychosocial history, and a systemic review.

The physical examination of a disabled patient/client includes conventional anatomic and pathologic data and information regarding the person's functional capacities. Basically the physical examination considers the disabled individual's general appearance, the head and the neck, the cardiovascular, respiratory, gastrointestinal, genitourinary, and the neuromuscular and locomotor systems. In cases of physical disability, the examining physician should include tests of muscle strength and range of motion of joints and an evaluation of the person's ability to perform daily living activities (Rusk, 1977).

The determination of rehabilitation program eligibility and subsequent services is the responsibility of the rehabilitation counselor in the federal-state program. Thus the state rehabilitation agencies employ medical consultants (M.D.s) to assist counselors. Consistent and regular medical consultation is needed during the rehabilitation process for clarification of terminology in reports, assessing medical feasibility and treatment results, and obtaining advice concerning medical management problems and the need for specialist exams.

Psychological evaluation. The primary purposes of psychological evaluations are to determine the nonphysical abilities and limitations of the disabled person and to identify attitudes, interests, motivations, and personality variables which will affect the formulation of an Individualized Written Rehabilitation Program and subsequent rehabilitation services. Psychological measures should be administered for specific purposes since not all abilities or all facets of personality are necessarily important for the rehabilitation of an individual (Rusk, 1977).

When psychological measures are used for determining rehabilitation potential and direction, it is important to remember that test information serves only as an aid in decision making. Thus the user of psychological information should attempt to cross validate information and seek patterns in the assessment data. It is generally useful to place test information for a client into perspective by including previous experiences and behavior. Many rehabilitation clients are also handicapped by emotional problems related directly or indirectly to their disability. The user of psychological information should then seek information regarding the client's reaction to the disability, feelings toward adjustment to the disability, and the effect of this disability upon his social adjustment in the community (McGowan & Porter, 1967).

Thus psychological evaluation involves assessing many variables which may help identify behavioral patterns and integrating this information into an Individualized Written Rehabilitation Program of services that can lead to successful adjustment and gainful activity by the client.

Sociocultural evaluation. Social and cultural information about a rehabilitation client is an integral part of planning in the rehabilitation process. A complete understanding of the client's disability necessitates learning the extent of disability and the nature of his reactions to this and other life experiences (McGowan & Porter, 1967).

A social and cultural evaluation generally involves obtaining a social history. This social history includes identifying information about the client, referral information, information about the client's present and previous medical history, a personal and family history (including information about the general climate of the home), an educational history, a work history, and information regarding the client's personality and habits and economic situation (McGowan & Porter, 1967).

When the total picture of the disabled person is being developed, it is also important to place all evaluation information into a cultural and environmental context. Individuals are a part of the constellation of factors inherent in their physical, social, and cultural surroundings and are influenced by the interaction between genetic endowments and the environment. Thus an understanding of a client's background and environment can help to more clearly discern the rehabilitation needs. Sociocultural information is usually obtained through an interview with the client. However, it can also be obtained, in part, by review of social service reports and anecdotal records that might be available. Additional sources are significant others in the disabled client's life: family, friends, teachers, and employers. The client's own social insights, skills, attitudes, and motivations are significant to an understanding of his self-perceptions and relationships to family members as well as to the community.

Vocational evaluation. In its broadest meaning, vocational evaluation includes all medical, psychological, social, cultural, vocational, and educational information which helps to define the rehabilitation client's problems and development of his vocational potential. As used here, however, it will pertain more narrowly to information and techniques for specifically assessing vocational aptitudes, potentials, and prognosis.

The best predictor of future performance is still past performance. Thus, for clients with a work history, information about previous jobs—including work habits, interests, attitudes, areas and degrees of responsibility, and relationships with other employees and with supervisors—represents very important pieces of vocational evaluation information.

For clients without a previous work history, the rehabilitation counselor must rely on assessments of the client's aptitudes and expressions of job interest and aspirations in predicting vocational potential. There are many paper-and-pencil measures and inventories to assess aptitudes and interests. In addition, there are work evaluation procedures which are helpful. The use of work samples, i.e., isolated work tasks that can be compared with standards for employed workers, is a common practice in rehabilitation. Situational assessment is another. The latter involves placing the rehabilitation client in a simulated or real work environment and assessing performance and behavioral adjustment. Another approach to vocational evaluation is to begin with an analysis of the job involving the identification of job requirements and the necessary worker traits for performance of the job and then relating the qualifications of the client to these requirements.

Perhaps the most useful approach to vocational evaluation is job-site rotation. When clients are placed in actual job situations for short evaluation periods, the advantages inherent in a previous work history are attained. Job-site evaluations offer the opportunity to test a client's interests, aptitudes, relationships to supervisors and other employees, and adjustments to varying work environments.

Educational evaluation. The educational evaluation process represents an attempt to identify the learning experiences of the disabled individual so his attitudes, knowledge, skills, and motivations can be understood. The primary purpose of an educational evaluation, of course, is to relate the disabled individual's repertoire of skills to vocational potential and goals. The educational evaluation for a client should include a determination of the attained level of education, including special areas of interest and achievement, an indication of learning capacity, information regarding study habits, an assessment of psychological reactions to educational situations, and information regarding extracurricular activities as they relate to learning.

In most cases, obtaining evidence of previous learning experiences will necessitate a visit to schools to examine school records and perhaps have conferences with school counselors and teachers. It may also necessitate administering educational tests to obtain a correct assessment of the individual's knowledge and capacities. Consideration of the individual's educational achievements in other than academic areas is also essential for evaluation of the client's potential for vocational adjustment and a fuller life after rehabilitation.

Extended evaluation

In the event that a determination of rehabilitation potential cannot be immediately made for an applicant but a physical or mental disability which is a handicap to employment has been established, the public program provides for an extended evaluation period. This extended evaluation cannot, however, exceed 18 months. By the end of 18 months, a decision must be made regarding an applicant's eligibility or ineligibility for rehabilitation services in the public program. Only one extended evaluation period can be permitted for each client unless a handicapped individual's needs have been determined to have significantly changed. In decisions of ineligibility, so the rights of individuals to service by the public program will be protected, it must be determined beyond any reasonable doubt that an applicant cannot be expected to benefit in terms of employability (Department of Health, Education, and Welfare, 1974).

Individualized Written Rehabilitation Program

The Individualized Written Rehabilitation Program (IWRP) is a plan jointly developed by the rehabilitation counselor and the handicapped person or, if the person is incapable of independent judgment, the parent, guardian, or appropriate representative. It is a continuously developed plan for each eligible applicant for rehabilitation services or individual in extended evaluation.

The primary emphasis in developing an IWRP is on the determination and achievement of a vocational goal. As a minimum, the IWRP includes (1) the basis for determination of eligibility or extended evaluation, (2) a long-range employment goal, (3) intermediate rehabilitation objectives related to the attainment of the employment goal, (4) identification of specific vocational rehabilitation services necessary to achieve the employment goal, (5) the expected date for initiation of each service and the anticipated duration of these services, and (6) a procedure and schedule for evaluation of progress toward the rehabilitation objectives and the employment goal. In addition, the client or an appropriate representative must be involved in the development of the plan and be informed of his rights and appeal procedures if dissatisfied (Department of Health, Education, and Welfare, 1974).

Counseling and guidance

Though counseling and guidance are integral parts of the provision of most services in rehabilitation, they may also be a distinct and separate service. As has been mentioned, when counseling is the only service needed by the client in addition to job placement the client is considered to be in status 14.

Counseling is the synthesizing function of the rehabilitation process (Malikin & Rusalem, 1969). It is the function which addresses the holistic nature of humans. It is also the counseling function that integrates separate disciplinary practice into a comprehensive approach for serving the individual. Though there are many counseling theories and techniques advocated, there are many more similarities than differences among these. The ultimate goal of counseling is a helping relationship between the counselor and the counselee culminating in improved client function.

Physical and mental restoration

Physical and mental restoration refers to health-related services that are important to correct physical or mental conditions which interfere with optimal functioning of the rehabilitation client. Examples might be medical, physical, and therapeutic treatment, and/or prosthetic appliances. It can include the many services of physical medicine, physical therapy, occupational therapy, communication therapy, rehabilitation nursing, orthotics and prosthetics, and psychiatry (Department of Health, Education, and Welfare, 1974; Rusk, 1977).

Training

In rehabilitation, training refers to the broad range of learning opportunities and experiences which will help the client progress to the employment goal of the Individualized Written Rehabilitation Program. Jarrell (1972) classifies rehabilitation training into four broad areas: (1) personal adjustment training, (2) prevocational training, (3) compensatory skill training, and (4) vocational training.

Personal adjustment training refers to the development of habits and attitudes which are related to adjustment in the world of work. Examples are dependability, responsibility to others, tolerance, consistency, and capacity for time considerations (Bitter, 1968). *Prevocational training* refers to the background knowledge needed to select and become ready for occupational skill development. It is a preparatory stage for vocational skill training. Program examples are familiarity with occupations through field tours, job-site rotation, and reading. It also includes learning to complete employment applications, using public transportation, and managing an income. Many work adjustment programs combine personal adjustment training and prevocational training. *Compensatory skill training* refers to the development of personal skills that compensate for disability and that may be important for employability. Examples are speech reading, gait training, and mobility training for the blind. *Vocational training* involves the development of specific job skills. These skills may be obtained in numerous ways—through trade and vocational schools, colleges and universities, apprenticeship programs, rehabilitation facilities, sheltered workshops, and on-the-job training.

Job placement

In a vocationally oriented program, job placement represents the culmination of the entire rehabilitation process. Job placement is important in the restoration of an individual to the highest level of functioning of which he is capable. To have been a successful process, the employment situation must be commensurate with the abilities, interests, and potential of the rehabilitated client. Job placement is very complex and often underrated, involving matching the individual to the appropriate job. The process necessitates recognizing relationships between client variables and work environment variables. The former include both personal factors and job skill factors; the latter are all the considerations inherent in the job.

No two work environments are exactly alike (Bitter, 1968). Thus effective job placement requires that the rehabilitation counselor or placement specialist have a thorough knowledge of the community and its resources. In addition, the professional worker must be skilled in job analysis to be able to understand the requirements of the job. Job engineering may also be involved, entailing minor job modifications to help the employer and client fully benefit from the client's skills. It should be noted, however, that job placement is a mutual responsibility of the rehabilitation counselor and client which is considered early in the rehabilitation process. The counselor and the client must work together if they are to effect a vocational outcome that will truly reflect the restoration of the client to his fullest level of vocational functioning.

Postemployment services

Postemployment services are provided in the rehabilitation process after clients are vocationally rehabilitated to assist them in maintaining employment. Postemployment service might be any rehabilitation service(s); but activities should be related to the client's original Individualized Written Rehabilitation Program.

At a minimum, continued counseling may be essential; however, postemployment service may also include any rehabilitation service that does not entail a complex or comprehensive new rehabilitation effort. Such postemployment services may be either a one-time performance or a combination extended over a period of time. There is no limit on the duration of postemployment services in the public rehabilitation program. Some examples of postemployment services are supplementary training resulting from a change in job requirements, health services, arrangements with other agencies for home help, wheelchair repair, and transportation subsidy if needed (Department of Health, Education, and Welfare, 1974; West Virginia Research and Training Center, 1975).

Other services

Maintenance support, through financial payments, may be made available to clients to cover their basic living expenses—including food, shelter, clothing, and any other subsistence that may be important for achieving the rehabilitation goal of the handicapped person.

Transportation support may also be provided to rehabilitation clients to make possible the provision of services. Relocation and moving expenses are also available if related to the achievement of rehabilitation goals.

Services to *family* members of a handicapped individual are oftentimes important for the adjustment of clients to their rehabilitation goals. This and any other *support* service may be provided in the public rehabilitation program if important to the individualized rehabilitation process. Examples of support services are supervision and management for small business enterprises (consultation, accounting, inspection, etc.), occupational licenses (needed to enter an occupation or a small business), tools, equipment, and supplies, interpreters for the deaf, readers and mobility service for the blind, technological aids and devices, and any assistance which might benefit the handicapped individual in achieving employability.

REHABILITATION PROGRAMMING
Client selection and priorities

The Rehabilitation Act of 1973 required that state rehabilitation agencies establish priorities for serving the handicapped. This, of course, is necessary only if the agency is unable to provide services to all who apply and are eligible or who are in need of an extended evaluation of rehabilitation potential to determine their eligibility. First priority must, according to legislation, be given to the most severely disabled. The 1973 legislation intended that this group should not be denied services or be delayed or deferred because of the complexity of the case, the cost, or the time it takes to successfully rehabilitate a severely disabled person. State agencies may, however, assign subsequent priorities to other disabling conditions, depending on local areas of concern.

Outcome and service goals

After the identification of client selection priorities, state rehabilitation agencies are required to establish outcome and service goals for each priority group. Thus, at a minimum, a state agency must establish such outcomes and service goals for the severely disabled. These must be stated in terms that are measurable. For example, if an agency goal is to expand rehabilitation services to spinal cord injured clients, then a measurable objective might be to serve 15% more severely disabled spinal cord injured clients during the next 12 months. To be useful, agency goals should generally be expressed in terms which can provide for service expansion or program improvement. An example might be to develop new service delivery resources or improve referral procedures or methods to expedite service delivery. Thus the establishment of outcomes and service goals becomes a policy and planning function of rehabilitation agencies (West Virginia Research and Training Center, 1974; Rehabilitation Services Administration, 1975a).

Individualized Written Rehabilitation Program

The Individualized Written Rehabilitation Program (IWRP) was mentioned earlier in this chapter under the "Sequence of Rehabilitation Services." The IWRP is a case planning and management tool. It identifies the basis for determination of eligibility or need for extended evaluation. It also identifies the terms and conditions of the program, for example, client financial participation, availability of rehabilitation funds, availability of class openings in training programs, any potential possibilities for delay in implementing the program and client responsibilities. If there is dissatisfaction with the provision of services, the rights of the client for an administrative review and a fair hearing are also noted. The IWRP is signed by the rehabilitation counselor or other representative of the agency and the client receives a copy. The IWRP may be amended with any appropriate change anytime during the rehabilitation process; again with client involvement.

The Individualized Written Rehabilitation Program represents a plan of action and a statement of mutual understanding. Though the client is not compelled to sign the IWRP or its amendments, the program should be developed with the client's full participation, understanding, and acceptance. In addition to specifying the basis for applicant eligibility for service, the IWRP contains five primary service-related content areas—including a long-range employment goal, intermediate rehabilitation objectives, specific rehabilitation services, duration of services, and evaluation of progress.

The *long-range employment goal* represents the aim of the rehabilitation process. It is the ultimate realistic vocational achievement of the client and should be based on his interests, abilities, and physical and mental potential. Formulation of a long-range employment goal offers the potential of a goal-directed activity which gives continuous consideration to job placement rather than serves merely as one step at the end of the rehabilitation process.

Intermediate rehabilitation objectives represent the series of steps designed to help the client achieve the long-range employment goal. Examples of objectives might be physical restoration, personal adjustment, and the development of vocational skills.

The IWRP also identifies *specific rehabilitation services* directly related to achievement of the intermediate rehabilitation objectives and the vocational goal. Examples might be physical therapy, adjustment counseling, vocational training, purchase of a wheelchair, or development of skills for independent living. However, where possible, the statement of rehabilitation services to be provided to the client should be specific.

The *duration of services* is also specified in the IWRP for each of the planned services. The anticipated date for initiation of each service should be identified and scheduled in a manner which will maximize the benefits of an orderly, sequential rehabilitation process.

The last content area of the IWRP is *evaluation of progress* toward attainment of the long-range employment goal. To be useful, the IWRP ought to outline the criteria for evaluating client progress. Factors that can be used to assess progress include counselor assessments, self-reports of the client, training progress reports, grades, and medical reports. A formal review of the IWRP is required by public program regulations at least annually. However, a review of progress should be a continuous process and formal sessions may be conducted at any time and may be initiated by either the counselor or the client. The results of such reviews should be recorded and the IWRP redeveloped or amended as appropriate. A number of alternatives are available in the event the client is not making satisfactory progress toward attainment of intermediate objectives and the long-range goal. The levels of achievement may be reconsidered, the appropriateness of the objectives may be reevaluated, the dates for achievement of objectives may be reset, or if necessary services may be terminated (Rehabilitation Services Administration, 1975b).

The following are examples of completed Individualized Written Rehabilitation Programs used in two state rehabilitation agencies:

State A
Individualized Written Rehabilitation Program

Client's name
1841 North 17th St.
City, State, Zip code

Date _____ 6-10-78
Elig. or EE date _____ 6-2-78
Disability code _____ 220
Approved by _____ J.B.
DOT code _____ 219.488

1. Vocational goal _Clerk accounting_
2. Tentative objectives for extended evaluation _N/A_

INTERMEDIATE REHABILITATION OBJECTIVES

1. Arrange for baby sitter for surgeries
2. Physical restoration
3. On-the-job training
4. _____

SUMMARY OF PLANNED SERVICES

Following is a list of some of the key services planned for the future. It does not include services already provided and may omit certain continuing services (such as counseling and guidance).

	Service	Projected date to begin	Cost
1.	Bilateral simple mastoidectomies	July 1978	$1033
*2.	Bilateral myringoplasties	Oct. 1978	$1050
3.	On-the-job training	Oct.-Dec. 1978	0
4.			

*To include fees for surgeon, anesthesiology, hospitalization.

Continued.

CLIENT PARTICIPATION IN COSTS OF SERVICES AND SIMILAR BENEFITS

Summary of the client's participation in the cost of planned services, or the availability of similar benefits for which the individual is eligible (i.e., VA, scholarships, etc.)

None

CLIENT'S VIEWS REGARDING GOAL, OBJECTIVES, AND SERVICES PLANNED

Without rehabilitation I could not restore my hearing and, perhaps, work. Knowing that there is still help for people like myself is greatly appreciated. Rehab has been very helpful to my family. Thank you. (written by client)

(Attach additional sheets, if necessary)

REVIEW AND EVALUATION OF PROGRESS

Procedure: Periodic review of progress toward intermediate vocational objectives and goal is made to determine case progression. The results of the scheduled reviews and evaluations of progress will be discussed with the client and summarized as an entry in the written program. For extended evaluation, a minimum of one review each 90 days is required; the total case must be reviewed annually.

Schedule	Criteria and outcome
4-79	Successful job performance as reported by employer and job satisfaction as reported by client.

(Attach additional sheets, if necessary)

EXPLANATION OF CLIENT RIGHTS

I have been informed of my rights and the manner in which I may appeal if I am not satisfied. I have actively participated in the development of my rehabilitation plan.

Signed: _____

Client—Parent or Guardian

June 14, 1978

Date

Counselor

State B
Individualized Written Rehabilitation Program

Program of services ☒ Extended evaluation ☐

Name _____(client)_____ Case no. __6734__ Soc. Sec. no. __342-61-9735__

Vocational goal ____Millwright foreman____ (DOT code) ____638.131____

When will vocational goal be reached? __September 1979__

Rehabilitation services	Projected date to begin	Anticipated duration	Vocational rehabilitation cost
Counseling and guidance	May 1979	4 mo	—
Job placement	May 1979	4 mo	—

Narrative explanation. Include how services are in accord with needs and limitations of client, long-range goal and intermediate objectives, client participation, and any additional pertinent information.

Client experienced cardiac infarction while working as a millwright and feels pessimistic about employment future. His physical condition is class II-C, which suggests some discomfort in ordinary activity and moderate restriction of physical activity. Present employer is willing to place him on light assembly work. Counseling and guidance service is intended to help client adjust to disability. Job placement discussions will be pursued with employer for light physical work and, possibly, employer preparation for foreman responsibilities. Client will be gradually reintegrated to full-time employment with employer and progress in terms of adjustment assessed by employer's reports of client's work record.

I have participated in the development of this program. The program will be renegotiated at the desire of either myself or my rehabilitation counselor. My rights have been explained to me and I am aware of the right to appeal grievances as well as the manner of appeal.

_____ _____May 4, 1979_____
Client signature   Date

_____ _____May 4, 1979_____
VR Counselor signature   Date

SUMMARY

The rehabilitation process is characterized by a goal-oriented, individualized, sequence of services. The process is standardized and facilitated in the public program through the use of service delivery status codes which, in effect, reflect client progress toward the rehabilitation goal.

Two diagnostic studies are conducted early in the rehabilitation effort. The *preliminary* diagnostic study is for the purpose of determining applicant eligibility for services. The *thorough* diagnostic study is intended to determine which services are needed by the individual to become rehabilitated. The latter evaluation may include medical, psychological, sociocultural, vocational, and educational assessments, depending on the client's need. If necessary, an extended evaluation period of up to 18 months can be provided for determining whether services will benefit an individual in terms of employability.

The Individualized Written Rehabilitation Program for clients is the heart of the rehabilitation process. The IWRP is a plan for client services. The program identifies a basis for service, an employment goal, intermediate objectives, rehabilitation services and their duration, and criteria for evaluation of progress. Services may include counseling and guidance only, or physical restoration, training, maintenance, transportation, family and other support services may be employed to assist the disabled person in achieving employability. After job placement any rehabilitation service which will assist a client in maintaining employment may be provided so long as it does not entail a new rehabilitation effort.

Due to 1973 rehabilitation legislation, the severely disabled must receive first priority for service. In addition, agencies must establish outcome and service goals for each priority group of disabled identified for service.

Thus the rehabilitation process represents a systematic approach to helping the disabled achieve the maximum independent functioning of which they are capable.

SELF-EVALUATION QUESTIONS

1. What are the characteristics of the rehabilitation process?
2. What are the four types of status codes which characterize the rehabilitation process?
3. Who may make a referral to the rehabilitation program?
4. What is the purpose of an extended evaluation period of up to 18 months?
5. What is status 08?
6. At what point (status code) does an individual become an active case?
7. What are the "administrative" status codes?
8. When would a client be in status 14?
9. When multiple services are provided simultaneously, which status code would generally be used?
10. How long must a client remain in employment before successful closure can be considered?
11. Service interruption is reflected by which status code?
12. What are the criteria for closing a client as successfully rehabilitated (status 26)?
13. What is the difference between status 28 and status 30?
14. What postemployment services (status 32) may and may not be provided?
15. What is the purpose of the preliminary diagnostic study?
16. What content areas should be considered in the thorough diagnostic study?
17. Why is a medical history an important part of the medical evaluation?
18. What are the primary purposes for employing medical consultants in the public rehabilitation program?

19. What are the primary purposes of psychological evaluation?
20. What are some ways in which sociocultural information about a client can be obtained?
21. What is the best predictor of future work performance?
22. What are some general ways to obtain vocational assessment information about a client?
23. What kinds of information about a client should be included in an educational evaluation?
24. What are the content requirements of the Individualized Written Rehabilitation Program?
25. What are the major types of training in the rehabilitation program?
26. What is job engineering?
27. What are some examples of support services?
28. To what group of applicants must rehabilitation agencies give first priority for service as required by the Rehabilitation Act of 1973?
29. In what form should outcome and service goals of an agency be stated?
30. Must the client sign the Individualized Written Rehabilitation Program?
31. How often is a review of the Individualized Written Rehabilitation Program for a client required?
32. What alternatives might be considered if a client is not making satisfactory progress toward his intermediate rehabilitation objectives and long-range employment goal?

REFERENCES

Bitter, J. A. Toward a concept of job readiness. *Rehabilitation Literature,* 1968, 29(7), 201-203.

Department of Health, Education, and Welfare. Vocational rehabilitation programs: implementation provisions, rules and regulations. *Federal Register,* 1974, 39(235), 42470-42507.

Jarrell, G. R. Selective training. In J. G. Cull & R. E. Hardy *Vocational rehabilitation: profession and process.* Springfield, Ill.: Charles C Thomas, Publisher, 1972.

Leary, P. A., & Tseng, M. S. The vocational rehabilitation process explained. *Journal of Rehabilitation,* 1974, 40(1), 9, 34.

Malikin, D., & Rusalem, H. *Vocational rehabilitation of the disabled: an overview.* New York: New York University Press, 1969.

McGowan, J. F., & Porter, T. L. *An introduction to the vocational rehabilitation process.* Washington, D.C.: Superintendent of Documents, Government Printing Office, 1967.

Rehabilitation Services Administration. *Guidelines: order of selection priorities and outcomes and service goals* (Draft). Washington, D.C.: RSA, Department of Health, Education, and Welfare, 1975a.

Rehabilitation Services Administration. Individualized written rehabilitation program. *Rehabilitation Services Manual* (Chapter 1507). Washington, D.C.: RSA, Department of Health, Education, and Welfare, 1975b.

Rusk, H. A. *Rehabilitation medicine.* St. Louis: The C. V. Mosby Co., 1977.

West Virginia Research and Training Center. *Understanding the guidelines for the Rehabilitation Act of 1973 on order of selection, priorities, outcomes, and service goals.* Institute, W. Va.: West Virginia Research and Training Center, 1974.

Wooster, J. H. *An introduction to rehabilitation counseling: a manual for counselors.* Helena, Mont.: Division of Vocational Rehabilitation, 1970.

ADDITIONAL READINGS

Gellman, W. Fundamentals of rehabilitation. In J. F. Garrett & E. S. Levine (Eds.), *Rehabilitation practices with the physically disabled.* New York: Columbia University Press, 1973.

Hardy, R. E. Vocational placement. In J. G. Cull & R. E. Hardy (Eds.), *Vocational rehabilitation: profession and process.* Springfield, Ill.: Charles C Thomas, Publisher, 1972.

Hoffman, P. R. Work evaluation: an overview. In J. G. Cull & R. E. Hardy (Eds.), *Vocational rehabilitation: profession and process.* Springfield, Ill.: Charles C Thomas, Publisher, 1972.

Institute on Rehabilitation Services. *Medical consultation in vocational rehabilitation* (Rehabilitation Services Series No. 65-46). Washington, D.C.: Rehabilitation Services Administration, Department of Health, Education, and Welfare, 1965.

McGowan, J. Referral, evaluation, treatment. In D. Malikin & H. Rusalem (Eds.), *Vocational rehabilitation of the disabled: an overview.* New York: New York University Press, 1969.

Sinick, D. Training, job placement, follow-up. In D. Malikin & H. Rusalem (Eds.), *Vocational rehabilitation of the disabled: an overview.* New York: New York University Press, 1969.

West Virginia Research and Training Center. *Understanding the guidelines for the Rehabilitation Act of 1973 on expanding and improving services to the severely handicapped: the referral process.* Institute, W. Va.: West Virginia Research and Training Center, 1975.

MEDIA RESOURCES

Visual

1. "The Vocational Rehabilitation Process" (140 slides with audiotape cassette, 30 minutes). Developed by the Vocational Rehabilitation Division Training Center, Department of Human Resources, 505 Edgewater, N.W., Salem, Ore. 97304.

    Provides an overview of the rehabilitation process, including referral, screening, intake, evaluation, eligibility determination, job placement, closure, and follow-up.

2. "Expanding and Improving Services to the Severely Handicapped as Covered in the Rehabilitation Act of 1973" (four-part slide-tape, study guide series, 60 minutes). Developed by the West Virginia Research and Training Center, University of West Virginia, Institute, W. Va. 25112.

    Describes approaches to evaluating rehabilitation potential, intake, and referral and identifying the severely handicapped.

3. "Understanding the Guidelines on the Rehabilitation Act of 1973 on Order of Selection, Priorities, Outcomes and Service Goals" (four-part slide-tape, study guide series, 60 minutes) Developed by the West Virginia Research and Training Center, University of West Virginia, Institute, W. Va. 25112.

    Interprets the Rehabilitation Act of 1973 guidelines in four parts: (1) Order of Selection and Priorities, (2) Disabled Public Safety Officers, (3) Administrative Concerns, (4) Outcomes and Service Goals.

4. "Understanding the Guidelines on the Rehabilitation Act of 1973 on the Individualized Written Rehabilitation Program" (slide-tape and study guide, 20 minutes). Developed by the West Virginia Research and Training Center, University of West Virginia, Institute, W. Va. 25112.

    An interpretation and suggested strategies for implementation of the Individualized Written Rehabilitation Program. The study guide contains examples and exercises.

5. "Understanding the Guidelines on the Rehabilitation Act of 1973 on Post-Employment Services" (slide-tape and study guide, 20 minutes). Developed by the West Virginia Research and Training Center, University of West Virginia, Institute, W. Va. 25112.

    An interpretation of the public rehabilitation program guidelines for postemployment services to successfully rehabilitated clients.

6. "Evaluating the Retarded Client" (16 mm color film). Developed by Audiovisual Center, Film Rental Services, University of Kansas, 746 Massachusetts, Lawrence, Kan. 66044.

    Illustrates the importance of utilizing various professionals for assessing medical, cognitive, emotional, and behavioral assets and limitations of clients as well as the need for continuously evaluating client progress.

7. "Training Resources and Techniques" (16 mm color film). Developed by Audiovisual Center, Film Rental Services, University of Kansas, 746 Massachusetts, Lawrence, Kan. 66044.

    Depicts the rehabilitation counselor as a coordinator for acquiring a variety of training resources in developing a comprehensive treatment plan for retarded clients.

8. "Placement: The Goal of Vocational Rehabilitation" (slides with audiotape cassette, 20 minutes). Developed by the West Virginia Research and Training Center, University of West Virginia, Institute, W. Va. 25112.

Overview of job placement as part of the rehabilitation process including client and job development, placement, postemployment services, and follow-up.

Audio

1. "Guide for Completion of the RSA-300" (audiotape cassette with programmed manual, 30 minutes). Developed by the West Virginia Research and Training Center, University of West Virginia, Institute, W. Va. 25112.

   Provides guidance in completing the RSA-300 form regarding client information in the rehabilitation process.

2. "Collecting Information from the Client" (audiotape cassette with printed transcript, 32 minutes). Available from Materials Development Center, University of Wisconsin–Stout, Menomonie, Wis. 54751.

   Describes approaches for obtaining client information.

3. "Casefinding and Referral: Getting the Deaf Client into Rehabilitation" (audiotape cassette, 45 minutes). Developed by Arkansas Rehabilitation Research and Training Center, Hot Springs Rehabilitation Center, P. O. Box 1358, Hot Springs, Ark. 71901.

   Discusses methods of getting deaf persons into the rehabilitation process.

REHABILITATION CLIENTS

The purpose of Section Two is to give the reader some understanding of the nature and effect of disability for rehabilitation clients.

There are two chapters. The first, Chapter 4, uses a common format for describing fifteen disabilities. Though these are not the only disabilities in rehabilitation programming, they are representative of those emphasized by the Rehabilitation Act of 1973 as potentially severe. A feature of this chapter is its focus on the vocational problems and rehabilitation service considerations for each disability. Also included is an explanation for the construction of medical terms and some common medical abbreviations. Chapter 5 gives a brief orientation to some adjustment considerations for the disabled and describes a sample of vocational adjustment approaches and programs.

4

Disabilities

OVERVIEW AND OBJECTIVES

This chapter presents the reader with a brief orientation to medical terminology and an overview of 15 disabilities commonly dealt with in rehabilitation. Each disability is described in terms of etiology, classifications, vocational problems, and rehabilitation service considerations. Major objectives of this chapter are to assist the reader to understand the structure of medical terms and become acquainted with basic information about various disabilities, particularly as they relate to the delivery of rehabilitation services.

MEDICAL TERMINOLOGY

Medical terminology facilitates communication within the medical community or profession. Though often confusing to the layman, medical terms are intended to offer preciseness in communicating about anatomical references and pathological conditions. In addition, many abbreviations are intended to provide some sort of organization to communication in medicine. However, there are inconsistencies in the system; and the layman would be well advised to utilize the context in which a word is presented as an aid to understanding. The availability of a good medical dictionary is indispensable to understanding medical reports, records, and communications.

Though medical terms have many origins, most come from Greek or Latin words. Many come from other languages—including German, Italian, Japanese, Chinese, and Arabic. Others come from the names of persons and places. Still others are fabricated by pharmaceutical firms (Felton, Perkins, & Lewin, 1966). It is not the intent of this section to offer a comprehensive glossary of medical terms and abbreviations. Rather, it is hoped that a brief orientation to vocabulary will assist the reader toward understanding medical terminology. An excellent text and student workbook for building a medical vocabulary is *Learning Medical Terminology Step By Step* by Young and Barger.

Analysis of terms

The structure of medical terms generally involves root words, prefixes, and suffixes. The root word, or stem, usually refers to some definite object, for example, a part of the body. The prefixes (which precede the root word) and the suffixes (which follow the root word) are modifying terms. The prefix usually defines the relationship of the root word to its environment. The suffix generally describes the condition or act formed on the root word. Examples of prefixes to root words are *hyper* (excessive) thyroid, *endo* (within) thoracic (chest), *micro* (small) hepatica (liver). Examples of suffixes and their relationship to root words are psych (mind) *ology* (knowledge), appendic (appendix) *itis* (an inflammation), crani (skull) *ectomy* (excision).

Prefixes. A prefix describes (1) a deviation from normal, (2) the relationship between the root word and its environment, or (3) the relationship of another object to the root word. Examples follow:

Word element	Meaning	Example
a	without; not	aphonia (without speech)
ab	from; off; away from	abduct (to draw away from center or median line)
ad	to	adduct (to draw toward center or median line)
antero	in front of	anteroposterior (directed from front toward back)
ana	upwards; again; backwards; excessively	anaphylaxis (excessive protective reaction)
bi	two	bicellular (made up of two cells)
dys	bad; difficult	dysentery (literally, bad intestine)
endo	within; inward	endotracheal (within trachea)
ex	out; away from	exhalation (expulsion from lungs)
exo	outside; outward	exophytic (growing outward)
hemi	half	hemicrania (pain affecting only one side of head or cranium)
homo	same; similar	homoplasty (transplantation of tissue of same source as tissue it replaces)
hyper	abnormally increased; excessive	hyperacidity (excessive acidity)
hypo	abnormally decreased; deficient	hyporeflexia (diminution or weakening of reflexes)
intra	in; within	intracerebral (within brain or cerebrum)
macro	large	macrocyte (abnormally large red blood corpuscle)
micro	small	microcoria (smallness of pupil)
mono	one	monogenic (pertaining to or influenced by single gene)
neur	nerve	neuritis (inflammation of nerve)
odon	tooth (dens)	odontology (sum of knowledge of teeth)
patho	disease; morbid condition	pathogen (any disease-producing agent or microorganism)
pan	all	panarthritis (inflammation of all joints)

Word element	Meaning	Example
para	beside	parasternal (beside sternum)
peri	around; near	periarterial (around artery)
post	after; behind	postcibal (after eating)
pre	before	preaxial (in front of axis of body)
sub	under; less than	subiliac (below ilium)
super	above; excessive	superficial (situated on or near surface)
thrombo	clot; thrombus	thromboplastic (causing clot formation in blood)

Suffixes. Generally a suffix describes a condition of, or an act performed on, the root word. Some examples are *itis,* meaning an inflammation; thus pancreatitis would refer to an inflammation of the pancreas. Similarly *otomy* refers to an incision. Pancreatotomy, then, would refer to an incision of the pancreas. Other common examples of suffixes, their meaning, and their use are the following:

Word element	Meaning	Example
algia	pain	myalgia (muscular pain)
emia	blood	hypoglycemia (deficiency of sugar in blood)
ectomy	excision; surgical removal	appendectomy (excision of vermiform appendix)
genic	giving rise to; causing	psychogenic (originating in mind)
iasis	condition of	mydriasis (great dilatation of pupil)
itis	inflammation	adenitis (inflammation of gland)
metry	measurement	pelvimetry (measurement of capacity and diameter of pelvis)
ology	knowledge	odontology (sum of knowledge of teeth; dentistry)
osis	disease; morbid state; abnormal increase	osteosclerosis (abnormal hardness of bone)
pathy	morbid condition or disease (generally used to designate noninflammatory condition)	neuropathy (any disease of nervous system, especially degenerative [noninflammatory] disease of nerve or nerves)
penia	poverty; scarcity	thyropenia (diminished thyroid secretion)
pexy	surgical fixation	nephropexy (surgical fixation of freely movable kidney)
plasty	formation or plastic repair of	hernioplasty (surgical repair of hernia, with reconstruction of muscle or tissue wall)
rhea	profuse flow	rhinorrhea (copious mucus discharge from nose)
scopy	examination of	bronchoscopy (inspection of interior of tracheobronchial tree with bronchoscope)

Many abbreviations are used in the medical field. The following represent some common examples. However, a word of caution is necessary. As with medical terms, it is important to decipher the meaning of abbreviations from the context in which they are used. In different locations abbreviations have varied meanings.

Abbreviation	Meaning
a̅a̅	of each
a.c.	before meal (ante cibum)
Aq.	water
b.i.d.	twice a day (bis in die)
B.P.	blood pressure
C.A.	chronologic age
cc	cubic centimeter
cg	centigram
C.N.S.	central nervous system
CVA	cerebrovascular accident (stroke); cardiovascular accident
ECG	electrocardiogram
EEG	electroencephalogram
E.N.T.	ear, nose, and throat
G.I.	gastrointestinal
gm	gram
GU	genitourinary
h.s.	at bedtime (hora somni)
I.M.	intramuscular
I.V.	intravenously
mm	millimeter
OB	obstetrics
O.D.	right eye (oculus dexter); Doctor of Optometry
O.S.	left eye (oculus sinister)
O.U.	both eyes together or each eye (oculus uterque)
p.c.	after meal (post cibum)
Q.	quadrant; electric quantity
q.s.	a sufficient amount (quantum satis)
R.B.C.	red blood cells; red blood (cell) count
ss	one half (semis)
T	temperature time

The foregoing abbreviations are certainly not exhaustive of those used throughout the practice of medicine; rather, they are intended to serve as a few examples. It is highly recommended that the practitioner in rehabilitation obtain a good medical dictionary which contains both medical terms and abbreviations as an aid in understanding and communicating about disabilities. A useful recommended edition is *Dorland's Pocket Medical Dictionary.*

The balance of this chapter will briefly describe 15 types of disability that are often served in rehabilitation programming: alcoholism, arthritis, blindness and visual impairments, cardiovascular disease, deafness and hard of hearing, developmental disabilities (cerebral palsy, epilepsy, mental retardation), drug abuse, neurological disorders, orthopedic disabilities, psychiatric disabilities, renal failure, speech impairments, and spinal cord conditions.

ALCOHOLISM

Alcoholism is considered an illness. It is characterized by excessive drinking which leads to intoxication and is a chronic and complex disease which interferes with an individual's health and his emotional, occupational, and social functioning. It can involve physiological, sociological, and psychological factors. Physiologically the individual loses the ability to metabolize alcohol. Sociologically alcohol may be a means for the individual to adjust to a social system. Psychologically the drinking may be an escape from underlying, stressful personality dynamics (Sixth Institute on Rehabilitation Services, 1968).

Etiology

Addiction to alcohol is a disease that can occur in many kinds of people. At the present time there are no known causes. There has been no agreement on the identity of personality factors or traits associated with alcoholics or that certain personality traits may be the cause or result of excessive consumption. Nor has there been research to indicate that physiological, nutritional, metabolic, or generic defects might explain the etiology of alcoholism. Though not yet determined, it is suspected that the process of addiction may be similar to the process in diabetes. The liver is involved, and it is possible that some people cannot correctly metabolize alcohol with increased consumption.

Higher incidence rates for alcoholism have been found in some ethnic groups —including the Northern French, Americans, Swedes, Swiss, Poles, and Northern Russians—yet low incidence rates in others have been noted—such as among Italians, some groups of Chinese, orthodox Jews, Greeks, Portugese, Spaniards, and Southern French. Also it has been found that the lowest incidence of alcoholism is generally associated with healthy and moderate attitudes toward drinking (Sixth Institute on Rehabilitation Services, 1968).

Classifications

The American Psychiatric Association (1968) classified drinking problems into three categories: *episodic excessive drinking,* which results in the individual becoming intoxicated as many as four times a year; *habitual excessive drinking,* when individuals are intoxicated more than twelve times a year or are under the influence of alcohol more than once a week; and *alcohol addiction,* which reflects a dependence on alcohol characterized by the appearance of withdrawal symptoms. Should continuous heavy drinking continue for more than 3 months, addiction to alcohol is presumed.

Vocational problems

Vocationally, excessive drinking results in absenteeism, tardiness, and a diminished quality in the performance of job-related responsibilities. Interpersonal relationships are also affected. Alcoholics often become impatient and lose their ability to communicate meaningfully with other people. They are, many times, unrealistic about their own aptitudes and their level of functioning. Some alcoholics are capable of giving the impression that they are much more skilled than they really are. Many do have skills but are unable to function up to capacity because of excessive drinking (Sixth Institute on Rehabilitation Services, 1968).

Rehabilitation service considerations

The Sixth Institute on Rehabilitation Services (1968) reported the following six major treatment approaches for alcoholism:

1. *Acute detoxification.* This is generally needed by most alcoholic clients. The treatment program usually involves about 1 week of treatment for acute withdrawal symptoms. Preferably it can be accomplished in a hospital, but treatment can also be conducted on an outpatient basis in a clinic or office. The alcoholic should be removed from crisis situations which could precipitate drinking and be involved in the planning for continued treatment. A thorough medical evaluation and treatment for anxiety or depression are generally necessary. Such treatment may be in the form of tranquilizers and/or antidepressants and could be expected to extend for two or three years.

2. *Chronic detoxification.* This involves continuous medical treatment following acute detoxification. Such medical treatment generally involves medication, diet, and laboratory studies every 2 months until the condition is stabilized or the individual has recovered. When the liver is involved, vitamin therapy administered intramuscularly is generally recommended twice weekly in the beginning, but decreasing to every two weeks after three months. Treatment for other physical disabilities, such as emphysema, anemia, ulcers, gastritis, should also be part of the treatment program. Clients requiring chronic detoxification are generally over 60 years of age and alcoholism has been a problem for more than fifteen years. Usually their drinking has plateaued and there is liver damage. Some associated characteristics include diabetes, anemia, emphysema, neuritis, and perhaps arthritis.

3. *Environmental restructuring.* This involves moving the client away from the conditions which are conducive to drinking. Such an approach attempts to break old patterns. It could involve moving the individual closer to the clinic or other treatment resources and arranging for positive contact with members of the helping professions—such as a minister, physician(s), rehabilitation counselor,

or Alcoholics Anonymous sponsor. Individuals most likely to benefit from such environmental restructuring include those who are homeless, unstable, in difficulty with the law, of limited intellectual capacity, or suffering from psychosis.

4. *Supportive therapy*. This consists of counseling and low-pressure support for individuals with dependency needs, social deprivation, depression, repression, or rigidity. Sometimes supportive therapy can be an important influence for individuals who are affected by a role change (for example, a divorce) or who have a symptomatic fixation (for example, backache, breathing difficulty, or fear of a heart attack). Supportive therapy can also assist the individual to remain on a job while adjustment and changes slowly evolve.

5. *Internal change therapy*. Such therapy might involve group therapy, individual counseling, orientations through movies and discussion, and social casework. Internal change therapy is often helpful for persons who drink only in sprees, show some evidence of job and family stability, or have the intellectual capacity for abstract thinking.

6. *Treatment for the counteralcoholic*. A counteralcoholic is the significant other person whose own needs are being met by the alcoholic's drinking behavior. Such an individual might be a spouse, parent, child, employer, or landlord. Treatment for the counteralcoholic is important to the recovery of the alcoholic and may include individual or joint interviews, involvement in group therapy, or involvement in Alcoholics Anonymous.

It is important to remember that alcoholics have individual differences. Each person with a drinking problem must be approached in an individualized manner. Physical or emotional addiction to alcohol exists in all kinds of people. Individuals who are to be effective helpers must be willing to accept these differences, must have considerable patience, must be willing to fail and to allow the client to fail, must be aware of their own emotional needs and defenses, and must be able to tolerate ambiguity from the client.

It is most important in the treatment of alcoholics that a comprehensive and coordinated approach to services be provided for each client. The treatment of alcoholism requires a multidisciplinary approach which might involve many helping professionals including physicians, psychologists, public health workers, social workers, ministers, employers, law enforcers, rehabilitation counselors, peers, and mental health workers. Since most treatment approaches seem to do some good, the alcoholic client must be assisted with a coordinated multidisciplinary program of rehabilitation.

ARTHRITIS

The term arthritis means inflammation of a joint. There are basically two pathological processes which affect joints: one is characterized by inflammation in multiple joints, which may spread to other parts of the body, as in rheumatoid arthritis; the other is characterized by deterioration of the cells which make up the structure of the joint, as in osteoarthritis.

Etiology

Rusk (1977) reports that there are more than a hundred different causes of arthritis. However, most arthritics can be identified by seven major causes: (1) arthritis due to specific infection, (2) arthritis due to rheumatic fever, (3) rheumatoid arthritis and rheumotoid spondylitis of unknown cause, (4) arthritis due to direct trauma, (5) arthritis due to gout, (6) degenerative joint disease (osteoarthritis) due to age or joint injury, and (7) nonarticular rheumatism due to emotional stress (Miller & Obermann, 1968; Rusk, 1977). Rheumatoid arthritis, degenerative joint disease, and nonarticular rheumatism account for at least two thirds of all arthritic disorders.

Classifications

The causes of arthritis also serve to classify the disease. Rusk (1977) lists thirteen classifications of arthritis and rheumatism accepted by the American Rheumatism Association:

1. Polyarthritis of unknown etiology—for example, rheumatoid arthritis
2. Connective tissue disorders
3. Rheumatic fever
4. Degenerative joint disease—for example, osteoarthritis
5. Nonarticular rheumatism
6. Diseases frequently associated with arthritis—for example, ulcerative colitis
7. Known infectious agents
8. Traumatic and/or neurogenic disorders
9. Known biochemical or endocrine abnormalities—for example, gout
10. Tumor and tumorlike conditions
11. Allergies and drug reactions
12. Inherited and congenital disorders
13. Miscellaneous disorders

Vocational problems

Arthritis is generally a progressive disease—that is, it worsens with time. The vocational problems presented by arthritis are due mainly to the limited range and motion of affected joints and muscle weakness. In addition, the emotional stress resulting from the disability and requirements of the job are important vocational considerations in job placement. The physical capacities of the worker should match the physical demands of the job. Some physical activity is necessary for muscles to be exercised and retain their strength since muscle weakness aggravates joint stability and contributes to the disability. A job which is too strenuous, however, can further irritate the disability and cause continued pain, inflammation, and destruction (Miller & Obermann, 1968).

Rehabilitation service considerations

The rehabilitation of the arthritic client involves a team approach to the whole individual and involves medical, psychosocial and vocational rehabilitation. Rusk (1977) lists seven factors that influence attainment of rehabilitation goals, including (1) medical control of the disease process, (2) the extent of damage to the joints, (3) the psychologic well-being of the client, (4) functional training for activities of daily living; (5) corrective surgery, if necessary, (6) the applicability of self-help devices, and (7) the vocational and socioeconomic resources of the client. Basically the medical objective for all arthritic individuals is to suppress the inflammation, control pain, maintain maximal functional range of motion in the joints, and preserve muscle strength (Hylbert, 1965; Miller & Obermann, 1968; Rusk, 1977). However, corrective surgery is sometimes helpful in protecting joints against further deterioration. Similarly the principal objectives for physical therapy are to maintain functional independence and protect the joint structures against further damage.

Functional training in activities of daily living is also important for helping the client to become maximally independent. If necessary, there are many self-help devices on the market for assisting arthritic clients—including devices for dressing, feeding, and sitting, wheelchairs, crutches, and implements to make work in the home easier (Rusk, 1977).

The psychological well-being of the arthritic client is essential for achieving rehabilitation goals. It is easy for an arthritic to become depressed and dependent. Thus there is a need for supportive counseling. The person will need emotional strength to cope with the stresses imposed by the disability (Felton, Perkins, & Lewin, 1966; Rusk, 1977).

Vocational considerations for arthritic clients must take into account that arthritis is most often a progressive disease; thus, it gets worse with time. Vocational evaluation should include an assessment of the individual's physical capacity including dexterity, eye-hand coordination, and ability to work in different positions. Certain types of work are generally unsuitable for arthritic persons—jobs that require temperature changes, work in inclement weather and humid situations, heavy physical labor or labor which requires excessive and repetitive use of the same muscles, work requiring performance of the same task for long periods of time, and work producing emotional stress for the client (Miller & Obermann, 1968; Graves & Bowman, 1974). Some clients also will have limited physical ability to use public transportation.

Rheumatoid arthritis presents the main vocational rehabilitation problem. Gouty arthritis does not cause severe disability. Osteoarthritis occurs in advanced ages. The rheumatoid arthritic, however, is often in the prime working years of life. Since such persons are likely to deny having a disability, they represent a real psychological challenge to the vocational rehabilitation professional (Felton, Perkins, & Lewin, 1966).

BLINDNESS AND VISUAL IMPAIRMENTS
Etiology

Rusher (1972) outlines six common causes of visual impairment: (1) hereditary conditions, (2) congenital conditions, (3) trauma, (4) infections, (5) metabolic conditions, and (6) degenerative conditions.

Blindness in infants is generally caused by congenital defects—for example, cataracts as a result of rubella (German measles) in the mother during the first 3 months of pregnancy. The rubella virus affects the eye of the embryo, causing lens defects.

The prevalent problem in children is injury to the eye, particularly between the ages of 5 and 15 years. Such injuries can be caused by wounds, chemicals, or any of many foreign objects in the eye.

In adults the most common disease of the eye is glaucoma, an internal eye disease in which the intraocular pressure is increased to the point of causing damage to the retina and optic nerve. The disease is generally categorized as primary, in which there is no antecedent ocular disease, and secondary, in which preexisting ocular disorders are present. Most glaucomas are caused by a defect in the mechanism of the eye that drains fluid and results in pressure on the retina leading to eventual destruction (Johnson, 1965; Felton, Perkins, & Lewin, 1966; Rusher, 1972).

Classifications

Legal blindness generally means that the central visual acuity of a person does not exceed 20/200 in the better eye with correcting lens. It can also mean that vision in the better eye is limited to a field less than 20° wide, called tunnel vision.

Visual impairments can be classified into (1) errors of refraction, including nearsightedness (myopia), farsightedness (hyperopia), astigmatism, and presbyopia (farsightedness due to loss of elasticity of the lens occurring with aging), (2) incoordination, as in crossed eyes (strabismus), (3) opacities, resulting from cataracts in the lens, inflammations that scar the cornea, or fibrous tissues behind the lens, (4) retinal disabilities, such as detachments of the retina or growths within the eye which interfere with the retina, and (5) miscellaneous conditions primarily injury, disease, or infection of the eye or parts (Hylbert, 1965).

Vocational problems

The blind or visually impaired person can be employed in many kinds of work, depending on his abilities, aptitudes, interests, and personality. Perhaps the most important consideration in the vocational adjustment and placement of the blind or visually impaired person is the psychological impact of the disability. If the individual's only disability is visual, the primary limitation may be general education, specific vocational training, and/or psychological adaptation to the disability (Felton, Perkins, & Lewin, 1966).

Rehabilitation service considerations

Paramount in the rehabilitation process is the acceptance and adjustment of the blind or visually impaired person to the disability. Blindness imposes many complications for an individual, particularly in terms of orientation, mobility, and communication. It is important for the individual to develop good space orientation and use the other senses to their maximum extent. Guidance and travel can be aided by the use of a long cane (red-tipped white), various electronic and mechanical sensory aids, seeing-eye dogs, or another person. Many if not most blind individuals learn to use a long cane for providing information about terrain. Use of a dog as a guide necessitates training the dog and the blind person.

Communication can be enhanced for blind individuals if they learn to read and write braille. Through braille and recorded talking books and taped materials the blind have access to literature. Learning to use the typewriter can also be an immense aid for communication. In addition, human readers for the blind are available through the public rehabilitation program. If possible, using a tape recorder in the performance of job or daily living activities can be of considerable help in everyday living (Hylbert, 1965; Johnson, 1965; Felton, Perkins, & Lewin, 1966).

Perhaps the most significant rehabilitation legislation for the blind authorized in the history of the United States rehabilitation program was the Randolph-Sheppard Act of 1936. This Act authorized states to license qualified blind persons to operate vending facilities such as cafeterias, snack bars, cart services, and vending machines in federal buildings. The Randolph-Sheppard Act was amended in 1974 to increase economic opportunities for the blind and to assist them in becoming self-supporting.

For the visually impaired, or partially sighted, person the primary rehabilitation objective is to protect present eyesight and facilitate the remaining sight with aids. The use of shields, goggles, glasses, and proper lighting is important for preventing further damage to the eyes. Optical aids are also available to the partially sighted—including eyeglasses, binoculars, and closed circuit television systems that permit them to see well enough to type from a printed or handwritten manuscript.

CARDIOVASCULAR DISEASE

Cardiovascular disease is a major rehabilitation problem. It is the primary cause of death in the United States. There are six primary types. *Arteriosclerotic* heart disease is the most common. It results from a narrowing of the coronary arteries and prevents the heart from getting sufficient blood to supply the needed oxygen. *Congenital* heart disease is a disorder resulting from a defect in the heart prior to birth. *Hypertensive* heart disease develops as a result of increased pressure in the arteries; this pressure increase puts added strain on the heart. *Rheumatic* heart disease generally occurs in childhood as a result of rheumatic fever and leads to heart valve abnormality. Rheumatic fever is a complication of streptococcal infection. *Congestive* heart failure is a complication of cardiovascular disease rather than a disease of the heart; it occurs when the heart is unable to pump sufficient blood to meet the requirements of the body.

Etiology

Cardiovascular heart diseases are caused by diabetes, high blood pressure, high cholesterol levels, and hypothyroidism. Other contributors to cardiovascular diseases are believed to exist—including sugars, cigarette smoking, obesity, and the absence of physical activity. There also seems to be a greater chance for cardiovascular disease if the person has a family history of heart disease.

However, the primary cause of cardiovascular heart disease is believed to be type A behavior, a complex of emotional reactions characterized by aggressiveness and a desire to achieve more and more in less and less time. The type A personality has a sense of urgency and an obsession with numbers, often resulting from attempting to accomplish too much in the time available. The type A personality also has much aggressive drive, reflecting itself in general hostility. Such a person tends to compete or challenge other people whether in business or in recreational activity. The opposite of type A behavior is type B. Though the type B person may be just as ambitious, this person is not plagued by the desire to obtain an increasing number of things in less and less time and thus may be less likely to develop cardiovascular disease (Friedman & Rosenman, 1974).

Vascular diseases relate to the arteries, veins, and lymphatic vessels. They are caused by a deficiency in the circulation of the blood due to narrowing of the vessels, obstruction in the vessels, inflammation caused by injury or infection, expansion of the vessel walls, or malfunction in the transfer of blood between the arteries and veins (Spodick, 1965).

Classifications

The New York Heart Association (1964) classified cardiovascular diseases into *functional* and *therapeutic*. The classifications are important for knowing what the client can do and for prescribing therapy.

There are four functional classes: class I suggests that ordinary physical activity does not cause undue fatigue or anginal pain, and thus there is no limitation of physical activity; class II may have a slight limitation of physical activity (these people are comfortable at rest; however, ordinary physical activity results in fatigue); a class III person is markedly limited in physical activity; though such a client may be comfortable at rest, less than ordinary physical activity causes fatigue, rapid heart beats, shortness of breath, or anginal pain; a class IV person is unable to carry on any physical activity without discomfort.

The therapeutic classes are as follows: class A—physical activity need not be restricted in any way; class B—ordinary physical activity need not be restricted, but the client should be advised against severe competitive efforts; class C—ordinary physical activity should be moderately restricted and more strenuous efforts discontinued; class D—ordinary physical activity should be markedly restricted; class E—complete rest, confined to bed or chair.

Vocational problems

Fear and depression are the major obstacles to a cardiac client's returning to employment. Though most cardiac clients require changes in their work habits, many believe they will be unable to ever work again. In addition, there is often a reluctance on the part of employers to hire a person with a cardiac disorder; such clients are believed to be a greater risk in terms of recurrence and possibly higher insurance rates.

Rehabilitation service considerations

As with other disabilities, cardiac rehabilitation involves a team approach. Because of the emotional aspect of cardiac disease, many cardiac clients will require supportive counseling. However, most of these people can return to their original occupation.

To aid in assessing and controlling the amount of work the heart does, physiologists have developed a measure called the *metabolic equivalent unit,* referred to as a "met." A met is a measurement unit of metabolic heat and is equal to 1.3 calories of effort in 1 minute. The system enables numerical values to be assigned to various activities. For example, doing desk work or sweeping the floor involves 2 or less mets. Bartending, auto repair, or light welding involves 2 to 3 mets. Bricklaying, cleaning windows, and stocking shelves involves 3 to 4 mets. This system can then be related to the functional classifications of the New York Heart Association. For example, if a client is classified as functional class I, his capacity is in the range of 6 to 9 mets, meaning he could probably undertake all physical activities, except competitive exertions. For a class II client the maximum expenditure of effort should be less than 4.5 mets. For class III clients it is 3 mets, and for class IV clients 1 to 1.5 mets (Franklin, Krauthamer, Razzak, & Pinchot, 1974).

Some examples of vocational and recreational activities classified by mets by Franklin et al. (1974) are listed on p. 72.

Mets	Vocational	Recreational
2 or less	Desk work	Walking 1 mph
	Driving	Playing cards
	Sweeping floor	Painting
2-3	Custodial	Walking 2 mph
	Typing	Bowling
	Peeling vegetables	Golf, riding cart
	Light woodworking	Fishing
3-4	Bricklaying	Walking 2½ mph
	Mopping	Pitching horseshoes
	Machine assembly	Volleyball, noncompetitive
	Wiring house	Golf, pulling cart
		Sailing small boat
4-5	Interior carpentry	Dancing
	Paperhanging	Gardening
	Raking leaves	Walking 3 mph
		Golf, carrying clubs
		Tennis, doubles
5-6	Light digging	Walking 3½ mph
	Shoveling	Ice skating
	General industrial labor	Bicycling 10 mph
	House construction	
6-7	Mowing lawn by hand	Walking 5 mph
	Splitting wood	Competitive badminton
	Shoveling snow	Tennis, singles
		Square dancing
		Water skiing
		Cross-country skiing
		Down hill skiing, slow
7-8	Digging ditches	Jogging 5 mph
	Carrying 80 pounds	Downhill skiing, vigorously
		Mountain climbing
		Basketball
8-9	Moving van work	Running 5½ mph
	Tending furnace	Handball and Squash
		Competitive basketball

Other considerations in cardiac rehabilitation are to avoid jobs with emotional stress, hot and cold extremes, and toxin-produced stresses. In addition, cardiac clients need to control their diet and weight by limiting caloric and fat intake, curtail the use of tobacco and alcohol, and get sufficient rest. If possible, the cardiac client must return to work. Returning to activity helps the individual cope with the situation realistically and maintain personal and family organization.

DEAFNESS AND HARD OF HEARING

Deafness refers to a total loss of hearing or such loss that the individual's hearing is nonfunctional for ordinary purposes of life. *Hard of hearing* refers to a partial loss. The person may have defective hearing but may be functional with or without a hearing aid (Felton, Perkins, & Lewin, 1966).

Etiology

Hearing disorders are classified into two types: *conductive loss* and *sensorineural loss*. A conductive loss is an impairment which affects the outer and middle ears in the sound conductive pathways; a sensorineural loss is an impairment which affects the inner ear or the auditory nerve.

The causes of conductive hearing loss are blockage, infection, and otosclerosis. Blockage is the most common and may result from a buildup of earwax, a swelling in the ear, or a growth. A conductive loss by infection is usually due to inflammation in the middle ear. The infection induces fluid to accumulate; the fluid creates pressure on the eardrum. In addition to pain, the pressure immobilizes the eardrum and the conductive hearing loss ensues. Otosclerosis is a hardening of the stapes (in the middle ear). The stapes is thereby prevented from transmitting sound vibrations.

Sensorineural hearing losses are caused by conditions affecting the nerve endings within the inner ear. As people become older, there is a natural deterioration of the sensory processes. Toxic conditions can also affect these sensitive nerve endings. Toxicoses can be produced by viral infections, including measles, scarlet fever, and mumps, or by drugs taken externally to treat some other condition. Toxins are carried to the inner ear by the circulatory system; there they affect the nerve endings in the cochlea. Another cause of sensorineural impairments is Meniere's disease. The origin of this disease is unknown; but fluid is produced and builds up in the inner ear, creating intense pressure that affects the sensitive nerve endings. Intense noise or a break in the bone surrounding the inner ear can also cause a sensorineural hearing loss. It is also possible to have a mixed hearing loss (i.e., conductive and sensorineural) resulting from a combination of causes (Storrs, 1973).

Classifications

Hearing impairments can be classified in several different ways: (1) deafness and hard of hearing, (2) conductive, sensorineural, and mixed hearing losses, or (3) prelingual and postlingual hearing losses.

To explain hearing loss, audiometric testing and evaluation are used. An audiometer measures the range of hearing in a scale represented by decibels. It is an electrical instrument that can provide pure tones of variable pitch and intensity. Zero on the decibel scale represents the threshold of hearing and is the smallest sound the normal ear can hear. Conversation heard from 12 feet repre-

sents about 50 decibels. The usual threshold for feeling discomfort is 110 decibels. A loss of hearing more than 80 decibels is profound loss; 60 to 80 decibels
is very severe loss; 40 to 60 decibels is moderately severe; 20 to 40 decibels,
moderate; and 15 to 20 decibels, only a slight loss which is probably insignificant
but should be monitored periodically.

Vocational problems

The major employment problem for the deaf is not unemployment but under-
employment (Eleventh Institute on Rehabilitation Services, 1973). Some of the
barriers to employment for deaf and hard-of-hearing persons are the requirements for normal hearing imposed by employers, entrance examinations which
emphasize verbal skills, and misunderstanding about the abilities of deaf people.
The most significant employment limitation affecting the deaf and hard of hearing, though, is being able to communicate with others.

The Eleventh Institute on Rehabilitation Services (1973) study group indicated that only 30% of spoken English is visible on the lips. This makes it very
difficult for deaf people, even with good speech-reading skills, to function in a
verbal environment. Such language barriers often contribute to educational
shortcomings during the formative years and place these people at a considerable
disadvantage in terms of employment. Consequently the life experiences of the
deaf are more restricted than are the life experiences of hearing persons. Language learning is made increasingly difficult if a child loses the ability to hear
before beginning to talk. Loss after the child has learned to speak, however, may
only involve basic learning skills upon which to build in a near normal fashion
(Costello, 1973).

The limited life experiences of the deaf also affect adjustment once the person has obtained a job. Cull and Hardy (1974) indicate that the greatest single
vocational problem for the deaf is not the acquisition of job skills but the adjustment problems on the job. Work habits and attitudes are important to success
in employment for the deaf. The nature of the job can also be an important con-
tributor to success or failure in employment. For example, many deaf persons
with sensorineural loss hear less well in noisy surroundings. Because sensorineural deafness frequently occurs in higher frequencies, speech is difficult to
understand. This hearing loss will be complicated by a noisy environment.

Rehabilitation service considerations

The extent of hearing loss is important to the nature of the rehabilitation services. A conductive loss sometimes will require only a hearing aid and some
speech-reading training. Sensorineural involvement may or may not be helped
with a hearing aid, and considerable speech-reading and auditory training may
be necessary. A mixed hearing loss involving both conductive and sensorineural
impairments will require more extensive services.

There are two frequently used tests to determine whether a hearing loss is conductive or sensorineural: the *Weber* and the *Rinne*.

The Weber Hearing Test utilizes a tuning fork which is set in motion and placed on the client's forehead. If both ears are equal in their hearing loss, the client will report the tuning fork as being in the middle of the head. If the client indicates that the tuning fork is heard in the poor ear, he has conductive deafness. If it is heard in the better ear, he has a sensorineural impairment.

The other test, the Rinne Hearing Test, also uses a tuning fork. The otologist sets the fork in motion and holds it close to the client's external ear. When it is no longer heard, it is placed on the mastoid process. If the client can again hear it, the loss is conductive. If the fork cannot be heard by bone conduction, the hearing loss is sensorineural (Walker & Holbert, 1973).

Surgery. Sensorineural deafness is generally irreversible. However, in the case of conductive deafness, surgery is possible to restore some or all of a persons hearing. This is true only if the loss is due to mechanical difficulty within the eardrum, the middle ear, or the ossicular chain. It is also now possible to replace with a biosynthetic eardrum hearing organs which have been ruptured through infection or an accident.

Hearing aids. For hard-of-hearing persons there are four types of hearing aids on the market—including aids which can be worn on the body, within eyeglasses, behind the ear, and in the ear.

The hearing aid worn on the body is a relatively large instrument capable of producing high levels of amplification. It is the most powerful of the hearing aids and can provide a wide frequency range for people with very severe hearing impairments. It is capable of a variety of power, volume, and tone-control settings. An advantage of the body hearing aid is that it can be adapted for telephone pickup.

The eyeglass hearing aid is intended for persons who wear glasses and have a mild to moderate loss in hearing. The amplifying unit is located in the bow of the glasses. It is capable of providing amplification for people with hearing losses up to 75 decibels. In this type of hearing aid, a short length of tubing connects the unit to an ear mold worn by the user.

The behind-the-ear hearing aid is also for mild to moderate hearing impairments. It consists of an amplifying unit molded to fit behind the ear of the user. When the microphone is placed at the ear level, the problem of clothing noise commonly encountered with the body hearing aid is reduced.

The in-the-ear hearing aid is a miniaturized unit that also can be used for mild to moderate hearing losses. Because of its size, it does not have a wide frequency band, is not as powerful as other types, and is limited in the quality of its sound. However, the in-the-ear hearing aid is helpful for persons who would not otherwise use a hearing aid (for cosmetic reasons) and for those who would use the hearing aid in some situations but not others (Walker & Holbert, 1973).

Communication training. Perhaps the greatest service need for the deaf and hard of hearing is in the area of communication training. There are three types: speech reading, auditory training, and sign language. Speech reading is the ability to read lips and other speech-related visual clues. The greater the hearing loss, the more valuable is speech reading to the hearing-impaired person. Auditory training attempts to help the individual become an attentive listener and is generally done in conjunction with a hearing aid. Emphasis is on discrimination and sound selection. Sign language is the use of manual symbols for communicating. It is an easily learned process that can facilitate communication among the deaf and between the deaf and normal-hearing persons. Many professionals working with the deaf believe "total communication," which involves all aspects of communication including speech reading, sign language skills, facial expression, and body language, facilitates communication with the deaf.

Employment. Persons with conductive hearing loss adjust more readily to noisy situations than do those with sensorineural impairments. Sensorineural impairments are usually accompanied by tinnitus (subjective ringing noises). The condition can be aggravated on noisy jobs. If dizziness or balance problems are associated with the hearing loss, employment in high places or around dangerous machinery is not advisable.

A rehabilitation program should not overlook emphasis on personal and social adjustment. This emphasis should be on the development of personal behavior patterns to facilitate effective relationships with others. Similarly the development of work attitudes and behaviors will not only stimulate the deaf person but also assist in the person's effort to become a more satisfactory employee.

DEVELOPMENTAL DISABILITIES

The term *developmental disabilities,* coined with the passage of the Developmental Disabilities Services and Facilities Construction Act in 1970 (Public Law 91-517), amended by the Developmental Disabled Assistance and Bill of Rights Act (Public Law 94-103), and again amended by the Rehabilitation Act Amendments of 1978 (Public Law 95-602), refers to a developmental disability as a severe chronic impairment that originates before the age of 22, continues indefinitely, and constitutes a substantial handicap (see page 10). In many cases these individuals do not have the potential for independent functioning and require lifelong services. The three primary groups of developmental disability described here are cerebral palsy, epilepsy, and mental retardation.

CEREBRAL PALSY

Cerebral palsy is a condition, not a disease, caused by damage to the brain. *Cerebral* refers to the brain, and *palsy* to the lack of control over the body's muscles.

Etiology

The condition known as cerebral palsy can happen at any time, but it generally occurs during the prenatal or paranatal period. Perhaps the chief cause is an insufficient supply of oxygen reaching the infant's brain. However, it can also result from an awkward birth position, labor that lasts too long, interference with the umbilical cord, or premature separation of the placenta from the wall of the uterus. Other causes are premature birth, blood type incompatibility between the parents, infection of the mother with German measles, or a viral disease during early pregnancy.

Postnatal causes of cerebral palsy are generally due to disease. Examples are meningitis, encephalitis, scarlet fever, rheumatic heart disease, tumors, toxins, and brain injury (McLarty & Chaney, 1974).

Classifications

Cerebral palsy is generally classified according to observable symptoms, ranging from mild to severely handicapping.

1. *Spastic*. Characterized by stiffness of the muscles and jerky movements. More than half the cases of cerebral palsy are estimated to be of the spastic type.
2. *Athetotic*. Characterized by slow wormlike involuntary movements of the extremities. It occurs in about 25% of cerebral palsy cases.
3. *Rigidity*. Limbs resistant to movement. This type of cerebral palsy is sometimes called "lead pipe" rigidity.
4. *Ataxic*. Characterized by an imbalance while walking.
5. *Tremor*. An uncommon type of cerebral palsy evidenced by rhythmic movements which are involuntary and uncontrollable.

Not all cerebral palsied individuals fall neatly into the five classifications; many have combinations of the foregoing types (Allen, 1962; Robinault & Denhoff, 1973; Rusk, 1977).

Vocational problems

The involuntary muscular movements of cerebral palsied individuals makes it difficult for them to find employment, particularly if physical work or movement is involved. The cerebral palsied individual is also often psychologically traumatized by the disability. Most suffer from emotional stress and have some sort of perceptual defect. In addition, many have speech problems or hearing defects. Vocational problems may include a low tolerance for the physical demands of work, poor interpersonal skills, and difficulty in mastering the activities of daily living (McLarty & Chaney, 1974).

Rehabilitation service considerations

Cerebral palsy is not a progressive disease. Sometimes surgery can help muscle coordination. Medication may reduce nerve damage symptoms like contractures, seizures, and tension. Braces can help reinforce muscles or correct deformities.

To prevent error in estimating the individual's full potential, a complete psychological evaluation is important. The adult cerebral palsied individual has probably experienced a life of attention to his physical development and neuromuscular needs. As a result his education and social experiences may have been somewhat neglected. Thus Denhoff and Robinault (1960) believe educational and social experiences should be a primary consideration, particularly as the individual progresses through school years into adulthood.

A rehabilitation program for the cerebral palsied should begin with prevocational activities, that is, efforts to help accomplish positive interpersonal relationships, independence, and attitudes of personal and social responsibility (Allen, 1962). The rehabilitation of the cerebral palsied necessitates a team approach involving physical, occupational, speech, and hearing therapy as well as very carefully planned programs of vocational and social adjustment.

EPILEPSY

Barnes and Krasnoff (1973) define epilepsy as a "chronic episodic disturbance in function of the central nervous system which is characterized by one or more of the following usually transitory features: disruption of consciousness, convulsions, and alteration in sensory, motor, autonomic, cognitive, and affective status."

There are as many different symptoms of epilepsy as there are epileptics. However, Rodin (1975) indicates that all epileptic seizures have the following characteristics in common:

1. They are involuntary.
2. They last less than a few minutes.
3. They are similar on various occasions.
4. They always involve purposeless stereotyped and repetitive behavior.
5. Consciousness is usually adversely affected.

Etiology

The onset of epilepsy can occur at any age. Though there is not conclusive evidence, some form of generalized seizures are thought to be inherited. However, focal seizures (i.e., partial seizures occurring in only a part or parts of the body) are more likely to be related to lesions in the brain. Epilepsy may also be caused during birth as a result of trauma, inadequate oxygen to the brain, blood incompatibility, low blood sugar, or maternal infection as by syphilis or German measles. Epilepsy may be acquired after birth due to infections of the nervous system or to toxins like alcohol and lead. The condition can result from head injury, brain tumor, or obstruction in an artery which results in the loss of blood to an area of the brain (Dreifuss, 1975).

Classifications

The most common types of seizures are (1) *grand mal,* (2) *petit mal,* (3) *psychomotor,* and (4) *focal motor*.

Grand mal seizures are the most common and also the most dramatic forms of attack. A grand mal seizure may last several minutes and is usually preceded by some sensory experience or warning. The epileptic may emit a cry at the start of the convulsion, lose consciousness, and fall. During this stage the muscles contract and the body stiffens. This is followed by muscular contractions in the form of jerky movements. Because an individual is unable to swallow during a seizure, there may be excessive salivation; when mixed with air, the saliva appears as foam. After the seizure there is a period of stupor or sleep which may last up to 4 hours. The individual often does not remember what occurred during the seizure and will usually have sore muscles and a headache and be very tired. Grand mal seizures may occur at any time and be as frequent as several times in one day or only once in several years (Barnes & Krasnoff, 1973; Wright, 1975).

Petit mal seizures are very brief losses of consciousness, lasting only a few seconds or, at most, 1 or 2 minutes. They may be very difficult to detect. A person with a petit mal seizure may stare into space, flick the eyelids, or have slight jerking movements. In contrast to grand mal seizures, petit mal seizures are quite frequent, occurring perhaps as often as a hundred times in one day. The onset generally is during childhood and tends to either disappear after age 18 or be replaced by other types of seizures such as grand mal (Barnes & Krasnoff, 1973; Wright, 1975).

Psychomotor seizures are thought to result from focal lesions in the temporal lobe of the brain. They affect both the motor system and the mental processes. The individual may stare or become confused and engage in purposeless motor movements such as running around in a circle. Some persons experience fear, alarm, irritability, or depression. Though the individual is not unconscious, generally the experience is not recalled (Barnes & Krasnoff, 1973; Felton, Perkins, & Lewin, 1966).

The fourth type of seizure, the focal type, may be convulsive movements that begin in one part of the body or on one side. The attack often occurs with the loss of consciousness and may be limited to one part of the body or may spread to other parts. Sometimes it precedes generalized seizures and a loss of consciousness. Focal seizures are most commonly found in adults (Grand & Grand, 1974; Wright, 1975).

Vocational problems

The most serious obstacle to rehabilitation of the epileptic is the stigma attached to epilepsy by public attitudes. Even among rehabilitation professionals, it has been found that there are inappropriate and negative attitudes toward epileptic clients (Jacks & Toubbeh, 1975). Both the general public and some rehabilitation workers would perhaps benefit from a general program of education with up-to-date information about epilepsy.

Though vocational problems for epileptics vary from one individual to another, it is generally true that epileptics should not work in high places or around moving machinery because of the potential danger to themselves. Epileptics are generally not permitted to operate motor vehicles, though this varies from state to state depending on the time period from the last seizure. However, even if a job does not require driving, employment opportunities are often dependent on being able to get to and from work. Additional vocational problems for the epileptic are the psychological responses to the disability. For some this may be reflected in self-doubt, seeking secondary gains from the illness, or taking a defeatist attitude. There is little evidence, however, to suggest that epileptics share a common personality. Depending on the location of the cerebral lesions, epileptics may have a greater incidence of personality disturbances; but personality patterns do not appear to be related to convulsive disorders per se (Barnes & Krasnoff, 1973; Risch, 1975; Rodin, 1975; Wright, 1975).

Rehabilitation service considerations

A diagnosis of epilepsy is made by the physician, usually with the help of an electroencephalogram (EEG). An EEG is a graphic tracing of electrical impulses from brain activity recorded on moving bands of paper. These tracings enable the physician to determine whether there are seizure disorders and may even identify the sites of lesions in the brain. The primary treatment for epilepsy is medication. Though it is not possible to cure epilepsy, it is possible to control seizures. The extent of control varies among individuals. EEG tracings can also be used to determine the effects of medication. In addition to medication, the lifestyle of the epileptic must generally be controlled by avoidance of fatigue, eating balanced meals, exercising, and getting enough sleep. For many epileptics a careful assessment of attitudes toward the disability is important. Counseling is a vital personal adjustment consideration.

Perhaps the most important rehabilitation service consideration, however, is the need to address reluctance by employers to hire individuals with a history of epilepsy. Rehabilitation professionals must engage in community education because the general public still has many misconceptions about the epileptic person's capabilities. In truth, the epileptic is no different in behavior, capabilities and emotions from nonhandicapped individuals. Nevertheless, rehabilitation workers must prepare their clients for reluctant employers.

To tell the employer about a history of epilepsy diminishes the possibilities of getting a job. However, it has also been found that persons who do not tell experience a greater likelihood of having a seizure at work, probably because of their anxiety in being found out, and often lose their jobs when they are discovered (Sinick, 1975). The decision to tell an employer about the condition is one that only the client can make. The rehabilitation worker can do little more than help the client understand the implications of either approach. Sometimes objections to employment can be worked through by arranging an on-the-job training situation for the client in which the employer has an opportunity to learn about the client and his capabilities.

In all job placements a primary consideration is the safety of the client and those around him. The rehabilitation of epileptics necessitates an individualized approach. Though it is potentially hazardous for an epileptic to work around power equipment and high places, generalizations should be made cautiously (Barnes & Krasnoff, 1973; Risch, 1975; Sinick, 1975).

MENTAL RETARDATION

Mental retardation is defined by the American Association on Mental Deficiency (AAMD) as follows: "Mental retardation refers to significantly subaverage general intellectual functioning existing concurrently with deficits in adaptive behavior, and manifested during the developmental period" (Grossman, 1973). According to the AAMD definition, mental retardation involves both subaverage intellectual functioning and deficits in adaptive behavior. Thus, unless there is impairment in both areas, the individual is not considered to be mentally retarded. Intellectual function is determined by psychological tests of intelligence—such as the *Wechsler Adult Intelligence Scale (WAIS)*. Significantly subaverage general intellectual functioning is considered to be more than 2 standard deviations below the population mean. On a *WAIS* this would be below a 70 intelligence quotient (IQ). Adaptive behavior, by contrast, refers to an individual's ability to relate to social responsibility and independent functioning. Deficits in adaptive behavior are considered in relation to cultural standards of personal independence and social responsibility which are appropriate for the person's age.

Measurement for adaptive behavior is not as advanced as measurement for intelligence, but the AAMD does have an Adaptive Behavior Scale for measuring social maturity. The developmental period referred to in the AAMD definition is intended to represent birth through 18 years of age. Emphasizing adaptive behavior as part of the condition of mental retardation means that rehabilitation and other helping professions can change the individual's disability status. If, through service intervention, rehabilitation can raise an individual's adaptive behavior to standards of normal independence and social responsibility, the disability has been successfully treated (Prehm, 1974; Brolin, 1976).

Etiology

The 1973 AAMD *Manual on Terminology and Classification in Mental Retardation* (Grossman, 1973) identifies ten groups of mental retardation causes: (1) infection and intoxication, (2) trauma or physical agents, (3) disorders of metabolism or nutrition, (4) gross brain disease (postnatal), (5) diseases and conditions due to known prenatal influence, (6) chromosomal abnormality, (7) gestational disorders, (8) retardation following a psychiatric disorder, (9) environmental influences, and (10) retardation resulting from other conditions such as biological influences.

Classifications

As just indicated, mental retardation is classified according to intellectual functioning and adaptive behavior. Using intellectual functioning as one criterion, the AAMD Manual identifies four levels of retardation—mild, moderate, severe, and profound. The mildly retarded person is at least 2 standard deviations below the population mean. On a *Wechsler Adult Intelligence Scale* this would be an IQ between 55 and 69; the moderately retarded person is more than 3 standard deviations below the mean or an IQ between 40 and 54; the severely retarded person is more than 4 standard deviations below the mean or an IQ between 25 and 39; and a profoundly retarded person would have an IQ of less than 25 or be more than 5 standard deviations below the mean. Most retarded individuals are classified as mildly retarded.

The adaptive behavior criterion for mental retardation is less precise and may depend, in large part, on practitioner judgment. The *Adaptive Behavior Scale* offered by the AAMD can help in making a diagnosis. In addition, the *Vineland Social Maturity Scale* may be used. However, clinical judgment based on the observations of a skilled practitioner is the most useful alternative for determining the degree to which an individual meets the personal, independent, and social responsibility standards expected of his age and cultural group.

Vocational problems

Many retarded persons lack the common experiences associated with maintaining a job, such as community and work exposure. They learn basically from concrete experiences and on a nonverbal level. They require continuous repetition and reinforcement in the learning process and have limited ability for transfer of learning from one situation to another (Bitter & Bolanovich, 1966). Since the mentally retarded generally think more slowly, it takes more time and patience on the part of the employer to get them started on activities. Some retarded persons must be told the simple things that others would pick up without having been told.

Rehabilitation service considerations

Bitter, Bolanovich, and O'Neil (1967) outlined some rehabilitation service considerations in programming for the moderately mentally retarded. Among the implications of their three-year school-work experience demonstration project conducted at the St. Louis Jewish Employment and Vocational Service were the following:

1. It is desirable to integrate habilitationing programming early in the school curriculum.
2. A reality-oriented production shop can provide an important vehicle for evaluation of work potential and orientation to the work environment.
3. The extension of habilitation services into the community is important for providing realistic experiential programming.
4. Specific job preparation and occupational training are desirable in a total vocational preparation sequence.
5. Industry is a potential training resource for retarded persons.
6. Continuous vocational evaluation utilizing a wide range of resources is desirable in habilitation programming.

DRUG ABUSE

Drug abuse is considered to be the illegal or improper use of a narcotic substance, including the illegal possession, transfer, or sale of drugs.

Etiology

There is no single cause of drug abuse. Many factors or conditions have been suggested as contributors, including changing mores, boredom, rebellion, desire for an experience, a search for philosophy, and escape. Drug abuse occurs at all social and economical levels. However, there are some social factors which are usually considered to be more closely associated with drug abuse than others— broken homes, absence of a father, and organized crime. Likely candidates for drug abuse are individuals who are unstable, easily frustrated, and emotionally depressed.

Classifications

Drug abusers vary in their degree of dependence on drugs, but drugs themselves can be classified into five major categories: marijuana, stimulants, depressants, hallucinogens, and narcotics (Ninth Institute on Rehabilitation Services, 1972).

Marijuana is a plant that grows in mild climates. When it is smoked, it enters the bloodstream and works on the brain and nervous system. It affects both the senses and the emotions. It can create distortions in one's perception of time, space, and sound; it also can result in dreamlike thoughts, laughter, or crying. Habitual users may exhibit antisocial behavior. However, marijuana is thought not to cause physical dependence; therefore, withdrawal from the drug does not produce a physical sickness.

Stimulants are drugs that directly stimulate the central nervous system. They produce increased activity and excitation. An example of a widely used stimulant is caffeine—found in coffee, tea, and other beverages. However, there are other stimulants commonly used in the practice of medicine that can also be abused.

Like marijuana they do not usually result in a physical dependence. Nevertheless, a psychological dependence can be developed.

Depressants are intended to relax the central nervous system. Common examples are those intended to help attain sleep. They slow down reactions, and their effects can resemble drunkenness. A physical dependence can materialize if depressants are excessively used. Tolerance for the drug can also develop, necessitating increasingly greater doses to achieve the same effect.

Hallucinogens produce hallucinations or illusions. The effects are unpredictable. A commonly known hallucinogen is LSD. Use of the drug results in a "trip" that causes visual alterations and changes in mood. One's perception of color, spatial arrangement, sound, touch, movement, and the size of objects may be distorted. The "trip" may last many hours, depending on the quantity of the dose. Hallucinogens do not create a physical dependence or a withdrawal syndrome. However, hallucinogens (particularly LSD) may be dangerous and their use has been known to result in inadvertent or intentional suicide.

Narcotics are the most dangerous drugs. They lead to physical dependence and produce withdrawal symptoms when not used. Narcotics depress the central nervous system, which results in a reduced sensitivity to pain. Narcotics have been valuable drugs in medical practice. However, the abuser of a narcotic becomes addicted and requires increasingly larger doses of the drug. Discontinuance leads to withdrawal symptoms of varying intensity depending on the degree of physical dependence and the amount of drug used. Heroin is perhaps the most dangerous of the narcotic drugs. It produces the greatest psychological and physical dependence of all drugs. Tolerance for the drug is developed quickly, and discontinuance induces severe withdrawal reactions. Heroin may be administered by snuffing the powder into the nostrils or by injecting it into the skin or directly into a vein.

Vocational problems

Drug abusers are often unaware of the need to develop acceptable work habits. Sometimes they may be too concerned with the habit and its continuance to prepare adequately for employment. In addition, they often lack self-confidence; they anticipate failure and disappointment. Because of the habit, abusers are often in trouble with family members and the law. Thus society and employers often have negative attitudes toward drug abusers. Many addicts are undertrained and undereducated for meaningful work, further reducing their effectiveness (Drug Abuse Council, 1972; Ninth Institute on Rehabilitation Services, 1972).

Rehabilitation service considerations

Treatment of the drug abuser should be matched with needs rather than on availability of the treatment system. Service must begin by breaking down physical and psychological dependency on drugs. Restoring the addict's self-confidence and respect and providing the necessary education and job skills to succeed in the vocational world follow.

There are basically three approaches to the treatment of a narcotic user: (1) the immediate elimination of the use of drugs, resulting in detoxification which is achieved only with considerable physical pain, (2) the substitution of less dangerous drugs like methadone or narcotic antagonists that are intended to block the effects of the drug, and (3) a multimodality treatment approach with a range of services provided, including detoxification, therapeutic environments, vocational training, group therapy, and instruction in the use of leisure time (Drug Abuse Council, 1972).

Therapeutic communities use a residential approach in which an individual lives with other addicts. The emphasis is on detoxification, coping with reality, and developing healthy human relationships and responsible behavior. The "therapeutic community" concept for drug addicts began with the founding of Synanon in 1958 by Chuck Dederick. Synanon was started as a nonmedical program of residential group living operated by recovered addicts. An outgrowth of the Synanon concept is a well-known program at Daytop Village in New York City. Daytop is similar to Synanon but differs in that it uses professional staff to assist in treatment programs. Similarly, self-help programs may involve outpatient services. These are commonly referred to as ambulatory programs; they offer therapy, crisis intervention, and counseling.

Rehabilitation really begins only after detoxification of the drug abuser. Chemical substitutes such as methadone are aids to detoxification; however, they can result in new addiction. The advantage of a methadone maintenance program is that it permits the user to function in a relatively normal manner. Treatment components in a multimodality approach include medical service, individual, group, and family counseling, educational services, job preparation and training, and therapy. Counseling detoxified addicts should focus on the here-and-now rather than on long-term plans. In addition, an emphasis should be on prevocational preparation for employment, including the building of self-confidence, adjustment to work, general work competencies, and specific job preparation. Equally important is assistance in the constructive use of leisure time (Drug Abuse Council, 1972; Ninth Institute on Rehabilitation Services, 1972).

NEUROLOGICAL DISORDERS

Neurological disorders relate primarily to the central nervous system, comprised of the brain and the spinal cord. There are 12 pairs of cranial nerves and 31 pairs of spinal nerves. Each pair consists of two roots: a sensory root and a motor root. Although the spinal cord is an integral part of the central nervous system, it will be discussed separately later in the chapter.

Etiology

The causes of neurological disorders are generally due to abnormal changes in the tissue of the body. These changes can result from (1) anoxia (i.e., oxygen deficiency to body tissues), (2) trauma such as severing, stretching, or crushing of nerves, (3) infections, (4) an insufficient blood supply to the brain, which leads to degeneration of brain tissue (unlike other tissues of the body, the brain is not capable of regenerating cells), and (5) either benign or malignant tumors. Tumors are an overgrowth of cells that multiply themselves and cause interference with the connecting nerve pathways.

In addition, peripheral nerve disorders can be caused by poisons and various deficiency states—such as vitamin deficiency and diabetes (Lorenze, 1965; Felton, Perkins, & Lewin, 1966; Rusk, 1977).

Classifications

Neurological disorders may be classified into cerebrovascular accidents, infectious diseases of the brain, diseases of unknown cause, and other conditions such as cerebral palsy, brain tumors, and epilepsy.

Cerebrovascular accidents. Cerebrovascular accidents are commonly called strokes and result from a destruction of brain tissue due to disturbances of blood circulation. They may occur in different ways; for example, a blood vessel may burst, or a blood clot may form in an artery and cause blockage of the blood supply.

Infectious diseases of brain. Infectious diseases may be caused by bacterial infection or viral disorders. An example is meningitis, which is an inflammation or infection of the covering of the brain and spinal cord (called the *meninges;* singular, *meninx*). Another example is encephalitis, an infection of the brain itself.

Diseases of unknown cause. Examples of neurological disorders of unknown etiology are Parkinson's syndrome and multiple sclerosis.

Parkinson's syndrome is a slowly progressive condition characteristically affecting the elderly. Tremors of the hand, muscle rigidity, and difficulty in making voluntary movements are outstanding symptoms.

Another progressive disease is multiple sclerosis. By contrast with Parkinson's syndrome, multiple sclerosis occurs in young adults. It results from a degeneration of the myelin sheath around the tracts of white matter of the central nervous system, causing destruction of nerve tissue. The person with multiple sclerosis may develop speech problems, paralysis of the extremities, emotional instability, mental retardation, and a variety of other sensory disturbances including blindness.

Other conditions. Other examples of neurological disorders are cerebral palsy, epilepsy, and brain tumors. Cerebral palsy and epilepsy were discussed earlier in this chapter. Brain tumors are abnormal overgrowths of cells that may be either benign or malignant. If benign, they are easily removed by surgery; if malignant, they have a tendency to spread. This overgrowth of cells can cause impairment of functions, depending on the location of the tumor. A tumor in some parts of the dominant temporal lobe can cause aphasia. Impaired vision may be caused by pressure from a tumor on the optic nerve. Some symptoms resulting from brain tumors are headaches, nausea, vomiting, drowsiness, changes in personality, and impaired mental functioning (Hylbert, 1965; Lorenze, 1965; Felton, Perkins, & Lewin, 1966; Rusk, 1977).

Vocational problems

An important consideration in the vocational rehabilitation of persons with neurological disorders is whether or not the disease is progressive, static, or regressive. Many neurological disorders are progressive in nature. Depending on the severity of the disease, the client's age, and his general physical condition, planning for many persons with neurological disorders must be conservative in nature. The effect of the disease will determine the nature of the vocational problem. As an example, a nerve injury in the upper extremity might involve a sensation loss which would preclude the client from a job requiring tactual sense. Each neurological disorder presents its own complication and thus its own vocational problem. Clients with neurological disorders are difficult rehabilitation cases because of the progressive nature of the diseases (Felton, Perkins, & Lewin, 1966; Rusk, 1977).

Rehabilitation service considerations

Rusk (1977) believes the primary emphasis in the rehabilitation of clients with neurological disorders should be toward the restitution of or substitution for the client's motor deficiency. The goal is to strengthen weak muscles through reeducation exercises with an emphasis on functional improvement.

In the case of cerebrovascular accidents, a primary emphasis is given to physical therapy for muscle reeducation. In addition, gait training is usually necessary. Because the destruction of brain tissue usually affects speech, speech therapy is often recommended. Sometimes drugs are prescribed to reduce the chances of further strokes. Vocational planning for clients with cerebrovascular accidents is often limited, however. If the client's age and general physical condition justify vocational planning, this may be possible (Felton, Perkins, & Lewin, 1966).

Treatment for clients with infectious diseases such as meningitis is primarily preventive. With infections due to bacteria, the effort is toward prevention of complications during the acute stage. Treatment following the acute stage depends on the residual disability.

Parkinson's syndrome, like multiple sclerosis, is a slowly progressive disorder. Because of muscular rigidity, the client is encouraged to keep physically active.

A program of general conditioning can help. Clients usually benefit from physical and occupational therapy.

Rehabilitation for multiple sclerosis victims is directed toward helping the person function in activities of daily living. The disease is slowly progressive, and any vocational planning should take into consideration the expected deterioration in the client's health.

The primary treatment for clients with brain tumors is surgical removal of the growth. If the tumor is benign and removed, there generally is little permanent loss of function. Malignant tumors are often inoperable. The rehabilitation considerations are thus directed toward psychological problems stemming from frustrations resulting from restricted activity (Hylbert, 1965; Felton, Perkins, & Lewin, 1966; Rusk, 1977).

ORTHOPEDIC DISABILITIES

Orthopedic disabilities are related to the musculoskeletal system—which is composed of bones, joints, and muscles.

Etiology

Orthopedic disabilities can occur from the following:
1. *Congenital deformities.* Examples are the absence of limbs at birth, bowing of legs, curvature of the spine, or spina bifida (a congenital gap in the vertebral column which permits the spinal cord to protrude).
2. *Trauma,* usually occurring as a result of injury or accident. Examples are fractures, dislocations, strains, sprains, and lacerations; however, trauma may also result from faulty posture, overweight, malalignment, muscular imbalance, and fatigue (Rusk, 1977).
3. *Vascular disorders* occurring as a result of inadequate blood supply to an extremity. This may result from a traumatic accident, arteriosclerosis (hardening of the arteries), diabetes, or other conditions such as Buerger's disease (a vascular disease characterized by rapidly progressive arteriosclerosis).
4. *Infections.*
5. *Tumors.*

Amputations in children are often due to congenital causes. Amputations for adults usually result from injury. Amputation for older individuals is most often because of disease such as diabetes and cardiovascular conditions.

Classifications

Orthopedic disabilities are usually classified according to the causes just mentioned. With amputation, however, they are classified according to the *location* of the amputation as follows (J. E. Hanger, Inc., 1972):

1. Lower extremities
   a. Partial foot

      b. Syme's amputation (ankle joint)
      c. Below knee (between ankle and knee)
      d. Knee disarticulation
      e. Above knee (between the knee joint and the hip)
      f. Hip disarticulation
  2. Upper extremities
      a. Partial hand
      b. Wrist disarticulation
      c. Below elbow (amputation through forearm and further classified as long, short, or very short depending on length of stump)
      d. Elbow disarticulation
      e. Above elbow (between the elbow joint and the shoulder)
      f. Shoulder disarticulation (removal of the entire arm)
      g. Forequarter (removal of clavicle and scapula)

Vocational problems

The vocational problems resulting from amputations are caused by two factors: (1) the functional limitation due to loss of a limb and (2) the psychological problems involved in coping with this loss. Generally the more joints lost through amputation, the greater is the functional limitation. Obviously a lower extremity amputee will be affected in walking, jumping, running, balancing, stooping, lifting, and carrying. Similarly an upper extremity amputee will be affected in throwing, pushing, handling, pulling, fingering, carrying, lifting, and foot-eye-hand coordination. However, depending on the individual's occupation, these may or may not constitute a vocational limitation. Individuals with a career which requires only thinking or speaking will be less affected than will those who are also dependent on physical performance. A lower extremity amputation is usually less limiting for most occupations than is an upper extremity loss (Fishman, 1962).

Of considerable importance in the rehabilitation of the amputee are the psychological problems that occur with the loss of a limb. In addition to learning how to get along without a particular extremity or with a prothesis (artificial device), the individual often experiences psychological problems resulting from a fear of inadequacy. Thus learning to use the prothesis can result in frustration, feelings of sensitivity, social inadequacy, insecurity, a lack of self-reliance and self-acceptance, and concern about the attitudes and perceptions of others toward him as an individual.

Rehabilitation service considerations

The most frequently employed therapeutic measures in physical medicine are heat, massage, and exercise. Heat can be applied through infrared radiation, hydrotherapy (water), or hot paraffin packs and moist packs. A deep heat beneath the skin can be applied with a short-wave, microwave, or ultrasound instrument.

Both physical therapy and occupational therapy are important in the applica-

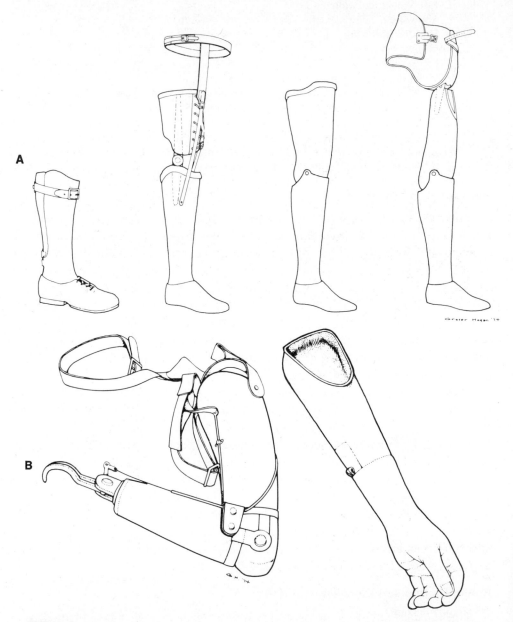

FIG. 4-1

Prostheses. **A,** Lower extremity prostheses for below the knee, knee disarticulation, above the knee, and hip disarticulation amputations; **B,** Upper extremity prostheses, including the conventional split hook and a myoelectric type. (From Hilt, N., and Schmidt, E. *Pediatric orthopedic nursing.* St. Louis: The C. V. Mosby Co., 1975.)

tion of physical medicine. Physical therapy is a science administered by a person trained in the application of heat, massage, and exercise. Occupational therapy is used to gain physical function through purposeful activity. For example, to regain function in a limb, the client might be purposely engaged in a meaningful activity such as woodworking or knitting. Occupational therapy also involves prevocational exploration, retraining for homemaking, and restoration of physical function for engaging in the activities of daily living. The physical therapist and occupational therapist also provide much of the training to amputees for using prosthetic and orthotic (correction) equipment (Rusk, 1977).

It is a common practice in leg amputation to immediately apply a plaster of Paris dressing in the form of a socket following surgery. A temporary and adjustable leg is then fitted to the individual to enable him to stand the very next day. The sutures from surgery are removed after approximately 2 weeks, and a new case socket is applied and kept in place for approximately 10 days after which a permanent prosthesis is fitted (J. E. Hanger, Inc., 1972).

Each amputee is an individual with unique needs. Thus a prosthesis should be developed and fitted to meet the individual's personal and vocational needs. In general, the lower the level of the amputation, the more functional is the stump. An exception is a below-knee amputation between the ankle and the knee because of poor blood circulation to this area.

The most functional hand substitute for arm amputations is the split hook. Though an artificial hand has cosmetic value, it does not have the general adaptability of the hook. The best results are attained when artificial limbs are fitted as soon as possible after surgery.

Instruction in the use of prostheses is generally conducted by a physical therapist or an occupational therapist. Physical therapists often instruct lower extremity clients. Though instruction is primarily for functional use of artificial devices, it can be extended to assist the client in adapting to job requirements. Of crucial importance in rehabilitation is a healthy self-concept. Personal counseling can help an amputee accept himself and the attitudes of others (Fishman, 1962; Felton, Perkins, & Lewin, 1966; J. E. Hanger, Inc., 1972; Lewis, 1973; Rusk, 1977).

PSYCHIATRIC DISABILITIES

Psychiatric disabilities are perhaps the most prevalent disorders in rehabilitation; yet psychiatric clients are, perhaps, the most difficult for rehabilitation (Micek & Bitter, 1974).

Etiology

Psychiatric disabilities can be caused by organic factors or psychological factors involving an interaction between the individual and the environment. Psychological factors are often considered functional disorders. Organic psychiatric disorders can be caused by infection as occurs in encephalitis, meningitis, and syphilis; or by poisons, tumors, brain injury, neurological diseases, or a malfunction in normal body processes (Felton, Perkins, & Lewin, 1966). Other causes are trauma, arteriosclerosis, and chronic alcohol or drug use. Organic disorders can be either acute (i.e., severe symptoms during a short course, which means the client will get better) or chronic (meaning the disability will continue and may even be progressive). Organic disorders are a result of damage to the brain.

Classifications

Functional impairments refers to psychological factors or emotions of a person rather than to physiological defects in the brain. Though there are other classification systems, functional disorders may be classified into three categories: neuroses, personality disorders, and psychoses.

Neuroses. Neuroses are usually the result of an individual's anxiety stemming from internal conflict. In a neurosis there is no gross personality disorganization or loss of contact with reality. Rather the neurosis may be reflected in a phobic reaction involving a localized fear of an object or situation. Examples are a fear of high places or closed places. A neurosis may be of the conversion type, in which an emotional reaction is converted into a body symptom (e.g., loss of voice or facial tics). Another type of reaction to distress is called "dissociative." Dissociative reactions are characterized by multiple personalities in an individual but without conscious awareness of this by the person. Still another neurotic reaction is obsessive-compulsive. An obsessive-compulsive person is characterized by irrational ideas. Though illogical, these ideas are persistent and the neurotic person experiences uncontrollable urges to perform acts that are usually against his ordinary wishes. The person may be obsessed with something specific, such as numbers, or may be a compulsive hand washer. Such persons are often rigid, orderly, cautious, and controlling.

Personality disorders. Personality disorders relate to the basic personality of an individual. They are a result of a lifelong pattern for coping with the environment and are usually difficult to change. Personality disorders are often classified according to primary characteristics. For example, the *obsessive-compulsive* personality disorder is characterized by strict adherance to schedules and rules. Such an individual is generally rigid and has an excessive concern for morality and authoritarian standards. The *hysterical* personality is very excitable, tends to overreact, and seeks attention. The *passive-aggressive* personality is highly dependent but is characterized by hostility, obstructionistic behavior, and general uncooperativeness. A *sociopathic* personality exhibits behavior patterns that are antisocial. Often the person with a sociopathic personality is of above average intelligence, but the behavior pattern is characterized by irresponsible activity, poor judgment, poor foresight, and a poor appreciation of the consequences of actions (Myers, 1965; Felton, Perkins, & Lewin, 1966).

Psychoses. Psychoses are a severe emotional disorder represented by a break with reality. Psychotic individuals have such severe personality disorganization that they cannot carry on even routine activities, including work and normal relationships with other people. The most common types of psychotic disorders are schizophrenia, manic-depressivism, and involutional depression.

Schizophrenia is the most frequent type of psychosis, whose primary features are ambivalent behavior and withdrawal from interpersonal relationships. Simple schizophrenic behavior is characterized by the loss of ambition and social withdrawal. The schizophrenic with a paranoid personality generally feels persecuted. The behavior pattern is dominated by delusions, often grandiose, in which reality is rationally misinterpreted. The catatonic schizophrenic exhibits abnormal motor behavior which may include excessive activity or inhibition including stupor (partial unconsciousness).

The primary features of a *manic-depressive* individual are the wide variations in mood, which may swing from hyperactivity to depression. In the manic state the individual is elated, excited, and hyperactive. He may have delusions of grandeur. In the depressed state the feelings are of withdrawal, sadness, and worthlessness; and the person may exhibit suicidal tendencies.

Involutional depression is a depressed state which generally occurs during a change of life period. It can occur in anyone and generally is associated with despair from feeling that one is growing old and the opportunity to achieve subjective goals is quickly passing by. An involutional psychotic reaction is a temporary disorder without previous psychosis (Myers, 1965; Felton, Perkins, & Lewin, 1966).

Vocational problems

Many times an individual's vocation is the source of adjustment problems. Conversely, the disorder interferes with functioning on the job. A particular area of difficulty is interpersonal relationships. Since positive relationships with others are important in most employment situations, the inability to bring about constructive social interactions can be a distinct vocational obstacle. How much of an obstacle an individual's psychiatric disability is to employment depends on the severity of the disorder. Persons with severe disturbances may require supervision and care in all areas of daily living, and perhaps, may engage in only limited productive activity such as in sheltered workshops. This would be particularly true if the client's behavior is disruptive to others. Persons with moderate disturbances may be capable of employment in situations involving limited stress. The potential vocational problems are hyperactivity, overreactions to situations, the possibility of misunderstanding instructions of supervisors, and withdrawal. Clients with only mild disturbances are often good candidates for competitive employment provided they can accept directions, maintain minimally adequate interpersonal relationships, and concentrate on the requirements of the job.

The extent of stress presented with the employment situation is a major consideration for predicting vocational adjustment.

Rehabilitation service considerations

The aim of rehabilitation for the psychiatric client is to enable the person to cope with life better. A comprehensive review of the literature between 1968 and 1972 by Micek and Bitter (1974) suggests that there are many rehabilitation approaches which have been used with psychiatric clients. Some approaches involve only verbal interaction between the therapist and the client. Other approaches involve a combination of verbal interaction and restructuring the client's environment. Examples are the use of sheltered workshops, halfway houses, and community living situations. Other forms of environmental restructuring include family therapy, behavior modification, and milieu therapy. Physical treatment is another approach to psychiatric disabilities. Drugs can be used for their tranquilizing effect and for treating depression. Electroconvulsive (shock) therapy, though decreasing in use, is generally intended to induce seizures for treating depression. Yet another approach to treatment is the use of group techniques—including group therapy, encounter groups, marathon groups, group living, and social clubs.

With most psychiatric clients the rehabilitation process is a slow step-by-step effort to reintegrate the individual into normal living patterns. Consideration must be given to the individual's tolerance for stress. The goal is to increase gradually the client's tolerance threshold and interpersonal skills and relationships. However, care must be taken to avoid developing or increasing dependency relationships. Felton, Perkins, and Lewin (1966) indicate that there is no type of job from which psychiatric clients need be prohibited; but each client is an individual, and what may be a stressful situation for one person may not be stressful for another. Considerable preparation of the psychiatric client for an employment situation and discussions with the employer by the counselor can facilitate successful rehabilitation.

RENAL FAILURE

Renal failure refers to a loss of function of the kidneys. The kidneys maintain a chemical balance in the body which helps other organs function correctly and remove body waste products from the bloodstream (Jones, 1974). Some symptoms of kidney disease are lethargy, inability to think, restlessness, decrease in appetite, anemia, high blood pressure, susceptivity to bruises, and bone disease due to a deficiency in vitamin D products.

Etiology

Jones (1974) lists the following causes of kidney disease: infection, hypersensitivity states, birth defects and hereditary diseases, circulatory conditions, tumors, metabolic diseases, and injuries.

Classifications

Renal failure may be classified as *acute* or *chronic*. In acute renal failure both kidneys temporarily stop forming urine. With treatment the kidneys may return to proper functioning. Chronic renal failure necessitates either a kidney transplantation or continuous treatment through hemodialysis. Hemodialysis is an artificial procedure which substitutes for the function of the kidney by removing waste products from the blood.

Another way to classify kidney diseases is by type. Hewitt and Lawlis (1973) have identified the following types of kidney disorders:

1. *Neuromuscular uropathy*. An abnormality in the urinary tract which interferes with the individual's ability to void.
2. *Glomerulonephritis*. Damage to the kidneys caused by bacteria toxins from acute infection in some other area of the body (e.g., a strep throat).
3. *Pyelonephritis*. An infection in the tissue of the kidney.
4. *Polycystic disease*. A hereditary disease in which normal kidney tissue is replaced by nonfunctioning cysts.
5. *Nephrosclerosis*. Hardening of the tissues (including the small blood vessels) of the kidney; may result from high blood pressure.
6. *Generalized arteriosclerosis*. Damage to the kidneys resulting from obstruction of blood flow to the kidney.
7. *Generalized diabetes*. An increase in urinary secretions which can destroy kidney tissue.
8. *Recurrent kidney stone formation*. An increased calcium excretion which can obstruct the elimination of urine from the kidneys.
9. *Congenital anomalies*. Supernumerary kidneys, obstructions in the lower urinary tract, abnormal position of the kidneys, and peculiar blood supplies.

In addition, acute renal failure can occur as a result of intake of poisons such as wood alcohol or antifreeze (ethylene glycol), surgical shock, heart attack, or severe systemic infections (Levinsky, 1965).

Vocational problems

Because renal failure is a terminal disease, the greatest vocational problem resulting from the disability is psychological. The fear of death can produce depression and feelings of inadequacy. Prior to treatment the individual may exhibit impaired judgment, drowsiness, and inability to concentrate. This results from brain dysfunction caused by the disorder. If the treatment of choice is a kidney transplant, the individual is highly subject to infection because of the large quantities of drugs needed to combat rejection. A job that is physically taxing could lower the client's resistance to disease and infection. A client treated by dialysis will, unless on a home dialysis plan, require 2 or 3 days during the work week for hospital dialysis. Not all jobs and employers lend themselves to such scheduling.

In addition, dialysis clients are often anemic and generally do better at non-physical jobs (Jones, 1974).

Rehabilitation service considerations

There are two treatments for renal failure: kidney transplant and dialysis.

A kidney transplant from one individual to another can restore the client to normal productive life. A difficulty in transplantation is that the body may reject the foreign organ. The closer the two persons are related, the better will be the chances for success. Thus the greatest success is with identical twins (Hewitt & Lawlis, 1973).

Hemodialysis is a process of cleaning the blood through an artificial kidney by removing waste materials. The process may take up to 6 hours. A piece of tubing is inserted into an artery, and another into an adjacent vein, creating a passage between the dialysis machine and the artery and vein. The process is known as a shunt. The shunt can be located anywhere on the individual's body but usually is in the arm. Hemodialysis is very expensive. Home dialysis can be cheaper in the long run than hospital dialysis, but the initial investment is large. The advantage of home dialysis is that the process can always be conducted during nonworking hours.

Another form of dialysis, peritoneal dialysis, is similar in principle to the artificial kidney. However, in peritoneal dialysis the client's own peritoneum (abdominal lining) serves as the filter. The impurities in the blood are passed through the peritoneum to a cleaning solution. This is in contrast to the artificial kidney, which uses synthetic membranes. Peritoneal dialysis is a more painful and more taxing process than hemodialysis.

Of particular importance in the rehabilitation of clients with renal failure is the supportive counseling they need to maintain ego strength in the face of a terminal disease. Since most renal failure clients will experience reduced sexual function, counseling for adjustment in this area may also be necessary. In addition, supportive counseling relative to dietary control will be necessary, since certain foods create extra work for the kidneys. Depending on the individual, the type of employment sought is an important consideration. As just mentioned, many dialysis clients may not be able to engage in physically strenuous activities. In addition, an employment situation with a tolerant employer will be important for clients who are receiving hospital dialysis (Hewitt & Lawlis, 1973; Jones, 1974).

SPEECH IMPAIRMENTS

According to Hall and Alexander (1974), "speech disorders are disabilities which impose limitations upon a person's ability to function in oral communication." A speech impairment can be a severe disability, psychologically, socially, educationally, and vocationally.

Etiology

There are many causes of speech impairment. Organic causes include brain damage, neurological disorders, congenital defects, structural irregularities to the teeth, lip, tongue, jaw, or palate, impaired hearing, tumors, and cerebrovascular accidents (stroke). Environmental causes are emotional maladjustments or conflicts, anxiety, poor speech models during childhood, and learned behavior.

Classifications

Speech impairments may be classified into disorders of speech development, articulation, phonation, fluency, and symbolization.

Speech development disorders may be a result of delayed speech from a lack of need to talk or poor speech models during early childhood. Usually speech development problems result in disorders of articulation.

Articulation disorders involve omission, substitution, distortions, or additions when pronouncing words (Gearheart & Weishahn, 1976). A cleft palate (a narrow slit in the roof of the mouth) most often results in articulation problems.

Phonation disorders involve problems of pitch, intensity, quality, or rate of speech. Acute laryngitis is an example of a phonation problem.

Fluency disorders relate to speech flow. The most common type of speech flow problem is stuttering. In stuttering, speech is characterized by repeated sounds or words, prolonged sounds, pauses, or blockages.

Symbolization disorders are due to injury in certain areas of the brain which result in communication difficulty. The process of translating thought into symbols is affected. Aphasia is a symbolization disorder. Aphasia may be expressive or receptive. In expressive aphasia the person is unable to speak coherently. In receptive aphasia the person is unable to process intelligently the sounds he hears (Felton, Perkins, & Lewin, 1966, Hall & Alexander, 1974).

Vocational problems

A person with a speech impairment is likely to have a low self-concept and low tolerance for frustration and is likely to be generally anxious in his relationships with others. Most social and work situations require verbal communication. If the person has a speech impairment, this can be a distinct disadvantage. Hall and Alexander (1974) believe speech impairments often lead to unemployment and underachievement.

Rehabilitation service considerations

Almost all clients with speech impairments will require the services of a speech-language pathologist. The speech-language pathologist attempts to improve the intelligibility of uttered words by improving the skills of articulation, phonation, and fluency. For some people, particularly those with a cleft palate or cleft lips, surgery can improve or correct the speech impairment. This might include oral surgery to correct the cleft, orthodontic treatment to realign teeth, and plastic surgery to correct cosmetic problems. Artificial appliances can sometimes be helpful. They are often used when it is difficult to close the cleft. Similarly, in laryngectomies an artificial larynx might be utilized.

Another important consideration in rehabilitation of persons with speech impairments is family and vocational counseling. Supportive efforts of the family can do much for the self-concept and emotional adjustment of the client and facilitate the rehabilitation process. Vocational counseling should, of course, take into consideration the personal communication requirements of the job.

SPINAL CORD CONDITIONS

The spinal cord is a mass of nerves extending from the base of the skull to the lower back. It conveys impulses from the brain to all parts of the body. It is responsible for sensory and motor functions and helps to maintain body processes.

Injury to the spinal cord affects the functioning of the sensory and motor control of the body from the site of injury down. Thus, if the damage is high in the spinal cord the individual may have partial or complete loss of functioning of the upper and lower extremities. Injury to the lower spinal cord can cause disturbed function of the lower extremities. The parts of the body affected and the extent of the functional loss depend on the level of injury to the spinal cord and the severity of the damage.

Etiology

Spinal conditions can result from trauma, infectious diseases, and congenital defects. The most common cause of traumatic injury to the spinal cord is automobile accidents. Sporting accidents are also frequent contributors to spinal cord injury—including diving accidents, gunshot wounds, and motorcycle, skiing, and football mishaps. Infection of the spinal cord can also occur either through the bloodstream or from infected areas near the spinal cord. Meningitis (inflammation of the membranes of the spinal cord) is an example. A rare congenital defect is spina bifida. Spina bifida is a defect of the vertebral canal in which the bones of the spine fail to close.

Classifications

The spinal cord consists of five divisions with a total of 31 pairs of nerves. Beginning at the base of the skull there are eight (8) cervical nerves, twelve (12) thoracic nerves, five (5) lumbar nerves, five (5) sacral nerves, and one (1) coccygeal nerve (Freed, 1965).

Lesions (i.e., disruptions in body tissues produced by disease or injury) to the spinal cord usually are classified according to location. Numbering for spinal cord segments is from the top down. Thus $C1$ to $C8$ refer to the cervical segments; $T1$ to $T12$ refer to the thoracic segments; $L1$ to $L5$ and $S1$ to $S5$ refer respectively,

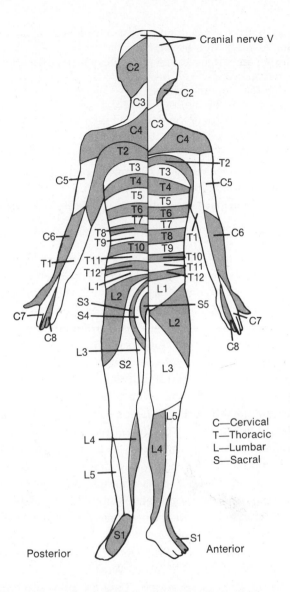

FIG. 4-2

Body surface represented for each spinal nerve. (From Boroch, R. M. *Elements of rehabilitation nursing: an introduction*. St. Louis: The C. V. Mosby Co., 1976.)

to the lumbar and sacral regions. Lesions to the first three cervical levels are usually rapidly fatal because respiratory difficulties result (O'Connor & Leitner, 1971).

Freed (1965) identified the following critical levels of spinal cord functioning. Each level includes all the functions above that level.

C5—Partial strength of shoulder motions and elbow flexion

> C6—Normal strength of shoulder and elbow flexion and wrist extension (permitting the person to grasp with the fingers)
>
> C7—Elbow flexion and extension and finger flexion and extension (enabling the person to grasp and release with his hands)
>
> T1—Complete use of arms and hands
>
> T6—Upper back muscle strength
>
> T12—Use of all the muscles of the thorax (chest), abdomen, and back
>
> L4—Hip motion and knee extension
>
> L5—Partial strength of all hip motions, knee flexion, and ankle and foot motions

Injury to the cervical levels results in quadriplegia, which is paralysis of all four body extremities. Individuals with injury from T1 down are usually called paraplegics. Such persons will normally have mobility in a wheelchair.

Vocational problems

With knowledge and technological advances in recent years the future of the spinal cord injured person has greatly improved. However, employment is a difficult rehabilitation process—particularly for people with limited use of all four extremities. Most successes have occurred in the professional, technical, and managerial areas (Poor, 1975). Because of the limited motor and muscular ability of spinal cord injured clients, job opportunities are generally limited to those which do not require physical activity; and educational level becomes important. Older clients generally have more difficulty adjusting to a change in life-style.

The primary areas of concern for employment of the spinal cord injured are motivation of the client, transportation needs to and from the job, mobility on the job, and bowel and bladder difficulties resulting from a loss of function. Understandably, spinal cord injured clients react to their disability with passivity, dependency, aggression, or compensation as a defense mechanism (Siller, 1969).

Transportation to and from the job is an important consideration. Depending on the severity of the disability, some people may be able to drive their own car with appropriate hand controls and devices; many, however, will find it necessary to be driven to their place of employment.

Mobility and the remaining muscle power of the individual are additional considerations for employment. The client with a cervical lesion will have only partial strength in the upper extremities. Thus he may be confined to a wheelchair and may require a full-time attendant. Homebound employment may be the limit of employment potential for many with a cervical lesion. If, however, the lesion is in the high thoracic area, the client will have upper extremity strength. Though forced to remain in a wheelchair such clients may have considerable independence in self-care activities and mobility. Sedentary jobs are possible for persons with a high thoracic lesion. Individuals with a midthoracic lesion have good upper extremity and thoracic stabilization. If the individual can manage transportation to and from a place of employment, work away from home is usually possible. Clients with a low thoracic lesion become excellent candidates for employment; and those with a low lumbar or sacral lesion are only moderately limited by deficiencies in ambulation and elevation activities (Long & Lawton, 1955).

An additional complication of spinal cord injury is loss of bowel and bladder control (incontinence). With excretory management and accessibility of toilet facilities at the place of employment, such problems can be minimized.

Rehabilitation service considerations

The medical treatment of the spinal cord injured person may involve traction applied to the spine or perhaps surgery. In all cases the client is immobilized and many of the functions of the body (e.g., bowel and bladder movements) are performed mechanically with the aid of medical staff. Many complications can arise during treatment of the spinal cord injured client. Pressure sores, called decubiti or decubitus ulcers, can develop as a result of lying in one position too long. In addition, the individual can develop respiration difficulties, blood abnormalities, and infections of the urinary and digestive systems (Sword & Roberts, 1974). The initial rehabilitation program may take 3 to 6 months and is very costly.

Immediately after the injury there is a period of spinal shock accompanied by a loss of reflex activity. This period may last anywhere from 2 to 8 weeks. With the return of the stretch flex may come spasticity, i.e., an increased resistance to movement. Physical activity is encouraged and physical and occupational therapy may be provided to increase strength and mobility. Elimination tract management involves bowel and bladder training and the use of a catheter. Prevention and control for decubiti can be accomplished by changing positions frequently and conscientious skin care. If blood pressure is a problem, elastic bandaging and/or the use of corsets helps to control pressure to extremities (O'Connor & Leitner, 1971).

In addition to being a severe and physically traumatic experience, spinal cord injury is also a tremendous psychological trauma. At first the individual is helplessly dependent for even the simplest of everyday tasks and may have little or no voluntary control over bowels or bladder. Such a blow to one's self-image can result in depression, frustration, feelings of inferiority, withdrawal from reality, or egocentricity. The person will experience not only anxiety but also psychological problems related to the loss of motor, bowel, bladder, and sexual function. However, personality does remain relatively constant and the client usually returns to his basic pretrauma personality within about 6 months following the injury. Counseling, physical therapy, and occupational therapy can contribute much to realignment of one's body image and acceptance of the disability (Mueller, 1962).

Besides assistance in overcoming the reaction of anxiety and depression to the physical disability, the spinal cord injured client will require assistance in

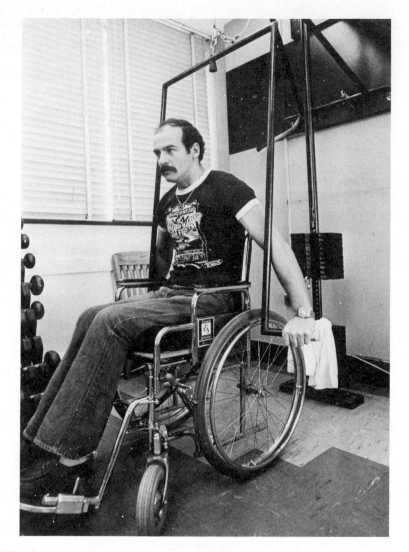

FIG. 4-3

Latissimus bar used in physical therapy for exercise. (From Rusk, H. A. *Rehabilitation medicine*. St. Louis: The C. V. Mosby Co., 1977.)

attending to the activities of daily living. Help is needed in eating, dressing and undressing, hygiene, developing socially acceptable bowel and bladder control, and mobility skills. Sexual function, which is significantly reduced, also becomes an important area for counseling. Long (1971) reports that "coitus is practiced with gratification by about a third of paraplegic men, and probably a higher percentage of paraplegic women." However, fertility in paraplegic men is low, although paraplegic women can conceive normally and bear children. The family is of extreme importance in the emotional adjustment of the individual as well as in the adjustment to mechanical devices for improving self-care and mobility. Training in the use of assistive devices and wheelchairs is mandatory for achieving a maximum level of functioning.

Though some spinal cord injured clients will be able to return to their former vocation, in general, the vocational outlook for the spinal cord injured is limited. Persons with cervical lesions will quite likely be limited to homebound occupations—bookkeeping, telephone services, and office responsibilities like typing and using office machines. Clients with thoracic lesions may be capable of employment outside the home dependent upon the level of the lesion. There is usually no limit of sedentary jobs for the T1 client. The T6 client will probably require a sedentary job but may be able to stand for periods of time. The T12 client should have only a few vocational limitations and may not even need a wheelchair for much of the day. The client with a lumbar lesion is almost completely independent in all activities; however, there are certain limitations—such as to jobs that require ambulation and elevation activities (Long & Lawton, 1955).

SUMMARY

A basic understanding of the construct of medical terminology can be a real aid to rehabilitation professionals. Medical terms can usually be analyzed in terms of root words, prefixes, and suffixes. The practitioner in rehabilitation would be well advised to obtain and use a medical dictionary which contains terms and abbreviations to facilitate communication with the medical community.

Fifteen severe disabilities were briefly described in this chapter in terms of the (1) potential causes of the disability, (2) methods for classifying the nature of the disability, (3) the vocational problems imposed by the disability, and (4) rehabilitation service considerations. A major underlying theme for service delivery of the disabled is the necessity for an interdisciplinary approach to serving individuals. Each client is unique; rehabilitation is rarely accomplished through the efforts of one profession or person. Effective service for attaining desired outcomes must involve the client and, hopefully, the family and can include physicians, psychologists, public health workers, social workers, rehabilitation counselors, ministers, employers, law enforcers, peers, mental health workers, and teachers. Thus rehabilitation involves a team approach to serving the whole person.

SELF-EVALUATION QUESTIONS

1. What are the purposes of prefixes and suffixes as components of medical terms?
2. What is alcohol "addiction"?
3. What are the vocational effects of excessive drinking?
4. What are some treatment approaches for alcoholism?
5. What are two pathological processes that affect joints in arthritis?
6. What is the purpose of physical therapy in treating arthritis?

7. Which type of arthritis presents the primary vocational rehabilitation problems?
8. What is glaucoma?
9. What is the criterion for legal blindness?
10. What is the purpose of the Randolph-Sheppard Act?
11. What is the primary cause of death in the United States?
12. What is the difference between type A and type B behavior?
13. What is the purpose of the functional and therapeutic classifications for cardiovascular diseases?
14. What are the potential vocational problems for cardiac clients?
15. What is a "met" (metabolic equivalent unit)?
16. What are the two types of hearing loss and where is the impairment located in each?
17. What is an audiometer?
18. What are (a) the major employment problem and (b) greatest vocational problem for the deaf?
19. What are the types of hearing aids?
20. How is cerebral palsy generally classified?
21. What is the most serious obstacle to rehabilitation of the person with epilepsy?
22. What is an electroencephalogram?
23. Can epilepsy be cured?
24. What are some implications of the American Association on Mental Deficiency definition for mental retardation?
25. What are the major categories of drugs?
26. What are the basic approaches to the treatment of drug abuse?
27. What are the two main components of the central nervous system?
28. What is another name for cerebrovascular accident?
29. Why is vocational planning for clients with neurological disorders often limited?
30. What is spina bifida?
31. How are amputations classified?
32. What are the vocational problems resulting from amputations?
33. Which is usually less limiting for most occupations, a lower or upper extremity amputation?
34. What is the difference between physical therapy and occupational therapy?
35. What are three functional psychiatric disorders and the differences between them?
36. What is an area of particular vocational difficulty for persons with psychiatric disorders?
37. What are the two treatments possible for renal failure?
38. What is the difference between hemodialysis and peritoneal dialysis?
39. What are five classifications of speech impairments?
40. What is aphasia?
41. What determines the *extent* of functional loss in spinal cord injury?
42. Why is a spinal cord injury to the first three cervicle levels usually fatal?
43. Below what level on the spinal cord does an injury permit complete use of arms and hands (paraplegia)?
44. What are the primary areas of concern for employment of the spinal cord injured?
45. How soon after a spinal cord injury does a client usually return to his basic pre-trauma personality?
46. What are the employment prospects for spinal cord injured clients with (a) cervical lesions, (b) thoracic lesions, and (c) lumbar lesions?

REFERENCES

Allen, R. M. Cerebral palsy. In J. F. Garrett & E. S. Levine (Eds.), *Psychological practices with the physically disabled*. New York: Columbia University Press, 1962.

American Psychiatric Association. *Diagnostic and statistical manual on mental disorders* (Rev. ed.). Washington, D.C.: APA, 1968.

Barnes, L., & Krasnoff, A. Medical and psychological factors pertinent to the rehabilitation of the epileptic. In A. B. Cobb (Ed.), *Medical and psychological aspects of disability*. Springfield, Ill.: Charles C Thomas, Publisher, 1973.

Bitter, J. A., & Bolanovich, D. J. Job training of retardates using 8 mm film loops. *Audiovisual Instruction*, 1966, *11*(9), 731-732.

Bitter, J. A., Bolanovich, D. J., & O'Neil, L. P. Some implications of the St. Louis Work Experience Center project. *Education and Training of the Mentally Retarded*, 1967, 2(4), 177-182.

Brolin, D. E. *Vocational preparation of retarded citizens*. Columbus, Ohio: Charles E. Merrill Publishing Co., 1976.

Costello, P. M. Educational and social factors in the rehabilitation of hearing disabilities. In A. B. Cobb (Ed.), *Medical and psychological aspects of disability*. Springfield, Ill.: Charles C Thomas, Publisher, 1973.

Cull, J. G., & Hardy, R. E. (Eds.). *Rehabilitation techniques in severe disability: case studies*. Springfield, Ill.: Charles C Thomas, Publisher, 1974.

Denhoff, E., & Robinault, I. P. *Cerebral palsy and related disorders: a developmental approach to dysfunction*. New York: McGraw-Hill Book Co., 1960.

Dorland's pocket medical dictionary. Philadelphia: W. B. Saunders Co., 1968.

Dreifuss, F. E. The nature of epilepsy. In G. N. Wright, (Ed.), *Epilepsy rehabilitation*. Boston: Little, Brown & Co., 1975.

Drug Abuse Council. *Federal drug abuse programs*. Washington, D.C.: Drug Abuse Council, 1972.

Eleventh Institute on Rehabilitation Services. *Rehabilitation of the deaf*. Hot Springs, Ark.: Arkansas Rehabilitation Research and Training Center, University of Arkansas, 1973.

Felton, J. S., Perkins, D. C., & Lewin, M. *A survey of medicine and medical practice for the rehabilitation counselor*. Washington, D.C.: Superintendent of Documents, Government Printing Office, 1966.

Fishman, S. Amputation. In J. F. Garrett & E. S. Levine, (Eds.), *Psychological practices with the physically disabled*. New York: Columbia University Press, 1962.

Franklin, M., Krauthamer, M., Razzak, T. A., & Pinchot, A. *The heart doctor's heart book*. New York: Grosset & Dunlap, Publishers, 1974.

Freed, M. M. The central nervous system: disorders of the spinal cord. In J. S. Myers, (Ed.), *An orientation to chronic disease and disability*. New York: The Macmillan Co. 1965.

Friedman, M., & Rosenman, R. H. *Type A behavior and your heart*. New York: Alfred A. Knopf, Inc., 1974.

Gearheart, B. R., & Weishahn, M. W. *The handicapped child in the regular classroom*. St. Louis: The C. V. Mosby Co., 1976.

Grand, S. A., & Grand, A. K. Epilepsy. In R. E. Hardy and J. G. Cull (Eds.), *Severe disabilities: social and rehabilitation approaches*. Springfield, Ill.: Charles C Thomas, Publisher, 1974.

Graves, W. H., & Bowman, J. T. Rehabilitation of persons with rheumatoid arthritis. In R. E. Hardy & J. G. Cull (Eds.), *Severe disabilities: social and rehabilitation approaches*. Springfield, Ill.: Charles C Thomas, Publisher, 1974.

Grossman, H. (Ed.). *Manual on terminology and classification in mental retardation*. (Rev. ed.). American Association on Mental Deficiency. Baltimore: Garamond/Pridemark Press, 1973.

Hall, P., & Alexander, G. Handicapping speech disorders. In R. E. Hardy & J. G. Cull (Eds.), *Severe disabilities: social and rehabilitation approaches*. Springfield, Ill.: Charles C Thomas, Publisher, 1974.

Hewitt, A. L., & Lawlis, F. Diseases of the kidney. In A. B. Cobb (Ed.), *Medical and psychological aspects of disability*. Springfield, Ill.: Charles C Thomas, Publisher, 1973.

Hylbert, K. W. *Medical information for counselors: an outline text*. State College, Pa.: Counselor Education Press, 1965.

J. E. Hanger, Inc. *Limb prosthetics* (3rd ed.). Denver: J. E. Hanger, Inc., 1972.

Jacks, J. C., & Toubbeh, J. I. The public vocational rehabilitation program and epilepsy. In G. N. Wright (Ed.), *Epilepsy rehabilitation*. Boston: Little, Brown & Co., 1975.

Johnson, D. S. Visual disorders. In J. S. Myers (Ed.), *An orientation to chronic disease and disability*. New York: The Macmillan Co., 1965.

Jones, E. End stage renal failure. In R. E. Hardy & J. G. Cull (Eds.), *Severe disabilities: social and rehabilitation approaches*. Springfield, Ill.: Charles C Thomas, Publisher, 1974.

Levinsky, N. G. Diseases of the kidney. In J. S. Myers (Ed.), *An orientation to chronic disease and disability*. New York: The Macmillan Co., 1965.

Lewis, R. C., Jr. Amputations and amputees. In A. B. Cobb (Ed.), *Medical and psychological aspects of disability*. Springfield, Ill.: Charles C Thomas, Publisher, 1973.

Long, C., II. Congenital and traumatic lesion of the spinal cord. In F. H. Krusen (Ed.), *Handbook of physical medicine and rehabilitation* (2nd ed.). Philadelphia: W. B. Saunders Co., 1971.

Long, C., II, & Lawton, E. B. Functional significance of spinal cord lesion level. *Archives of Physical Medicine and Rehabilitation*, 1955, *36*, 249-255.

Lorenze, E. J. The central nervous system: disorders of the brain. In J. S. Myers (Ed.), *An orientation to chronic disease and disability*, New York: The Macmillan Co., 1965.

McLarty, C. L., & Chaney, J. A. The cerebral palsied. In R. E. Hardy & J. G. Cull (Eds.), *Severe disabilities: social and rehabilitation approaches*. Springfield, Ill.: Charles C Thomas, Publisher, 1974.

Micek, L. A., & Bitter, J. A. Service delivery approaches for difficult rehabilitation clients. *Rehabilitation Literature*, 1974, *35*(9), 258-263, 271.

Miller, L. A., & Obermann, C. E. *The arthritides (Studies in continuing education for rehabilitation counselors)*. Menomonie, Wis.: Materials Development Center, University of Wisconsin–Stout, 1968.

Mueller, A. D. Psychologic factors in rehabilitation of paraplegic patients. *Archives of Physical Medicine and Rehabilitation*. 1962, *43*, 151-159.

Myers, J. S. Emotional disorders. In J. S. Myers (Ed.), *An orientation to chronic disease and disability*. New York: The Macmillan Co., 1965.

New York Heart Association. *Diseases of the heart and vessels: nomenclature and criteria for diagnosis* (6th ed.). Boston: Little, Brown & Co., 1964.

Ninth Institute on Rehabilitation Services. *Rehabilitation of the drug abuser*. Washington, D.C.: Rehabilitation Services Administration. Department of Health, Education, and Welfare, 1972.

O'Connor, J. R., & Leitner, L. A. Traumatic quadriplegia: a comprehensive review. *Journal of Rehabilitation*, 1971, 37(3), 14-20.

Poor, C. R. Vocational rehabilitation of persons with spinal cord injuries. *Rehabilitation Counseling Bulletin*, 1975, *18*(4), 264-271.

Prehm, H. J. Mental retardation: definition, classification and prevalence. In P. L. Browning (Ed.), *Mental retardation: rehabilitation and counseling*. Springfield, Ill.: Charles C Thomas, Publisher, 1974.

Risch, F. Rehabilitation planning for the epileptic client. In G. N. Wright (Ed.), *Epilepsy rehabilitation*. Boston: Little, Brown & Co., 1975.

Robinault, I. P., & Denhoff, E. The multiple dysfunctions called cerebral palsy. In A. B. Cobb (Ed.), *Medical and psychological aspects of disability*. Springfield, Ill.: Charles C Thomas, Publisher, 1973.

Rodin, E. A. Medical considerations. In G. N. Wright (Ed.), *Epilepsy rehabilitation*. Boston: Little, Brown & Co., 1975.

Rusher, W. D. Eyes and vision. In R. E. Hardy & J. G. Cull (Eds.), *Social and rehabilitation services for the blind*. Springfield, Ill.: Charles C Thomas, Publisher, 1972.

Rusk, H. A. *Rehabilitation medicine*. St. Louis: The C. V. Mosby Co., 1977.

Siller, J. Psychological situation of the disabled with spinal cord injuries. *Rehabilitation Literature*, 1969, *30*(10), 290-296.

Sinick, D. Job placement and post-placement services for the epileptic client. In G. N. Wright (Ed.), *Epilepsy rehabilitation*. Boston: Little, Brown & Co., 1975.

Sixth Institute on Rehabilitation Service. *Rehabilitation of the alcoholic*. Washington, D.C.: Rehabilitation Services Administration, Department of Health, Education, and Welfare, 1968.

Spodick, D. H. Diseases of the heart and peripheral blood vessels. In J. S. Myers (Ed.), *An orientation to chronic disease and disability*. New York: The Macmillan Co., 1965.

Storrs, L. A. Rehabilitation medical aspects of hearing disorders. In A. B. Cobb (Ed.), *Medical and psychological aspects of disability*. Springfield, Ill.: Charles C Thomas, Publisher, 1973.

Sword, S., & Roberts, M. M. The spinal cord injured patient. In R. E. Hardy & J. G. Cull (Eds.), *Severe disabilities: social and rehabilitation approaches*. Springfield, Ill.: Charles C Thomas, Publisher, 1974.

Walker, M. L., & Holbert, W. *Medical aspects of rehabilitation*. Knoxville, Tenn.: University of Tennessee Center for Extended Learning, 1973.

Wright, G. N. Rehabilitation and the problem of epilepsy. In G. N. Wright (Ed.), *Epilepsy rehabilitation*. Boston: Little, Brown & Co., 1975.

Young, C. G., & Barger, J. D. *Learning medical terminology step by step*. St. Louis: The C. V. Mosby Co., 1975.

ADDITIONAL READINGS

Anthony, W. A. *The principles of psychiatric rehabilitation*. Amherst, Mass.: Human Resource Development Press, 1978.

Bolton, B. *Psychology of deafness for rehabilitation counselors*. Baltimore: University Park Press, 1976.

Bregman, S. *Sexuality and the spinal cord injured woman*. Minneapolis: Sister Kenny Institute, 1975.

Committee on Nomenclature and Statistics of the American Psychiatric Association. *Diagnostic and statistical manual of mental disorders*. (2nd ed.). Washington, D.C.: American Psychiatric Association, 1968.

Cull, J. G., & Hardy, R. E. (Eds.). *Types of drug abusers and their abuses*. Springfield, Ill.: Charles C Thomas, Publisher, 1974.

Hardy, R. E., & Cull, J. G. (Eds.). *Drug dependence and rehabilitation approaches*. Springfield, Ill.: Charles C Thomas, Publisher, 1973.

Mooney, T. O., Cole, T. M., & Chilgren, R. A. *Sexual options for paraplegics and quadriplegics*. Boston: Little, Brown & Co., 1975.

Perlman, L. G., & Pietsch, S. C. *The person with epilepsy: lifestyle, needs, expectations*. Chicago: National Epilepsy League, 1977.

Sands, H., & Minters, F. C. *The epilepsy fact book*. Philadelphia: F. A. Davis Co., 1977.

Schlesinger, L. E., & Frank, D. S. *On the way to work: a guide for the rehabilitation counselor*. Washington, D.C.: Epilepsy Foundation of America, 1976.

Smith, L. G., & Davis, P. E. *Medical terminology: a programmed text* (3rd ed.). New York: John Wiley & Sons, Inc., 1976.

Task Force on Concerns of Physically Disabled Women. *Toward intimacy: family planning and sexuality concerns of physically disabled women*. Everett, Wash.: Planned Parenthood of Snohomish Co., Inc., 1977.

Task Force on Concerns of Physically Disabled Women. *Within reach: providing family planning services to physically disabled women*. Everett, Wash.: Planned Parenthood of Snohomish Co., Inc., 1977.

Young, C. G., & Barger, J. D. *Medical specialty terminology: pathology, clinical cytology, and clinical pathology* (Vol. 1). St. Louis: The C. V. Mosby Co., 1971.

Young, C. G., & Likos, J. J. *Medical specialty terminology: x-ray and nuclear medicine* (Vol. 2). St. Louis: The C. V. Mosby Co., 1972.

MEDIA RESOURCES

Visual

1. "Institute on Alcoholism" (ten ½" videotape series, 30 to 60 minutes per tape). Developed by the Division for Research and Training in Rehabilitation, School of Medicine, University of Southern California, 1739 Griffin Ave., Los Angeles, Calif. 90031.

   Ten videotapes that provide an overview of alcoholism from a medical, psychological, social, and vocational perspective.

2. "The Fifteenth American" (16 mm films). Available from Hofstra University Instructional Communication Center, 1000 Fulton Ave., Hempstead, Long Island, N.Y. 11553.

   A series of eight 16 mm films on alcoholism rehabilitation entitled (1) Group Therapy, (2) Lay Treatment Procedures, (3) Rehabilitation of the Alcoholic through Individual Therapy, (4) The Interdisciplinary Approach to Rehabilitation, (5) The Counselor in Various Rehabilitation Settings, (6) Case Study, (7) A Survey of Rehabilitation, and (8) It's Up to You.

3. "One of Sixteen Million" (16 mm film, 20 minutes). Available from Alabama Department of Public Health, Film Librarian, Bureau of Primary Prevention, Room 204, State Office Building, Montgomery, Ala. 36104.

   An animated film which describes arthritis—including prevalence, types, symptoms, effects, and methods of treatment.

4. "Not Without Sight" (16 mm film, 20 minutes). Available from American Foundation for the Blind Film Library, Public Education Division, 15 West 16th St., New York, N.Y. 10011.

   Describes five types of visual impairment: glaucoma, cataract, macular degeneration, retinitis, pigmentosa, and diabetic retinopathy. Each impairment is simulated for the viewing audience.

5. "Views of Impaired Vision" (16 mm film, 43 minutes). Available from Film Distributors Supervisor, Ohio State University, Dept. of Photographs and Cinema, 156 West 19th Ave., Columbus, Ohio 43210.

   The psychological effects of visual impairment and blindness shared by participants in the film.

6. "Meeting the Challenge of Blindness" (16 mm film, 26 minutes). Available from The Seeing Eye Inc., Office of Public Information, 9 Rockefeller Plaza, New York, N.Y. 10020.

   Depicts how four blind people—a homemaker, a husband and wage earner, a retired businessman, and a young working woman—deal with blindness.

7. "What Do You Do When You See a Blind Person?" (16 mm film, 13 minutes). Available from American Foundation for the Blind Film Library, Public Education Division, 15 West 16th St., New York, N.Y. 10011.

   Describes how to help blind persons in various situations.

8. "Heart of the Matter" (74 slides with audiotape cassette). Produced by Sister Kenny Institute, Chicago Ave., at 27th St., Minneapolis, Minn. 55407.

   Description of the cardiovascular system, coronary heart disease, and social attitudes about heart attacks.

9. "Medical Aspects of Heart Disease" (two-part videotape available in 2″, 1″, ½″; 58 minutes each). Produced by Department of Physical Medicine and Rehabilitation, University of Colorado Medical Center, 4200 E. 9th Ave., Denver, Colo. 80220.

   Lectures by H. L. Brammel for rehabilitation workers. Part 1 reviews the types of heart disease and its relevance to the rehabilitation process. Part 2 suggests how to rehabilitate the cardiac patient.

10. "Cardiac Rehabilitation Research Project—Implications for the Myocardial Infarction Patient" (videotape available in 2″, 1″, ½″; 34 minutes). Produced by Department of Physical Medicine and Rehabilitation, University of Colorado Medical Center, 4200 E. 9th Ave., Denver, Colo. 80220.

    Lecture by H. L. Brammel that emphasizes rehabilitation of the whole person, beginning with hospitalization and continuing through reintegration in the community.

11. "Cardiac Patient—a Team Responsibility" (videotape available in 2″, 1″, ½″; 41 minutes). Produced by Department of Physical Medicine and Rehabilitation, University of Colorado Medical Center, 4200 E. 9th Ave., Denver, Colo. 80220.

    The fourth in a series of lectures by H. L. Brammel, that emphasizes a team effort involving physicians, nurses, therapists, and vocational rehabilitation personnel for rehabilitation of cardiac patients.

12. "No Whistles, No Bells, No Bedlam (16 mm film, 20 minutes). Available from National Technical Institute of the Deaf, Rochester Institute of Technology, 1 Lomb Memorial Dr., Rochester, N.Y. 14623.

    Describes some myths associated with employment of the deaf.

13. "Training Cerebral Palsy Patients" (16 mm film, 9 minutes, silent). Produced by RT-2, University of Minnesota, Medical Rehabilitation Research and Training Center, 860 Mayo Building, Minneapolis, Minn. 55455.

    Demonstration of a team approach to working with a cerebral palsy patient.

14. "Modern Concepts of Epilepsy" (16 mm film, 25 minutes). Available from University of Iowa, Division of Extension and University Services, Audio-Visual Department, Iowa City, Iowa 52240.
    Provides facts about epilepsy, types, seizure examples, and methods of alleviating the possibility of seizures.
15. "Institute on Epilepsy" (fourteen ½" videotapes, 30 to 60 minutes each). Produced by Division for Research and Training in Rehabilitation, School of Medicine, University of Southern California, 1739 Griffin Ave., Los Angeles, Calif. 90031.
    Series of videotapes that describe the history, causes, treatment, and educational, psychological, and social implications of epilepsy.
16. "A General Orientation to Mental Retardation" (two 140-slide trays with audiotape). Produced by Research and Training Center in Mental Retardation, Texas Tech University, P. O. Box 4510, Lubbock, Texas 79409.
    Provides a historical and legislative background to services for the mentally retarded, a description of the AAMD definition, evaluation services, and programs including recommendations for working with the retarded.
17. "Selling One Guy Named Larry" (16 mm film, 17 minutes). Available from Associated Films, Inc., 600 Madison Ave., New York, N.Y. 10022.
    A portrayal of the mentally retarded at work.
18. "Drug Abuse" (16 mm film, 5 minutes). Available from General Services Administration, Sales Branch, National Audiovisual Center, Washington, D.C. 20409.
    An overview of the types of drugs and the effects on individuals.
19. "Drugs and the Nervous System" (16 mm film, 16 minutes). Available from Florida State University, Media Center, Tallahassee, Fla. 32306.
    Animated demonstration of how a common drug, aspirin, can affect the nervous system. The effects of various narcotics on the nervous system are then described.
20. "User's Point of View—Recovered Drug Addict" (½" videotape, 60 minutes). Produced by RT-13, Arkansas Rehabilitation Research and Training Center, Hot Springs Rehabilitation Center, P.O. Box 1358, Hot Springs, Ark. 71901.
    Discussion by a recovered drug addict of his personal experience in using drugs and his experience in working with drug abusers.
21. "House on the Beach" (16 mm film, 60 minutes). Available from University of California Extension, Media Center, 2223 Fulton St., Berkeley, Calif. 94720.
    Description of Synanon House in Santa Monica, California, and its program for rehabilitating narcotic addicts.
22. "Let's Start Again, Mr. Wilson" (16 mm film, 24 minutes, with printed discussion guide). Produced by Sister Kenny Institute, Chicago Ave. at 27th St., Minneapolis, Minn. 55407.
    Portrays the medical aspects, services, and vocational potential of stroke clients.
23. "Causes and Effects of Stroke" (36 slides with tape cassette). Produced by Sister Kenny Institute, Chicago Ave. at 27th St., Minneapolis, Minn. 55407.
24. "Rehabilitation of the Stroke Patient" (38 slides with tape cassette). Produced by Sister Kenny Institute, Chicago Ave. at 27th St., Minneapolis, Minn. 55407.
    Emphasizes the team approach to rehabilitating stroke clients—including physician, nurse, physical therapist, occupational therapist, speech-language pathologist, psychologist, social worker, and vocational counselor.
25. "Vocational Rehabilitation of the Stroke Patient" (43 slides with tape cassette). Produced by Sister Kenny Institute, Chicago Ave. at 27th St., Minneapolis, Minn. 55407.
    Describes evaluative placement and follow-up services of the vocational rehabilitation counselor.
26. "Amputations and Prosthetics" (100 slides). Available from RT-6, Emory University, Regional Rehabilitation Research and Training Center, Woodruff Memorial Building, Atlanta, Ga. 30322.
    Describes patient evaluation and care involving amputation procedures, stumps, and prosthetic devices.
27. "To Be Somebody Again" (16 mm film, 18 minutes). Available from Mental Health Association of Erie County, Inc., 1200 Elmwood Ave., Buffalo, N.Y. 14222.
    Narrated by Glenn Ford, describes the effects of stress on mental health. A team treatment approach is emphasized.

28. "Journey" (16 mm film, 28 minutes). Available from Mental Health Association of Erie County, Inc., 1200 Elmwood Ave., Buffalo, N.Y. 14222.

    Provides insight relative to stresses which affect all people. A team approach to rehabilitation is emphasized.

29. "Speakers with Cleft Palates" (16 mm film, 30 minutes). Available from University of Iowa, Division of Extension and University Services, Audio-Visual Department, Iowa City, Iowa 52240.

    Describes some physiological characteristics of speech and their effects for individuals with cleft palates.

30. "Changes" (16 mm film, 28 minutes). Available from Everest & Jennings, Inc., 1803 Pontius Ave., Los Angeles, Calif. 90025.

    An overview of spinal cord injury and its effects physically, psychologically, and socially as told by patients of Craig Hospital in Denver.

31. "Institute on Spinal Cord Injury" (series of ten ½″ videotapes, 30 to 60 minutes each). Produced by Division for Research and Training in Rehabilitation, School of Medicine, University of Southern California, 1739 Griffin Ave., Los Angeles, Calif. 90031.

    Emphasizes three areas of spinal cord injury: (1) anatomy, physiology, and treatment, (2) the roles of the physical therapist, occupational therapist, and nurse, and (3) the psychological, social, and vocational implications.

32. "Telling It Like It is—Spinal Cord Injury" (½″ videotape, 90 minutes). Produced by RT-13, Arkansas Rehabilitation Research and Training Center, Hot Springs Rehabilitation Center, P.O. Box 1358, Hot Springs, Ark. 71901.

    Discussion by a panel of spinal cord injured persons who share their perceptions of rehabilitation services.

33. "Sexuality and Spinal Cord Injury" (½″ videotape, 90 minutes). Produced by RT-13, Arkansas Rehabilitation Research and Training Center, Hot Springs Rehabilitation Center, P.O. Box 1358, Hot Springs, Ark. 71901.

    A lecture on sexual aspects of spinal cord injury—including attitudes, capabilities, and adjustment.

34. "Spinal Cord Injury Team" (1″ videotape, 24 minutes). Produced by RT-2, University of Minnesota, Medical Rehabilitation Research and Training Center, 860 Mayo Building, Minneapolis, Minn. 55455.

    Presents actual examinations of a quadriplegic man by a team consisting of a nurse, social worker, occupational therapist, physical therapist, psychologist, vocational rehabilitation counselor, and psychiatrist. Recommendations are formulated in a team conference.

35. "Medical Aspects of Rehabilitation" (eight slide-tape learning units with script, study guide, instructor's guide, and multiple-choice questions). Available from Center for Extended Learning, Division of Continuing Education, University of Tennessee, Room 447 Communications and Extension Building, Knoxville, Tenn. 37916.

    Presents eight areas of study designed for individualized instruction: (1) musculoskeletal disorders, (2) cardiovascular disorders, (3) digestive disorders, (4) respiratory disorders, (5) neurological disorders, (6) hearing disorders, (7) endocrine disorders, and (8) developmental disorders.

36. "Management of Spinal Cord Injury" (12 audiotape cassettes and album of over 300 miniature photographs). Available from Texas Institute for Rehabilitation and Research, 1333 Moursund Ave., Houston, Texas 77030.

    Describe in detail the critical phases of spinal cord injury rehabilitation, e.g., admission, acute management, intermediate care, discharge, and follow-up. In addition to the photographs, supplementary material includes a home care plan, descriptions of the care process for nurses, physical therapists, occupational therapists, and social service staff, and vocational placement material.

37. "Access" (16 mm film, 23 minutes). Available from Polymorph Films, 331 Newbury St., Boston, Mass. 02115.

    Depicts the personal experiences of two disabled individuals as they struggle to conquer their physical and emotional problems and make the transition from total disability to contributing members of society.

Audio

1. "New Direction—Alcoholism" (nine audiotapes). Available from Faces West Productions, 170 Ninth St., San Francisco, Calif. 94103.

   A series of audiotapes each presented by a different professional. Titles include The Alcoholic Script, Drinking Practices and Drinking Problems, Diagnosis and Referral, The Differential Selection of Alcoholics for Differential Treatment, A Realistic Consideration of Alternatives to Abstinence, The Physician's Role in the Treatment of Alcoholism, The Treatment of Alcoholism by Acupuncture, Training in Alcoholism, and The Non-degreed Professionals in the Treatment of Alcoholics.

2. "Rehabilitation of the Patient with Rheumatoid Arthritis" (four-track audiotape, 58 minutes). Available from Learning Resources Facility, Audiovisual Utilization, 550 First Ave., New York, N.Y. 10016.

   Describes the diagnosis, treatment, and rehabilitation of arthritic patients.

3. "Rehabilitation of Persons with Auditory Disabilities" (four-track audiotape, 89 minutes). Available from Learning Resources Facility, Audiovisual Utilization, 550 First Ave., New York, N.Y. 10016.

   Describes problems and solutions for congenital and adventitious hearing losses.

4. "Sex Problems in Paraplegia" (four-track audiotape, 90 minutes). Available from Learning Resources Facility, Audiovisual Utilization, 550 First Ave., New York, N.Y. 10016.

   A panel of medical specialists chaired by Howard A. Rusk discusses the implications of spinal cord injury on sexual function.

5. "Medical Terminology: An Individualized Approach" (nine body system modules with 22 audiotape cassettes, instructional supplement, supplemental modules for medical records training). Available from Westinghouse Learning Press, 770 Lucerne Dr., Sunnyvale, Calif. 94086.

   A package for learning medical terminology. Material is presented in terms of the nine major body systems. The learner studies the written material, completes brief exercises, and then listens to the tapes to identify, pronounce, spell, and transcribe medical terminology. The cassette tapes present key terms in three types of audioexercises: as a list, in context in a paragraph, and as found in a medical report.

6. "Stigma, Part One: What It's Like To Be Disabled" (audiotape, 60 minutes). Available from Center for Independent Living, 2539 Telegraph Ave., Berkeley, Calif. 94720.

   First person accounts of how it feels to be physically disabled.

7. "Stigma, Part Two: The Physically Disabled and the World" (audiotape, 60 minutes). Available from Center for Independent Living, 2539 Telegraph Ave., Berkeley, Calif. 94720.

   Discussion by disabled members of the Center for Independent Living in Berkeley, California, of architectural barriers, transportation difficulties, social interaction problems, and programs for the disabled.

5

Psychological and vocational adjustment of the disabled

OVERVIEW AND OBJECTIVES

This chapter provides the reader with a brief orientation to adjustment aspects of disability. It is divided into two major sections: (1) adjustment to disability and (2) a brief description of some vocational adjustment theories and practice.

Objectives of this chapter are to familiarize the reader with some psychological aspects of adjustment to disability in terms of self-concept, interpersonal relationships, and coping behaviors, to offer a concept of job readiness, to explain the Minnesota Theory of Work Adjustment, to provide an overview of work adjustment approaches, including the use of sheltered workshops, community job sites, and behavior modification techniques, and to present examples of vocational adjustment programs.

ADJUSTMENT TO DISABILITY

McDaniel (1976) reports that the disabled do not share common personality patterns even within disability categories. Though disability is often accompanied by difficulties in personal adjustment, there is not a common personality pattern which differentiates between disability groups.

Nevertheless, psychological effects are indeed associated with disability. These can arise directly from the disability, for example, damage to the central nervous system which results in a behavioral disorder. Psychological effects can result from an individual's attitude toward a disability based on what he knows about it, his prior experiences, and his aspirations. Effects can also stem from the attitudes of others toward a disability (McGowan & Porter, 1967). Knowing which factors affect psychological adjustment of disabled individuals the most is difficult. We do know that for amputees, psychological and physical adjustment is related to the severity of the disability. We also know that a sensory loss leads to a relatively high rate of social and occupational maladjustment (McDaniel, 1976).

Self-concept

Charles (1976) describes self-concept as the totality of what one believes to be true about himself and the value he places on those beliefs. What a disabled indi-

112

vidual believes to be true about himself is a product of his self-image and the viewpoints of, and interactions with, others. The value the individual places on these beliefs, or perceptions, determines whether he has a good or a poor self-concept. A good (i.e., positive) self-concept reflects satisfaction with self-perceptions that are important to the individual at the time.

Physically disabled persons frequently react to disability by showing an increased preoccupation with physical needs, depression, and a tendency to exaggerate sensations (McDaniel, 1976). However, the self-concept of the disabled individual will change over time as a result of learning and experience. Not only will the person learn what to expect of himself, he will also learn the attitude expectations of others.

Interpersonal relationships

There is evidence to indicate that the greater one accepts oneself the greater one is able to accept others and to feel accepted by others (Wright, 1960). Negative attitudes of others are usually toward the condition of the disability rather than the individual. Though there is no universal stereotype of the disabled, the severity of the disability may influence the perception others have toward the disabled and the degree of this acceptance will vary with sex, age, maturity, and possibly education (McDaniel, 1976). The self-concept of the disabled individual will also be a determinate of the nature of interpersonal relationships. The reactions of others may result from the disabled person's expectation of certain attitudes and feelings toward himself.

The attitudes of employers toward the disabled have been found to be similar to those of the general public. For example, negative attitudes are more related to the disability, per se, than to the individual. The more highly visible the functional disability is, the greater is the reluctance on the part of an employer to hire the handicapped. Positive attitudes on the part of an employer are often based on past experience with the disabled, the individual's competence, and the degree of sociability (McDaniel, 1976).

Helpful for interacting with some disabled persons is to talk about the disability but only if the disabled individual brings the subject up and wants to talk about it (Wright, 1960).

Coping behaviors

The way in which a physically disabled individual copes with a disability is dependent not only on the deficiency but on personal and environmental characteristics. After the initial shock to an individual, there is usually a denial reaction to a disability. The individual may first deny that he is disabled. This is usually followed by denial of the permanence of the disability. Depression is commonly experienced by the individual with the realization that the disability will be permanent. Such depression may vary in intensity and duration from person to person. The symptoms may be feelings of hopelessness, worthlessness, inactivity, and preoccupation with the disability; or there may be somatic symptoms like insomnia and weight loss. Hopefully depression is followed by personal and physical adjustment. Many coping behaviors may be exhibited during the adjustment process—(1) repression, which is selective forgetting (e.g., repressing negative attitudes toward the disability and the disabled), (2) reaction formation, which is adopting behavior opposite one's attitude (e.g., an overconcern for independence), (3) rationalization, i.e., attempting to provide logical reasons for behavior, and (4) projection of qualities that are perceived by the disabled to be unacceptable in himself onto others. An example of projection might be for the disabled to indicate that society feels he is inferior. On the more positive side, the disabled individual will begin to compensate for his limitations and channel his resources and energy toward personal strengths (Cull, 1972). Emphasis in the rehabilitation process is on rechanneling activity and attention toward occupational goals which capitalize on strengths and minimize limitations.

VOCATIONAL ADJUSTMENT THEORIES AND PRACTICE

As indicated in Chapter 1, vocational (or work) adjustment is a process of learning the meaning, value, and demands of work, of modifying or developing attitudes, personal characteristics, and work behavior, and of developing the functional capacities required to obtain the optimum level of vocational development (Tenth Institute on Rehabilitation Services, 1972). It is a learning process leading up to job readiness.

Concept of job readiness

Job readiness is defined as the attainment of performance patterns that will conform to those required by a work environment. Three considerations are important for an understanding of one's job readiness: first, there are individual performance patterns, in both behavior and skill, that affect employability; second, each job has its variables and no two work environments are exactly alike; and, third, job readiness involves a relationship between the job and the worker.

Worker variables include personal factors and job skill factors. Personal worker variables relate directly to individual behavior. Though they may affect job performance, they are really "life" adjustment factors—such as emotional maturity and stability, sensitivity, judgment, honesty, health and physical capabilities, and adaptive capacity. Some personal variables are more specifically important than others to demands of the work environment and are perhaps more amenable to development. Examples would be dependability, responsibility to others, tolerance, consistency, capacity for time considerations, attitudes, and interests. Job skill factors refer primarily to specific job knowledge and ability. The skilled trades are an example. A person cannot be considered "job ready" for work as a television technician unless he has the skills of a television technician. The more complex the job, the greater is the importance of job skills.

Work environment factors are all the variables inherent in a job and can include the type, kind, and size of the business, the type and amount of supervision, the working conditions (including hours, terms, and physical considerations), and the relationships among workers. It is the constellation of variables involved in any given job that constitutes a work environment and that is very important to determination of a person's job readiness. Any change in the constellation of these factors (e.g., a new worker) changes the work environment.

The range of work environment demands is considerable. Even within sheltered environments there are considerable differences. The range from the most simple of sheltered jobs to the most complex and demanding competitive work situations makes up a continuum. The theoretical point between sheltered and competitive environment is a matter of conjecture and will vary depending on such factors as the locality, labor market, and the economy. If labor is difficult to secure, employers will be more tolerant of the help they have. The opposite is true in a period of recession (Bitter, 1968).

Minnesota Studies in Vocational Rehabilitation

The Minnesota Studies in Vocational Rehabilitation were conducted between 1957 and 1972 at the University of Minnesota. Emphasis in the studies was on a theory of work adjustment. The Minnesota Theory of Work Adjustment is based on the idea of correspondence between the individual and the environment. The individual adjusts to work based on an interaction between his work personality and the work environment. Work personality is represented by an individual's vocational ability and vocational needs. The work environment is made up of ability requirements and reinforcer systems. Work adjustment, then, is a function of the worker's satisfaction with the job and the satisfactoriness of the worker in the job. A correspondence between the worker's vocational needs and the occupational reinforcers of the job is used to predict job satisfaction. A correspondence between the worker's abilities and the ability requirements of the job is used to predict job satisfactoriness. Considering both satisfaction and satisfactoriness can be used to predict job tenure (Lofquist, Dawis, & Hendel, 1972).

The Minnesota Studies also produced a number of measurement instruments for applying the theory's concepts. To measure the outcomes of work adjustment, i.e., satisfaction and satisfactoriness, the *Minnesota Satisfaction Questionnaire* and the *Minnesota Satisfactoriness Scale* were developed. The *General Aptitude Test Battery (GATB),* a standard measure of general abilities, is used to measure vocational abilities. The *Occupational Aptitude Patterns* developed through the U.S. Training and Employment Service is utilized to measure ability requirements. In addition, the *Minnesota Importance Questionnaire (MIQ)* was developed to measure vocational needs of potential workers; and the *Occupa-*

tional Reinforcer Patterns was published as a basis for determining the reinforcer systems of the job (Lofquist, Dawis, & Hendel, 1972).

The Minnesota Theory of Work Adjustment provides rehabilitation workers
with a systematic framework for thinking about vocational rehabilitation. It defines the goal of vocational rehabilitation as finding a job in which the disabled
person is satisfied and performs satisfactorily, with a high probability for staying
a reasonable length of time. Application of the Minnesota Theory of Work Adjustment and its instruments can be helpful in terms of vocational counseling,
development of work personality, and job placement.

VOCATIONAL ADJUSTMENT APPROACHES

Many rehabilitation programs include what is referred to as work adjustment
training in their programming for the purpose of preparing clients to become "job
ready." Usually this is taken to mean the development of personal variables like
responsibility and tolerance for work environments. Sankovsky (1971) identifies
three basic types of adjustment services in a rehabilitation setting: personal adjustment, social adjustment, and work adjustment. All three are conducted
within the context of vocational adjustment. A vocationally related adjustment
curriculum can include material ranging from personal appearance and hygiene
to the use of leisure time and community living, (such as shopping, budgeting,
and banking). Emphasis, however, is on the provision of vocational information
and the development of work habits like tolerance, consistency, capacity for time
considerations, and responsibility to others.

Dunn (1974) has identified three primary approaches to vocational adjustment. These are verbal, situational, and environmental approaches.

1. Verbal approaches can include individual counseling, group counseling,
videocounseling, and instruction. Individual counseling is intended primarily to
assist with personal adjustment. Group counseling, on the other hand, is intended to help with problems involving interactions with others. Videocounseling, i.e., videotaping samples of client behavior, can be an effective tool for providing feedback about behavior. Instruction, both individual and classroom, is
utilized in adjustment programs for providing clients with knowledge or information. Instructional approaches can be particularly helpful when a large number
of clients need the same information.

2. Situational approaches in vocational adjustment provide experiential opportunities for clients and include the use of production work in a sheltered environment, community job-site assignments, and behavior modification techniques.
These will be described in more detail.

3. Still another approach to vocational adjustment is environmental manipulation. Dunn (1974) refers to the elimination of job-site *barriers* and the use of
prosthetics for maximizing the efficiency of persons as two approaches to environmental manipulation. Barrier elimination includes (a) eliminating archi-

tectural features which prevent a handicapped individual from having access to a place of work, (b) eliminating work rules or other organizational controls which make it difficult to accommodate a disabled individual at the work site, and (c) eliminating job design hinderances. These three approaches to the elimination of barriers concentrate on the job and are often referred to as job engineering. They make it possible for the disabled person to do the work. Use of prosthetic strategies which attempt to maximize the behavior efficiency of disabled persons includes job performance aids like an artificial limb or some other device that enables the individual to perform certain tasks.

Medical therapists can also be important for the vocational adjustment of disabled clients. The occupational therapist, for example, can aid the client in adjusting to activities of daily living including self care, walking, getting in and out of chairs or automobiles, using kitchen equipment, and using the wheelchair or prosthesis. Therapists can also help a client increase his work tolerance and ability to lift objects and can adapt work equipment and work methods to fit the disabled person's limitations. The physical therapist can contribute to a client's work adjustment plan by aiding physical restoration through exercise, massage, and the use of mechanical apparatuses. Speech-language pathologists can aid the client in developing confidence and self-expression (Baker & Sawyer, 1971).

According to the 1978 *Standards Manual for Rehabilitation Facilities* offered by the Commission on Accreditation of Rehabilitation Facilities, vocational adjustment programs must develop individualized written work adjustment plans for each client. Such plans should include the behaviors to be worked with, the methods and techniques to be used, the persons responsible for implementation of the plan, the work assignment or environment where the plan is to be implemented, and a review or evaluation method for observing planned progress (Esser, 1975).

Three common situational approaches to vocational adjustment, particularly for the mentally disabled, are sheltered workshops, community job sites, and behavior modification.

Sheltered workshops

The sheltered workshop is a frequently used approach to vocational adjustment. As described in Chapter 1, a sheltered workshop is a rehabilitation facility, or part of such a facility, that utilizes production and work experience in a controlled environment for developing work habits and attitudes commonly expected in community employment. Sheltered workshops very much resemble light production industrial settings. Much of the work conducted by most sheltered workshops is of the bench assembly variety. Clients usually stand or sit at benches and assemble light appliances, package, sort, collate, or conduct work of a similar nature. Most contract work in a sheltered workshop is simple, repetitious, and of short duration. Work is usually obtained by making bids on jobs. However, some sheltered workshops engage in the production of their own products and the marketing of those products.

A usual difference between sheltered workshops and community employment is that most of the people making up the work force in a sheltered workshop are unstable, unskilled, and unprepared for work. When they become good workers, they are ready to enter competitive employment. This is in contrast to competitive industry, where the employer retains and rewards good workers and eliminates poor ones (Campbell & O'Toole, undated).

Workshop models. There are four basic models for rehabilitation programs utilizing workshops.

1. The first is the *long-term* facility. In this type of sheltered workshop, clients can work for a wage in an understanding and unpressured environment. Clients in such a workshop seldom require preparation for advancement to the employment market. The long-term workshop generally assumes that a sheltered environment is the extent of the client's capability for vocational and economic usefulness. There are two primary types of long-term facilities: one emphasizing remunerative employment with supportive rehabilitation services, the other emphasizing work activity for its therapeutic value supported by services for developing the client's independent living skills.

2. The *transitional* workshop goes a step further by introducing the professionally trained rehabilitation counselor. The function of the rehabilitation counselor is to effect behavioral change and prepare the client for community employment. This added dimension is primarily a casework process of relatively short duration and involves role training. The transitional workshop for clients is intended to provide the counselor with an opportunity for evaluation of employment potential, adjustment counseling, and selective job placement.

3. A third model is the *clinically oriented* workshop, which is in effect, a psychological laboratory. The clinically oriented workshop differs from the transitional workshop in that it uses professional vocational counselors in both the counseling role and the workshop supervisor role. Organizing the workshop in this manner involves the workshop to a greater degree as a rehabilitation instrument with the focus on psychosocial components of work. The distinguishing feature of the clinically oriented workshop is the use of professionally trained counselors as workshop supervisors. In the position of supervisor, the counselor can better control the client's workshop environment to bring about adjustment to psychosocial and physical elements of work.

4. A fourth model for sheltered workshops is the *habilitation* facility in an experience center approach. In the experience center approach the workshop is only one of many resources in the process of vocational adjustment. The professional vocational counselor serves as the client's case manager. In managing a client's program, the counselor may draw upon various resources which he deems appropriate to the educational, psychological, and social development of the client for future employment. The sheltered workshop is one of these re-

sources. It is like the transitional shop. It places emphasis on industrial conditions approximating those in business operations in the community. The workshop supervisor is usually an experienced industrial person familiar with production, time-and-motion studies, work contracting, employee relations, and supervision. His primary motivation is management of the workshop and total production control, that is, the control of material, machinery, labor, time, quantity and quality, and cost. This balance between the counselor, who can understand behavioral dynamics and relate them to general employment requirements, and the supervisor, who is on the job with the client, offers a way for the workshop to make a major contribution as a realistic rehabilitation tool. Thus the sheltered workshop takes on an integral role in the developmental process and may be used by the counselor at any time.

Each of these workshops has a place in the vocational rehabilitation of the disabled. Long-term shops meet the needs of specific types of clients, primarily the severely mentally disabled. The transitional workshop provides an opportunity to help clients adjust to their disability as it relates to the work world on an ego-supportive level. The clinically oriented workshop is an excellent resource for emotional and social adjustment problems in which work is a therapeutic medium. The habilitation workshop provides an educational experience to the vocationally unsophisticated, such as the mentally retarded and the school dropout, who have had little or no previous contact with the work world.

In summary, the long-term workshop can provide stable productive employment for disabled clients who generally cannot be restored to normal community living; the transitional workshop assists in restoring employment to disabled clients requiring a relatively short period for adjustment training; the clinically oriented workshop can help disabled clients with more serious psychosocial difficulties return to employment; and the habilitation workshop can focus on vocational education and experiences for disabled persons who have never known the work world (Bitter & Bolanovich, 1966).

Sheltered workshop training. Two recent efforts to train the severely handicapped, particularly the severely retarded in long-term workshops, are worthy of note. One represents the work of Marc W. Gold at the University of Illinois in Urbana-Champaign; the other is the work of G. Thomas Bellamy and his associates at the University of Oregon. Both approaches emphasize a form of task analysis.

For Gold (1976), the task analysis approach for assembly jobs comprises the following: (1) selection of a method for performing the task, (2) dividing the method into content steps, and (3) designing strategies for teaching the content, including a presentation format, feedback methods to clients, and training procedures. If a client is unsuccessful in achieving the desired results with Gold's plan, systematic adjustments can be continually made in the method, content, or teaching strategies until a way is found for the client to succeed.

For Bellamy, Inman, and Horner (1977), the task analysis (breakdown of a job into small functional steps) is placed in the context of an organizational structure, a work flow system, individualized treatment plans, and a data collection system. The authors refer to it as the "specialized training program" model. Organizationally the model can be implemented within a sheltered workshop or in an industry with a core staff who know the model's procedures. In the work flow system a contract job is selected based upon its availability and economic value rather than on its simplicity. A task analysis is then performed for each task or major component of the contract job, and clients are individually trained to do the job. Supervisors (seven clients per supervisor) provide needed job parts, social consequences for task attending and task completion, quality control, records of productivity, and token reinforcements. A treatment plan is developed for each client which identifies objectives, treatment procedures, and client evaluation methods. The data collection system for management of the model program includes production records, client task and treatment behavior information, and financial record-keeping.

Community job sites

Community job sites can be an important benefit to the vocational adjustment of the rehabilitation client. Though a sheltered workshop can provide an environment and the setting for social dynamics, it is a setting generally limited to work of the bench assembly variety and to working with others who are handicapped. Some of the advantages of extending this vocational adjustment experience into the community with actual employers and their place of business are as follows:

1. The experience is real and concrete. On an actual job site the client can work with real associates in related activities and can experience job changes, production demands, and a hierarchy of supervision. At a job site the client has an opportunity to demonstrate and test his abilities or lack of them in a setting and on activities similar or identical to those faced in future job placement.

2. The job site also provides for a functional appraisal of the behavior dynamics on the job by both the counselor and the employer. With the help of the employer, a counselor can realistically and objectively observe and evaluate strengths, weaknesses, and potentials of a client. In addition, the community job site affords an opportunity to compare the rehabilitation client's performance with that of regular employees, based on standards which the employer has established.

3. By using a variety of community job-site assignments, the rehabilitation client can experience an immediate perception of likes and dislikes in terms of areas of employment.

4. The client and counselor obtain an immediate perception of client capabilities and limitations. Through the experience the client can develop a more adequate self-concept, as a person and as a productive worker (Bitter, 1967).

Using employer job sites can have some disadvantages. For example, an employer may be too sympathetic toward the client and thus limit the effectiveness of a real and objective experience. It is also possible that the employer will not have enough time available to give the close supervision necessary with many rehabilitation clients, particularly during the early stages of the experience, even though he is more than willing to cooperate in such a program. A client's enthusiasm may distort an employer's evaluation of the client, thus minimizing the potential benefit of a vocational adjustment experience. However, these disadvantages can be minimized by an experienced rehabilitation counselor through employer orientation, care in the selection of a job site, and cooperation with the employer in providing the climate for evaluation and vocational adjustment (Bitter, 1967).

Behavior modification

Behavior modification has become increasingly used in recent years as an adjustment technique in rehabilitation. Behavior modification assumes that behavior can be changed, modified, or developed by systematically reinforcing a person's responses. It operates on the premise that observable actions can be increased or decreased by application of appropriate reinforcement methods. Reinforcers are consequences of behavior. Reinforcers for increasing behaviors may be either positive or negative. Positive reinforcers are agreeable. Negative reinforcers are disagreeable. Negative reinforcement involves *removal* of disagreeable reinforcers. An example is to remove a client from a work task which the client does not like and which results in disruptive behavior. Removing the client from the work task (negative reinforcement) can result in a desired behavior (influencing the client to be less disruptive) when the disagreeable work task is removed (Dunn, 1974).

Reinforcement for desired behavior is usually offered according to one of four common schedules. It can follow a certain number of responses (a ratio schedule) or a certain amount of time (an interval schedule). Both the number of responses and the amount of time can be either fixed or variable. In a *fixed ratio* schedule the reinforcement is offered after a given number of responses; in a *variable ratio* schedule the presentation of the reinforcement varies; in a *fixed interval* schedule the reinforcement is offered for a response after a specified period of time; and in a *variable interval* schedule the schedule is based on time but the ratio of the reinforcement varies. Fixed schedules are usually used at the beginning of a behavior modification program. Variable schedules are then used to maintain a level of response after an acceptable level of response has been attained (Walker & Shea, 1976).

Two other concepts that are important to the understanding of behavior modification are generalization and discrimination. Generalization represents a transfer of learning wherein a behavior, which was reinforced in the presence of one stimulus, will also be exhibited in the presence of another stimulus. Discrimination is the process of learning to act some way in one situation and another way in a different situation (Walker & Shea, 1976).

It was noted that there are two reinforcement methods for increasing behavior, i.e., positive reinforcement and negative reinforcement. Walker and Shea (1976) outline four of the most common behavior modification techniques for increasing desired behavior: shaping, modeling, contingency contracting, and token economy. Shaping is a systematic approach to reinforcing successive approximations of a behavior until the behavior is established. Modeling is the process of imitation in which the person learns or changes behavior as a result of observing another person perform that behavior. Contingency contracting involves establishing conditions for which a client can get something by exhibiting a required behavior. A token economy system employs a uniform reinforcer such as tokens, points, trading stamps, or play money. The tokens have a value in securing other types of reinforcers (e.g., recreation opportunities, tangible objects, or other individualized reinforcers).

Campbell (1971) describes an example of contingency contracting. In her example a client was permitted to do a preferred job task contingent upon increasing production on a job he did not like and on which he performed poorly. Campbell reports that this approach resulted in increased production on both. In addition, the client increased his ability to deal with job changes and job flexibility.

An example of a token economy approach is also described by Campbell (1971). Point cards were used. These could be exchanged for activities which vary in value. The activities included bus tours to plants, race tracks, and TV stations; entertainment by local celebrities; a canteen; and an opportunity to purchase overtime work or counseling. Implementation of the token economy system first involved establishing a baseline for each client during a 2-week practice period. This was done to establish point values. Clients would then receive points for actual outputs and could exchange them for the available activities. The results suggested that the token economy system improved productivity of the group and was maintained after the reinforcement contingency was discontinued. Similarly such approaches can be applied to other areas of work adjustment—including work habits, appearance, and other behaviors.

Walker and Shea (1976) offer six ways to decrease or eliminate undesirable behavior: (1) extinction, (2) time out, (3) satiation, (4) punishment, (5) reinforcement of incompatible behaviors, and (6) desensitization. *Extinction* is the removal of a reinforcer for a behavior. *Time out* removes the individual from a situation that reinforces undesirable behavior; presumably the individual is put in a setting which will be less conducive to the undesired behavior. *Satiation* is decreasing or eliminating unacceptable behavior by overreinforcing it. *Punishment* involves an adverse reaction to unacceptable behavior; punishment, however, is a relatively ineffective method for long-term changes in behavior since it tends to suppress rather than eliminate behavior. (A more effective approach is extinction, applied systematically.) *Reinforcement of incompatible behaviors* hopes to decrease an undesirable behavior by reinforcing some behavior that might be in opposition to the undesired behavior; an example is separating two workers who constantly argue with each other (the distance between the individuals is supposedly incompatible with arguing). *Desensitization* is a systematic process of reducing a learned fear in an individual; it involves relaxation training, a hierarchy of anxiety-evoking stimuli, and counterposing relaxation and the anxiety-evoking stimuli (Walker & Shea, 1976).

The use of behavior modification in rehabilitation and work adjustment raises some ethical issues. Roos (1974) identifies three behavior modification methods which could disregard some human rights of individuals. One is the use of adverse conditioning (e.g., painful stimuli, the loss of earned tokens, or the use of time-out procedures). A second is control of behavior, especially as it relates to attempting to effect change in attitude or personality. A third is selection of goals for behavior modification, particularly when done without involvement of the client (as usually happens for many severely disabled clients and very young children). Roos (1974) suggests, however, that recognizing such potential intrusion on human rights is a first step toward minimizing or avoiding dilemmas.

SOME VOCATIONAL ADJUSTMENT PROGRAMS
Vocational Guidance and Rehabilitation Services, Cleveland, Ohio

Vocational Guidance and Rehabilitation Services (VGRS) is a voluntary non-profit agency which offers vocational and educational counseling, vocational, educational, and psychological testing, employment counseling, group counseling, job placement, medical evaluation, physical therapy, activities of daily living, work evaluation, work adjustment, and skill training. It is located in a large Cleveland rehabilitation complex that includes many other people-oriented agencies.

Campbell and O'Toole (undated) describe the VGRS work adjustment program, which began as a five-year federally supported project. The project was established to provide services to clients who failed to learn the habits necessary to be good workers. Characteristics of this group were lack of confidence, fear of failure, and poor interpersonal relationships. Included in the group were people with emotional disabilities, physical disabilities (e.g., hemiplegia, epilepsy, birth injury, cerebral palsy, and amputations), and mental retardation. The goals of the VGRS work adjustment project were to improve self-esteem, work confidence, interpersonal relationships, physical stamina, grooming and dress, concentration, and vocational goal planning. At VGRS the sheltered workshop was the predominant work adjustment approach.

Techniques at VGRS for improving client self-esteem included role playing in group counseling sessions, a supportive attitude on the part of the counselor, client group discussions, visits to plants and factories, and a frequent change in workshop jobs. For building clients' work confidence, real work experiences were offered toward the end of the program in such areas as maintenance, shipping and receiving, food service, packing, clerical work, receptionist duties, and attending parking lots. Principal techniques for developing interpersonal relationships were group counseling and on-the-spot counseling for crisis situations. Counseling was also used for developing client concentration.

VGRS had a physical fitness area for improving stamina. There were a running machine, a rowing machine, bicycles, pool and Ping-Pong tables, weights, and punching bags. Though not required, clients were able to use this equipment during their work breaks. VGRS had a grooming clinic operated by volunteers for helping clients with personal appearance. In addition, clients were taken to the local vocational high school for hair cutting, styling, shampooing, and setting. Grooming kits were provided to male clients.

VGRS assumed the responsibility for placing the clients it served in jobs. The agency employed placement counselors whose responsibilities were to develop community resources, provide preplacement counseling for clients, and conduct job-readiness programs. Job-readiness programming involved learning to complete job application forms, becoming familiar with personnel testing procedures, and developing the ability to anticipate employer expectations; clients also learned about union membership, taxes, social security, fringe benefits, payroll methods, and check cashing. Much of the preparation for employment involved role playing; and in addition, the placement counselor arranged for employment interviews.

As a five-year federally supported project, the VGRS work adjustment program served a total of 300 clients. During the project's operational period it was successful in placing three fourths of its clients in competitive employment. Upon follow-up, only 18% of the clients served were found not to have worked since leaving the work adjustment program. The average stay in the program was approximately 16 weeks. VGRS considered two key factors to be important to the results of the program—the work adjustment counselor and the sheltered workshop, the counselor acting as a milieu therapist and dealing with problems as they arose in the workshop, the sheltered workshop providing clients with an opportunity to relate to concrete work and receive feedback on the results of their behavior and effort.

Work Experience Center, St. Louis Jewish Employment and Vocational Service

Bitter and Bolanovich (1966) describe another approach to vocational adjustment conducted as a demonstration project at the Work Experience Center (WEC) of the St. Louis Jewish Employment and Vocational Service. This experience center approach was based, in part, on the innovations of Kolstoe and Frey (1965) and utilized various resources for the educational, psychological, and social development of the client for future employment. The sheltered workshop was one of these resources. Another major resource was the employer and his place of business, referred to in the program as a "job site." These job sites were used for evaluation and training in a milieu of direct work experience. Cooperating employers would let clients work or train at their location for varying lengths of time as prescribed by counselors for specific training objectives. The sites differed greatly, not only in their job duties but also in terms of responsibility, psychosocial complexity, and work pressure. The rehabilitation counselor was in a position to employ situations and environments that could offer maximum opportunity to develop vocational potential of a particular client. For example, if the client needed a closely supervised domestic situation under the direction of an understanding female supervisor it was possible to arrange such a situation. On the other hand, if a situation was needed in an industrial setting with opportunity for initiative and responsibility, this too was possible.

In addition to traditional counseling approaches with clients, a wide range of resources were available to the Work Experience Center program. Some of these were group instruction, job rotation, orientation programs, field tours, and audiovisual training situations. The Work Experience Center program was described in five phases:

> *Phase 1* stressed intramural evaluation and general vocational adjustment. The main training vehicle was the WEC habilitation workshop. Each client was given appropriate experiences to provide him with a realistic orientation to employment and give the counselor a sound basis for evaluation of work potential.
>
> *Phase 2* was an extension of phase 1, continuing the emphasis on vocational evaluation and adjustment. However, in this phase the client's major experiences occurred during short job-site assignments with actual employers.
>
> During *phase 3* the client was given specific job preparation or occupational training. This preparation could take place in the workshop, at job sites, or in trade schools.
>
> When the client was prepared for a specific job situation, he was advanced to *phase 4,* which included a full-time or part-time job tryout with an employer. Ultimate employment in these assignments was contingent upon the client's performance.
>
> The client in *phase 5* of the program was considered officially employed. Postcurricular counseling continued with the client, the employer, and significant others until a satisfactory adjustment and acceptable level of job stability were in view.

At the completion of the project, 56% of the clients were community employed with an additional 23% employed in sheltered environments (Bitter, Bolanovich, & O'Neal, 1967).

Center for Developmental and Learning Disorders, University of Alabama, Birmingham

An example of the token economy system applied to rehabilitation is one conducted at the University of Alabama in Birmingham. Though the program is applicable to all handicapping conditions, the three-year project conducted during 1970-1973 at the Center for Developmental and Learning Disorders was for the rehabilitation of mentally retarded young adults. The Center's project defined the rehabilitation process of evaluation, adjustment, and training as a single procedure. Clients came to the facility for 6 hours a day. Target behaviors of the project were the handicapped person's inability to follow directions and remain with a task, academic incompetence, and inappropriate job behaviors. Six behaviors were identified as targets of the token economy system: (1) auxiliary work, (2) work, (3) academic, (4) direction following, (5) motivation, and (6) home-making.

The central operational concept of the Center's project was the job description. It provided a vehicle for describing jobs, job duties, and the training and evaluation of clients. It also incorporated a method for recording data about behavioral change.

The primary behavior modification method used in the Birmingham Center program was the contingency reinforcement approach. Tokens were given for positive increases in performance by the client. These tokens could, in turn, be exchanged for various positive reinforcers like candy, crackers, gum, television time, utilization of the telephone, lunch, and free time. The collection of information about clients included a period of observation without treatment (baseline) and then a period of treatment in which any decrease or increase in performance could be observed. During the project, observations and information were collected about each client on a daily basis. Implementation of the job description involved breaking each job down into its specific behaviors and dividing each specific behavior into its component elements. These component elements then became the objectives to be reached by the client. The system employed the concept of successive approximation, positively reinforcing each step of development toward an end goal.

Another behavior modification concept applied in the program was called fading. The concept of fading involved gradually increasing the amount of behavior for the same amount of reward. Thus, as each client completed step one, then step two, etc., he no longer was rewarded for the successful completion of each step but rather for the steps not yet perfected. Hopefully the successfully learned behavior would continue without the need for reinforcement.

The purpose of using tokens was to allow clients to choose their own positive reinforcers. The token system allowed clients to purchase almost any primary reward by exchanging the token for the reward desired. This personalized the system. Paper tokens functioned much like cashier checks. The token was made out to the client in his name with the date and the supervisor's name also showing. It also indicated a time period for which it could be exchanged. In addition to tangible reinforcements for appropriate behavior, the staff used praise and contact with the client.

As another step toward community adjustment, the fading procedure was again employed. A point system was substituted for the token economy. Instead of being paid tokens for the completion of jobs, a client accumulated points and was paid money at the week's end. The application of this approach helped the client make the transition from a token economy to job placement and a money economy.

Another dimension of the Birmingham program was the use of contingency contracts for after-program hours and minor home problems. The contract was used to identify reward points and appropriate behaviors after program hours. Such contracts were initiated between the client and a significant other (e.g., parents). Points earned and points spent were kept by the significant other and returned to program staff on a weekly basis.

Results of the three-year project were similar to the results of other rehabilitation programs for retarded clients. Of the 22 clients reported as data, 50% were employed either full-time or part-time at the end of the project. An excellently detailed book is available which describes the token economy system implemented at the Center (Welch & Gist, 1974). The volume offers excellent examples and illustrations of behavior modification principles applied in an open token economy system.

Job Survival Skills Program, Singer Company

The Singer Education Division of the Singer Company in Rochester, New York, has developed a Job Survival Skills Program package for training individuals in the personal and interpersonal aspects of employment. The program utilizes the group approach to preparing the client for survival in employment and is intended to complement educational and vocational training for jobs.

Group interaction is the primary method for skill development in the program, which is divided into 15 informational units and includes 42 activities: puzzle assembly, simulation games, brainstorming sessions, group discussions, role playing, peer evaluations, and individual assessment. There are film strips for 13 of the 15 units. The Singer Company program can be used with as few as eight participants and requires approximately 25 hours of classroom instruction. Basic concepts for most of the units are introduced by a sound filmstrip presentation. These concepts are then reinforced through the use of a variety of activities that involve participants. Units' emphases include (1) the what and why of job survival skills, (2) the relationship between education and training and reaching job-oriented goals, (3) differing points of view and how needs, roles, and attitudes affect a person's point of view, (4) the relationship between a positive self-concept and successful employment, (5) the communication process and its implications in the work environment, (6) common supervisor-employee problem areas, (7) the effect of co-worker relationships on job satisfaction, (8) behaviors conducive to job success, (9) techniques for locating employment, (10) the importance of personal appearance, (11) how to prepare a resumé, (12) how to complete an employment application, (13) effective interview techniques, (14) a program summary and review, and (15) participant peer evaluation of employment strengths and weaknesses.

The program needs a skilled group leader who serves as a catalyst. The leader introduces skill units, leads discussion and brainstorming sessions, directs role playing, and summarizes and supervises individual and peer assessment activities.

Singer received a grant for evaluation of the program's effectiveness. Results indicated high program acceptance by both participants and group leaders. When a reaction scale of 1 to 5 was employed, strong positive feelings (5 rating) concerning the program were indicated by 85% of the participants. An additional 7% of participants in the program rated it a 4. Similarly, 80% of the group leaders rated the program either a 4 or 5.

SUMMARY

Though there are not common personality patterns that differentiate disability groups, disability does indeed have psychological effects. Important to the disabled person's psychological adjustment are his self-concept, interpersonal relationships, and coping behavior. Learning and experience affect one's self-concept and interpersonal relationships. However, the more one is able to accept oneself, the more one is able to accept others and feel accepted. Coping behaviors during the personal and physical adjustment process may include repression, reaction formation, rationalization, or projection. The goal of vocational rehabilitation is to constructively guide the client toward positive occupational goals which will capitalize on strengths and minimize limitations.

Vocational adjustment is a process of learning to effectively function in a work environment. Job readiness is attained when the performance patterns of an individual conform to the requirements of a work environment. The Minnesota Studies in Vocational Rehabilitation developed a theory of work adjustment involving an interaction between the vocational abilities and needs of the individual and the ability requirements and reinforcers of the work environment. Work adjustment then becomes a function of the satisfaction of the job to the worker and the satisfactoriness of the worker in the job.

Three primary approaches to vocational adjustment are verbal, situational, and environmental. Verbal approaches include individual and group counseling and instruction utilizing personal and video modalities. Situational approaches might involve the use of production work in a sheltered workshop, community job sites, and behavior modification. Environmental approaches necessitate changing the work environment to accommodate the client's disability or creating some prosthesis, device, or other job-performance aid for maximizing the client's efficiency in the work environment. The occupational, physical, and speech therapies can also be most helpful in assisting the adjustment process for disabled clients.

Three commonly used situational approaches in the vocational adjustment of rehabilitation clients, particularly for the mentally disabled, are sheltered workshops, community job-site assignments, and behavior modification efforts. A sheltered workshop uses production work in a controlled environment, primarily for developing work habits and attitudes usually expected in community employment. Community job-site assignments represent a vocational adjustment experience with community employers in their place of business. Behavior modification is an approach which assumes that a person's behavior can be changed, modified, or developed by systematically reinforcing particular responses.

Four vocational adjustment programs are described in this chapter.

1. The program at Vocational Guidance and Rehabilitation Services in Cleveland, Ohio, utilized a transitional sheltered workshop as the predominant approach complemented by a wide range of supportive techniques coordinated by a work adjustment counselor for developing habits necessary to be a good employee.

2. The Work Experience Center of the St. Louis Jewish Employment and Vocational Service used an experience center approach involving primarily a "habilitation" sheltered workshop and community job-site assignments as techniques for vocational adjustment of clients. As in the VGRS program, these two resources were complemented by a wide variety of supportive service resources.

3. The program at the Center for Developmental and Learning Disorders of the University of Alabama in Birmingham represented a contingency reinforcement approach using a token economy system. Tokens were given for positive increases in performance by clients and could be exchanged for other positive reinforcers.

4. The Job Survival Skills Program developed by the Singer Company is a packaged multimedia approach to training individuals in the personal and interpersonal aspects of employment. It involves 15 informational units and 42 structured activities requiring about 25 hours of instruction. The primary approach is group interaction led by a skilled group leader.

Each of these programs represents some of the more common techniques for addressing the psychovocational aspects of disability in a rehabilitation context.

SELF-EVALUATION QUESTIONS

1. What are some potential causes of psychological effects of disability?
2. What is the definition for self-concept?
3. What are two determinates of others perceptions of the disabled?
4. What is the usual reaction pattern to severe physical disability?
5. What are some coping behaviors that may be exhibited by the physically disabled during the adjustment process?
6. What is the difference between vocational adjustment and job readiness?
7. What are the considerations for an understanding of one's job readiness?
8. What are the worker and work environment concepts in the Minnesota Theory of Work Adjustment?
9. What are three potential applications of the Minnesota Theory of Work Adjustment?
10. What are the primary approaches to vocational adjustment?
11. How can the medical therapies aid the vocational adjustment process?
12. What is the primary purpose of a sheltered workshop in vocational adjustment programming?
13. How do the four basic models for sheltered workshop programming differ?
14. What are the limitations of sheltered workshops for vocational adjustment?
15. What are the advantages and potential disadvantages to using community job sites in a vocational adjustment program?
16. What is the basic premise underlying the use of behavior modification techniques?
17. What is the difference between negative reinforcement and punishment in behavior modification?
18. What are the definitions for the most common reinforcement schedules in behavior modification?
19. What are the most common behavior modification techniques for increasing desired behavior?
20. What are some behavior modification techniques for eliminating behavior?
21. What are three ethical issues associated with behavior modification that may potentially disregard some human rights of individuals?
22. What type of sheltered workshop was used in the Cleveland Vocational Guidance and Rehabilitation Services' work adjustment program?
23. What was the relationship between the sheltered workshop and the job site in the St. Louis Work Experience Center program?
24. Why is the primary behavior modification approach applied by the Center for Developmental and Learning Disorders at the University of Alabama in Birmingham considered a contingency reinforcement approach?
25. What are the techniques used for learning in the Singer Company's Job Survival Skills Program?

REFERENCES

Baker, R. J., & Sawyer, H. W. *Adjustment services in rehabilitation: emphasis on human change.* Auburn, Ala.: Rehabilitation Services Education, Department of Vocational and Adult Education, Auburn University, 1971.

Bellamy, G. T., Inman, D. P., & Horner, R. H. *Design of vocational habilitation services for the severely retarded: the specialized training program model.* Eugene: Center on Human Development, University of Oregon, 1977.

Bitter, J. A. Using employer job-sites in evaluation of the mentally retarded for employability. *Mental Retardation,* 1967, 5(3), 21-22.

Bitter, J. A. Toward a concept of job readiness. *Rehabilitation Literature,* 1968, 29(7), 201-203.

Bitter, J. A., & Bolanovich, D. J. The habilitation workshop in a comprehensive philosophy for vocational adjustment training. *Rehabilitation Literature,* 1966, 27(11), 330-332.

Bitter, J. A., Bolanovich, D. J., & O'Neil, L. P. Some implications of the St. Louis Work Experience Center project. *Education and Training of the Mentally Retarded,* 1967, 2(4), 177-182.

Campbell, N. Techniques of behavior modification. *Journal of Rehabilitation,* 1971, 37(4), 28-31.

Campbell, J. L., & O'Toole, R. *Work adjustment: a dynamic rehabilitation process.* Cleveland: Vocational Guidance and Rehabilitation Services, undated.

Charles, C. M. *Individualizing instruction.* St. Louis: The C. V. Mosby Co., 1976.

Cull, J. G. Adjustment to disability. In J. G. Cull & R. E. Hardy (Eds.), *Vocational rehabilitation: profession and process.* Springfield, Ill.: Charles C Thomas, Publisher, 1972.

Dunn, D. J. *Adjustment services: individualized program planning, delivery, and monitoring.* Menomonie, Wis.: Research and Training Center, University of Wisconsin–Stout, 1974.

Esser, P. J. *Individualized client planning for work adjustment services.* Menomonie, Wis.: Materials Development Center, University of Wisconsin–Stout, 1975.

Gold, M. W. Task analysis of a complex assembly task by the retarded blind. *Exceptional Children,* 1976, 43(2), 78-84.

Kolstoe, O. P., & Frey, R. M. *A high school work-study program for mentally subnormal students.* Carbondale, Ill.: Southern Illinois University Press, 1965.

Lofquist, L. H., Dawis, R. V., & Hendel, D. D. *Application of the theory of work adjustment to rehabilitation and counseling.* Minneapolis: Industrial Relations Center, University of Minnesota, 1972 (Minnesota Studies in Vocational Rehabilitation: XXX; Bull. 58).

McDaniel, J. W. *Physical disability and human behavior* (2nd ed.). New York: Pergamon Press, 1976.

McGowan, J. F., & Porter, T. L. *An introduction to the vocational rehabilitation process.* Washington, D.C.: Superintendent of Documents, Government Printing Office, 1967.

Roos, P. Human rights and behavior modification. *Mental Retardation,* 1974, 12(3), 3-6.

Sankovsky, R. Adjustment services in rehabilitation. *Journal of Rehabilitation,* 1971, 37(4), 8-10.

Tenth Institute on Rehabilitation Services. *Vocational evaluation and work adjustment services in vocational rehabilitation.* Washington, D.C.: Rehabilitation Services Administration, Department of Health, Education, and Welfare, 1972.

Walker, J. E., & Shea, T. M. *Behavior modification: a practical approach for educators.* St. Louis: The C. V. Mosby Co., 1976.

Welch, M. W., & Gist, J. W. *The open token economy system: a handbook for a behavioral approach to rehabilitation.* Springfield, Ill.: Charles C Thomas, Publisher, 1974.

Wright, B. A. *Physical disability—a psychological approach.* New York: Harper & Row, Publishers, 1960.

ADDITIONAL READINGS

Bitter, J. A., & Bolanovich, D. J. Job training of retardates using 8 mm film loops. *Audiovidual Instruction,* 1966, 11(9), 731-732.

Brickey, M. Normalization and behavior modification in the workshop. *Journal of Rehabilitation,* 1974, 40(6), 15-16; 41, 44-46.

Bruch, M. A., Kunce, J. T., Thelen, M. H., & Akamatsu, T. J. *Modeling, behavior change and rehabilitation.* Columbia, Mo.: Regional Rehabilitation Research Institute, University of Missouri–Columbia, 1973.

Carrison, M. P. The perils of behavior mod. *Phi Delta Kappan,* 1973, 54(9), 593-595.

Cobb, A. B. (Ed.). *Medical and psychological aspects of disability.* Springfield, Ill.: Charles C Thomas, Publisher, 1973.

Cushing, M. When counseling fails—then what? *Journal of Rehabilitation,* 1969, 35(4), 18-20.

Dickerson, L. R., & Andrew, J. D. (Eds.). *Work adjustment: a resource manual.* Menomonie, Wis.: Research and Training Center, University of Wisconsin–Stout, undated.

Durfee, R. A. Another look at conditioning therapy. *Journal of Rehabilitation,* 1969, 35(4), 16-18.

Esser, T. *A structured guide for selecting training materials in adjustment services.* Menomonie, Wis.: Materials Development Center, University of Wisconsin–Stout, 1977.

Esser, T. J., & Botterbusch, K. F. (Eds.). *Token economics in rehabilitation (a book of readings)*. Menomonie, Wis.: Materials Development Center, University of Wisconsin–Stout, 1975.

Garrett, J. F., & Levine, E. S. (Eds.). *Psychological practices with the physically disabled*. New York: Columbia University Press, 1962.

Goffman, E. *Stigma: notes on the management of spoiled identity*. Englewood Cliffs, N.J.: Prentice-Hall, Inc., 1963.

Gold, M. W. Stimulus factors in skill training of the retarded on a complex assembly task: acquisition, transfer and retention. *American Journal of Mental Deficiency*, 1972, 76(5), 517-526.

Greenleigh Associates, Inc. *The role of the sheltered workshops in the rehabilitation of the severely handicapped*. New York: Greenleigh Associates, Inc., 1975.

Miller, N. E., & Dollard, J. *Social learning and imitation*. New Haven, Conn.: Yale University Press, 1941.

National Rehabilitation Association. The work adjustment profile. *Journal of Rehabilitation*, 1971, 37(4), whole issue.

National Rehabilitation Association. Adjustment services for the severely handicapped. *Journal of Rehabilitation*, 1978, 44(1), whole issue.

Neff, W. *Work and human behavior*. New York: Atherton Press, 1968.

Payne, J. S., Mercer, C. D., & Epstein, M. H. *Education and rehabilitation techniques*. New York: Behavioral Publications, Inc., 1974.

Pigot, R. A. Behavior modification and control in rehabilitation. *Journal of Rehabilitation*, 1969, 35(4), 12-15.

Sankovsky, R., Arthur, G., & Mann, J. (Eds.). *Vocational evaluation and work adjustment (a book of readings)*. Auburn, Ala.: Alabama Rehabilitation Media Service, Auburn University, undated.

Stubbins, J. (Ed.). *Social and psychological aspects of disability: a handbook for practitioners*. Baltimore: University Park Press, 1977.

Ullman, L. P., & Krasner, L. (Eds.). *Case studies in behavior modification*. New York: Holt, Rinehart & Winston, 1965.

Wehman, P. Toward a social skills curriculum for developmentally disabled clients in vocational settings. *Rehabilitation Literature*, 1975, 36(11), 342-348.

Wright, B. A. Social-psychological leads to enhance rehabilitation effectiveness. *Rehabilitation Counseling Bulletin*, 1975, 18(4), 214-223.

MEDIA RESOURCES

Visual

1. "Like Other People" (16 mm film, 37 minutes). Available from Perennial Education, Inc., 1825 Willow Rd., P.O. Box 236, Northfield, Ill. 60093.

    Explores the personal aspects of being severely physically disabled and the disabled's interactions with others. Emphasizes that the disabled have the same needs as others.

2. "The Eye of the Beholder" (16 mm film, 24 minutes). Produced by Stuart Reynolds Productions, Inc., 9465 Wilshire Blvd., Beverly Hills, Calif. 90212.

    Illustrates how perceptions differ and "no two people see the same thing in the same way."

3. "A Question of Attitude" (16 mm film, 12 minutes). Available from Australian News and Information Bureau, 636 Fifth Ave., New York, N.Y. 10020.

    Examines the reluctance of many employers to hire the physically disabled.

4. "Motivation Through Job Enrichment" (16 mm film, 28 minutes). Available from Pennsylvania State University, Audio-Visual Services, University Park, Pa. 16802.

    Frederick Herzberg discusses his "Motivation-Hygiene Theory," which emphasizes that the need for accomplishment can be found in the job. Various ways in which routine jobs can be enriched to provide motivation are illustrated.

5. "Psychology of Severe Physical Disability" (¾" videotape cassette; 58 minutes). Available from RT-19 University of Alabama, Medical Rehabilitation Research and Training Center, 1717 6th Ave., South, Birmingham, Ala., 35233.

    A lecture by Stanley J. Smits on the psychological adjustment of disability. Stages in adjust-

ment are outlined including denial, depression, and adjustment. Coping behaviors discussed include repression, day dreaming, and rationalization.

6. "Helping: a Behavioral Approach" (eight learning modules, slides with audiotape cassettes and study guides). Produced by West Virginia Research and Training Center, West Virginia Rehabilitation Center, Institute, W. Va. 25112.

   An introduction to learning principles for understanding motivation and behavior as they relate to the disabled. Covers behavioral interpretation, behavioral disability, laws of behavior, reinforcers, behavior problems, modeling, generalization and discrimination, and steps to helping.

7. "A Demonstration of Behavioral Processes" (16 mm film, 28 minutes). Available from Appleton-Century-Crofts, 440 Park Ave., South, New York, N.Y. 10001.

   B. F. Skinner demonstrates his classic principles of operant conditioning.

8. "Behavior Modification in Rehabilitation-Increasing Desired Behaviors, Decreasing Undesired Behaviors" (½″ videotape, 70 minutes). Produced by RT-13 Arkansas Rehabilitation Research and Training Center, Hot Springs Rehabilitation Center, P.O. Box 1358, Hot Springs, Ark. 71901.

   A presentation of behavior modification principles with rehabilitation examples.

9. "Prevocational Token Economy Program" (38 slides with tape cassette; 10 minutes). Produced by RT-15 University of West Virginia Research and Training Center, Institute, W. Va. 25112.

   Describes a program involving a token economy system for increasing motivation.

10. "Principles of Learning Applied to Motor Training" (16 mm film, 21 minutes). Produced by RT-2 University of Minnesota Medical Rehabilitation Research and Training Center, 860 Mayo Building, Minneapolis, Minn. 55455.

    Illustrates analysis of motor repertory of disabled patients, identification of measurable goals, and motor training utilizing conditioned learning by reinforcement.

11. "Personal Adjustment Training in a Sheltered Workshop" (16 mm film, 27 minutes). Available from Indiana University, Audio-Visual Center, Bloomington, Ind. 47401.

    Describes practices and techniques used in sheltered workshops for providing personal adjustment training. Emphasizes a team approach involving vocational evaluators, psychologists, social workers, and medical personnel in the delivery of adjustment services.

12. "Training for Tomorrow" (16 mm film). Available from Hillsborough Association for Retarded Children, Inc., P.O. Box 22125, Tampa, Fla. 33622.

    Describes the work adjustment program at the McDonald Training Center in Florida.

13. "Sheltered Workshop" (16 mm film, 5 minutes). Available from Pennsylvania State University, Audio-Visual Services, University Park, Pa. 16802.

    Describes the use of subcontract work in a sheltered workshop for disabled clients.

14. "Try Another Way" (16 mm film, 27 minutes). Available from Film Productions of Indianapolis, 128 E. 36th St., Indianapolis, Ind. 46205.

    An overview of Marc Gold's training methods for teaching complex assembly tasks to severely mentally retarded individuals.

15. "Dr. Marc Gold's Film Training Series" (16 mm film). Available from Film Productions of Indianapolis, 128 E. 36th St., Indianapolis, Ind. 46205.

    a. "Task Analysis: an Introduction to a Technology of Instruction" (18 minutes). *Describes a seven-phase sequence for doing task analysis.*

    b. "Content and Process: Two Components of Task Analysis" (12 minutes). *Illustrates that the subdivision of steps may be different for individual clients.*

    c. "Formats for Single Pieces of Learning: Subcategories of Process Task Analysis" (13 minutes). *Gold explains and demonstrates the details of various teaching options.*

    d. "Format for Multiple Pieces of Learning" (22 minutes). *An explanation of approaches to the logical connections between single pieces of learning for total task presentation.*

    e. "Feedback—General Issues" (20 minutes). *A discussion of the various facets of feedback.*

    f. "Feedback—Specific Issues" (15 minutes). *Five specific rules for spontaneous implementation of feedback are discussed.*

    g. "Reinforcement and Influence" (15 minutes). *Discusses "process influence" and "content influence."*

16. "The Work Adjustment Program: an Overview" (80 slides with tape cassette; 27 minutes). Available from Materials Development Center, University of Wisconsin–Stout, Menomonie, Wis. 54751.

    Provides guidance in the development of work adjustment services and programs. The development of written individualized client adjustment plans based on specific client needs is emphasized.

17. "Modeling: a Work Adjustment Technique" (79 slides with tape cassette; 18 minutes). Available from Materials Development Center, University of Wisconsin–Stout, Menomonie, Wis. 54751.

    Emphasizes the value and describes with examples modeling as a form of learning in rehabilitation programming.

Audio

1. "Psychological and Psychiatric Factors in Rehabilitation" (audiotape; 116 minutes). Available from Learning Resources Facility, Audiovisual Utilization, 550 First Ave., New York, N.Y. 10016.

    Describes the psychological effects of physical disability.

2. "Psychological Aspects of Disabilities" (audiotape cassette with printed transcript, 35 minutes). Available from Materials Development Center, University of Wisconsin–Stout, Menomonie, Wis. 54751.

    Explores some points of view and some conclusions concerning the psychological implications of disability.

3. "Principles of Work Adjustment" (audiotape cassette, 37 minutes). Available from Materials Development Center, University of Wisconsin–Stout, Menomonie, Wis. 54751.

    Rene Davis discusses the Minnesota Theory of Work Adjustment.

REHABILITATION METHODS

The purpose of Section Three is to present the reader with an overview of some of the many methods, techniques and approaches utilized with clients in the rehabilitation process.

There are five chapters in this section. Conceptually the chapters on casework methods (Chapter 6) and counseling approaches (Chapter 8) go together. However, they are organized and presented separately to reflect more closely the sequential nature of the rehabilitation process.

In addition to casework principles, Chapter 6 emphasizes interviewing methods and some guidelines for case recording. Chapter 7 encourages a comprehensive approach to the vocational evaluation of rehabilitation clients. Brief descriptions of the most common measures and techniques for evaluation are presented and organized in terms of psychological tests, work samples and situational assessment methods. Chapter 8 describes the basic concepts and applications for 12 counseling approaches which seem most applicable for many rehabilitation clients. No single counseling approach is advocated as most appropriate in rehabilitation; rather an eclectic approach is suggested because of the wide range among rehabilitation clients in functional capabilities. In addition, a brief overview of group counseling is presented. Chapter 9 addresses job placement techniques and emphasizes job placement as a consideration throughout the rehabilitation process. Various counselor approaches, or roles, to this function are described, along with some information and techniques for obtaining a successfully rehabilitated client in employment. A special feature of Chapter 9 is a description of the United States Employment Service's *Dictionary of Occupational Titles*. The last chapter (no. 10) gives an overview of the many community resources available for rehabilitation programming—and in so doing, gives ample demonstration of the diversity and flexibility of rehabilitation programming and the necessity for teamwork among professions and professionals.

6

Casework methods

OVERVIEW AND OBJECTIVES

Casework is an activity engaged in by all social science workers. This chapter is intended to provide the reader with a brief orientation to casework methods in rehabilitation. (Counseling, which is a part of casework, will be discussed in Chapter 8.) The chapter will provide an orientation to (1) casework principles, (2) interview methods, (3) case recording techniques, and (4) caseload management.

The objective of the chapter is to acquaint the reader with casework methodology as part of the service-delivery process in rehabilitation.

CASEWORK PRINCIPLES
Relationship

The casework relationship involves a "dynamic interaction of attitudes and emotions between the caseworker and the client" (Biestek, 1957). The development of rapport involving confidence and understanding between the caseworker and the client is important in casework. Rapport building begins with the introduction and should continue throughout the casework process. It necessitates an interest in the client and responsiveness to client needs on the part of the caseworker. It occurs in a permissive atmosphere in which the client feels comfortable and free to express himself.

Biestek (1957) identifies seven principles for good casework relationships. These seven principles for caseworkers (and the needs of clients on which they are based) are as follows:

1. Individualization (a need to be treated as a unique individual)
2. Purposeful expression of feelings (a need for freedom to express feelings)
3. Controlled emotional involvement (a need to get a sympathetic response to problems)
4. Acceptance (a need to be recognized as a person of worth)
5. Nonjudgmental attitude (a need to not be judged)
6. Client self-determination (a need to feel free to make choices and decisions)
7. Confidentiality (a need to be able to keep secrets about one's self)

Recognition of these seven principles in the casework relationship involves treating the client as a responsible person, being considerate of attitudes and feelings, remaining objective, being patient, being sensitive to the timing of questions and comments, and using critical and sympathetic comments only as tools in the casework process (Miller & Obermann, 1968). An effective relationship involves an attitude of caring and caring always includes helping (Schulman, 1974).

Communication

Johnson (1972) defines communication as "a person sending a message to another individual with the conscious intent of evoking a response." Effective communication necessitates interpretation of a message in the same way in which it was intended. To achieve such accuracy in communication is very difficult. Intentions are by their nature private and known only to the person sending the message. Since the sender's intent is not always clear to the receiver of information, there can be considerable discrepancy between what the sender communicates and what he intends to communicate. Similarly the receiver of the information may distort a message to match his expectation. To establish meaningful communication between persons requires an atmosphere of mutual trust and the correction of distortion in communication through feedback. The lack of trust is a major cause of communication distortion. The caseworker can help develop trust through acceptance and by being sensitive to his own and to the client's feelings and knowing that these feelings influence both perceptions and communications. As a receiver of information it is important for the caseworker to listen from the other person's point of view. Feedback, verbal and nonverbal, by the receiver of information offers the sender of a message some insight about how the message was received. It enables him to modify the message to more accurately communicate with the receiver. Continuous two-way communication can thus facilitate accuracy and understanding. Without feedback the sender of information has no way of knowing how the message was interpreted by the receiver (Johnson, 1972; Nylen, Mitchell, & Stout, undated).

Individualization

Biestek (1957) defines individualization as "the recognization and understanding of each client's unique qualities and the differential use of principles and methods in assisting each toward a better adjustment." He identifies six ways in which to individualize casework service: (1) be thoughtful in detail (e.g., make appointments that are convenient to the client's schedule), (2) provide privacy in interviews, (3) take care in keeping appointments, (4) come prepared for interviews, (5) involve the client (i.e. assist him to do for himself and engage him in the goal setting and service delivery process), and (6) be flexible (in other words, be willing to adjust goals and service delivery methods based on continuous development and changes in the client's situation).

Charles (1976) suggests that the development of specific behavioral objectives for clients and learning experiences tailored just for the individual are additional strategies for individualizing the service delivery process.

Participation

Active participation in the casework process by the client is important to the success of services. Not only does the client have the right to make his own decisions, but the more active he is in self-determination the more likely he is to develop the capacity to make decisions and achieve success in the rehabilitation process. The caseworker's role is to guide and promote change in client functioning. The caseworker helps the client to think things through for himself and to accept responsibility for formulating his own ideas. Some clients have a greater capacity for self-direction and self-determination. However, the caseworker's responsibility is to promote active participation in the decision-making process to whatever extent clients are capable. The ultimate goal, of course, is for the client to function as independently as possible of professional assistance.

INTERVIEW METHODS

Interviewing is done by everyone. It involves communication between two people. However, interviewing is something more than just conversation. It is a purposeful activity that intends to give or get information. In vocational rehabilitation a primary objective of interviewing is to obtain factual information regarding the client's vocational circumstances.

Preparing for the interview

Preparing for the interview involves having or developing a genuine interest in helping the client, identifying a purpose for the interview, knowing what information is already available and what information is still needed, and creating a physical environment that is conducive to a good relationship with the client.

Benjamin (1974) identifies two internal factors of the counselor as basic to the helping interview: (1) be oneself and (2) desire to help clients as much as possible. Taking such an attitude will help the caseworker develop trust, confidence, and rapport with clients.

Establishing a purpose enables the interview to take a meaningful direction. Interviewing is a time-consuming way to gather information; thus identifying a purpose for the interview will help use this valuable time to maximum advantage. The counselor can benefit himself and the conduct of the session by telling the client in advance how much time is available. Handled tactfully, such information will communicate to the client that his time is considered important and will also convey the interest of the counselor in the client.

Preparing for an interview involves reviewing already available information such as reports from other agencies, questionnaires, and test information. Reviewing this material in advance of the interview will conserve interview time and eliminate unnecessary duplication of effort. In addition, it will make the identification of needed information much easier.

Though good interviewing can take place almost anywhere, the physical environment can be important in realizing the full potential for interaction between caseworker and client. Of primary importance is that there be some degree of privacy. The interview should be free of interruptions—telephone calls, secretaries wishing a signature, knocks on the door—so that a feeling of respect for the client and a genuine interest in helping him will come across. It helps if the physical setting conveys a comfortable relaxed atmosphere conducive to communication. It is unnecessary to remove things that normally belong to an office; but, at the same time, the room should have a "professional" appearance. The caseworker's lunch and information about other clients should be put away. It is good practice to arrange the chairs so there are no obstacles between the counselor and the client. Placing chairs at a 90-degree angle to each other allows the client to regard the counselor yet does not require eye contact. However, it is sometimes helpful to have a table or desk nearby for writing.

FIG. 6-1

Interview rapport can often be aided by removing obstacles between the counselor and client and placing chairs at a 90-degree angle to each other. A table nearby for writing when needed is also helpful. (From: Chinn, P. C., Winn, J., & Walters, R. H. *Two-way talking with parents of special children*. St. Louis: The C. V. Mosby Co., 1978.)

Building the interviewing relationship

Building the interviewing relationship requires respect for the client, acceptance, understanding, empathy, and humanness. *Respect* entails having a sincere interest in the client. *Acceptance* means treating the client as an equal by regarding his ideas and feelings with respect. *Understanding* involves attempting to know what it is like to be the other person. Though such a goal is impossible to achieve, genuine listening can help. The counselor should avoid preoccupation and distractions and should make every effort to hear what the client is saying. *Empathy* is similar to understanding—attempting to understand the internal frame of reference of the client, i.e., imagining oneself in the other person's situation while at the same time remaining the helper. *Humanness* should signify a genuine and sensitive interest. A facade can lead to distrust; being oneself will help the client trust the caseworker (Benjamin, 1974).

By now the reader can see that the interview involves more than information gathering. It also involves some elements of a social relationship. However, the interviewer must know when to make social talk. If the client has difficulty expressing himself or is anxious, support and verbal encouragement can be an aid. Sometimes, if the interaction or subject is particularly difficult, casual chatting about the weather, sports, or any subject of common interest can be helpful in maintaining or building the interview relationship. The basic purpose of social talk in the interview situation is to facilitate the primary role relationship.

Other ways to develop the role relationship between caseworker and client is to use *echos* (repeating client verbatim), *extensions* (expanding on client comments), *clarifications* (explanations), and *summaries* (Richardson, Dohrenwend, & Klein, 1965). This is particularly true in the early stages of an interview when the caseworker may know very little about the client. The caseworker must direct the interview throughout. He must know when to listen, when to intercede, what to observe, and when to redirect the client. The goal is to help the client assist himself.

Establishing interview goals

Though rehabilitation is an employment-oriented program, specific interview goals will vary from client to client. Goals may include identifying client interests and vocational, physical, and mental potential; or they may involve a plan for resolving personal problems that are barriers to the rehabilitation process. The interview goal has been established when both interviewer and interviewee understand and agree on what is to be discussed. If they do not agree, there is no point in conducting the interview (Benjamin, 1974).

Guiding the interview

The interviewer needs to understand the problem of the client. To do so, he or she must permit the client to express himself in sufficient detail to make this happen. However, the caseworker must assume leadership in providing healthy guidance throughout the interview process. With the talkative client the interviewer may have to attempt to redirect the conversation by asking leading questions. With the reluctant client the interviewer may have to provide responses and leads which stimulate discussion. Benjamin (1974) identifies the following responses and leads that are frequently used: silence, mm-hm, restatement, clarification, reflection, interpretation, explanation, encouragement, assurance-reassurance, suggestions, advice, urging, moralizing, agreement-disagreement, approval-disapproval, opposition, criticism, disbelief, contradiction, denial, and rejection. In responding it is important to remember that the purpose of the interview relationship must always be to constructively give and get information to help promote the rehabilitation goals of the client.

Probing

Probing should stimulate discussion. It is intended to motivate the client to enlarge on what he said, clarify his comments, or explain reasons for what was said. It also helps to focus the discussion on relevant content. Some responses or leads just mentioned are also types of probes. For example, an "mm-hm," repeating a question, making a neutral comment, or asking for further clarification is usually intended to motivate the client to respond more fully (University of Michigan Survey Research Center, 1969).

The primary technique for probing is questioning. Benjamin (1974) suggests the following guidelines in using questions:
1. Questions should be as *wide open* as possible (i.e., they ought to permit the respondent to answer in a manner comfortable to him).
2. Questions should be *simple* (e.g., "What are your vocational interests?"), and should not force the client to choose between alternatives (e.g., "Are you interested in drafting or mechanics?").
3. Questions should be stated as *distinctly* as possible.
4. Questions should be *indirect* rather than direct (e.g., requiring only a *yes* or *no* response).
5. Questions should be followed by a *pause* to allow time for an answer.

Questions are appropriate when the caseworker has missed some information, when clarification is called for, when it is necessary to assist the client in exploring a thought, and when the client is finding it hard to talk but seems to have more to say (Benjamin, 1974).

Closing the interview

Benjamin (1974) considers two factors basic to closing the interview. One is that both the caseworker and the client should know when the closing is taking place and accept this fact. The other is that new material should not be introduced during the closing phase.

The responsibility for seeing that these principles are put into practice lies with the interviewer. The intent, however, is to close the interview without compromising rapport with the client. The client should have a positive feeling about the time spent and feel that it was a purposeful activity. A few techniques for closing the interview are to make some concluding statement of the discussion, to summarize the discussion thereby ensuring that both the caseworker and the client have understood each other, to ask the client to indicate his understanding of what went on during the interview, to summarize subjects that were brought up during the discussion but for which there was not adequate time for closure and suggest these as future topics, and to review the definite plans made during the interview and confirm follow-through activity relative to these plans (Benjamin, 1974).

Recording the interview

Everyone has his own style for taking notes of an interview or discussion. Taking notes can serve a very useful function—helping to refresh one's memory and documenting action steps which are agreed upon. Generally, the longer one takes to record observations after an interview the less likely he or she is to be accurate in remembering. Note taking during the interview, however, should not interfere with the helping relationship. Benjamin (1974) offers a few "don'ts" in recording an interview.
1. Don't use note taking as an escape from meaningful participation in the interview.
2. Don't use note taking as a form of cross-examination by pointing out inconsistencies in reactions.
3. Don't permit recording to interfere with the flow of the interview.
4. Don't be secretive about taking notes.

After termination of the interview, it is usually helpful to summarize. A summary which synthesizes information helps to consider how, what, and under what circumstances information was provided (Multi-Resource Centers, Inc., 1972).

CASE RECORDING
Purpose

Recording information about a client can serve a number of purposes: synthesizing information which permits the caseworker to understand the client better, documenting evaluation information and services rendered, and justifying the determination of eligibility or the extended evaluation of a client for eligibility in the public rehabilitation program. Other purposes are periodic case review of client progress, program monitoring, evaluation and planning, and to provide continuity in the rehabilitation program.

Recording methods

McGowan and Porter (1967) identify five forms of recording: (1) recording on established forms, which are usually required for case uniformity within agencies, (2) summary recording, which condenses case information into brief accounts of what happened, (3) process recording, which is usually very detailed and provides a complete record of the client's rehabilitation process, (4) research recording, which is intended to gather data or information about cases in a prescribed format, and (5) narrative recording, which gives a relatively brief account of the client's total situation.

Content guidelines

The following is information which should, as a minimum, appear in a rehabilitation client's case record:

1. Eligibility or ineligibility of the client applicant
2. Client's perception of his rehabilitation problem
3. New information significant to the client's rehabilitation
4. Evaluation information (including medical, educational, psychological, social, and vocational information)
5. Client's planned rehabilitation program and amendments to the program
6. Service provisions (including provisions to the client and his family members and postemployment services)
7. Interruptions to the client's program or loss of contact with the client
8. Readiness for employment, and the job placement plan
9. Closure of the case

CASELOAD MANAGEMENT

The Third Institute on Rehabilitation Services (1965) defined caseload management as "the use of techniques (methods or details of procedure) to control the distribution, quality, quantity, and cost of all aspects of case work activities in order to accomplish the program goals of the agency." Caseload management involves work planning by the caseworker and includes planning the work day and a pattern of work activities for greatest efficiency. It also involves concerned decision making by the rehabilitation worker and the client to provide the most effective service to the client. Attention must be given to referral practices, resources, service arrangements, length of service, and costs. Good caseload management also requires that the counselor have an organized approach to maximizing the use of limited resources for accomplishing service outcomes for clients.

The Rehabilitation Act of 1973 placed a priority for case selection on severely disabled applicants, assuring that an increasing number of these persons would enter into rehabilitation caseloads. State rehabilitation agencies can give a second priority to target groups of their choice. State rehabilitation counselors must consider such priorities in the management of caseloads.

The rehabilitation worker is the central figure in caseload management. However, other factors also affect the management and delivery of services to clients: agency goals, procedures for processing cases, budget, number of staff, size of caseloads, personnel performance, the nature of client problems, and program efficiency (Third Institute on Rehabilitation Services, 1965).

SUMMARY

Casework is an activity common to all social science professions. Principal casework activities include interviewing, case recording, and caseload management. The individualized casework relationship begins with the development of rapport between caseworker and client. It is highly dependent upon active participation of the client and accurate two-way communication between caseworker and client.

A primary objective in vocational rehabilitation interviewing is to obtain factual information regarding the client's vocational circumstances. Good interviewing involves preparation and client acceptance, empathy, interview goal setting, and the ability to guide the discussion toward achievement of those goals.

Case recording serves a number of purposes in rehabilitation—including synthesis and documentation of information, case review, and service continuity. Because rehabilitation workers often have sizable client caseloads, caseload management is generally an overlooked skill. It necessitates planning, priority setting, and organization by the caseworker.

SELF-EVALUATION QUESTIONS

1. What are some principles for good casework relationships?
2. What are two ingredients for meaningful communication between persons?
3. What are some ways to individualize casework service?
4. Why is it important for clients to actively participate in the casework process?
5. What is a primary objective of vocational rehabilitation interviewing?
6. What does preparation for an interview involve?
7. What is empathy?
8. What are some responses or leads which the interviewer might use for stimulating or redirecting discussion?
9. What are the guidelines for using questions in probing during an interview?
10. What are some techniques for closing an interview?
11. What are the reasons for doing case recording in rehabilitation?
12. What are some methods for case recording?
13. What information should appear in a rehabilitation client's case record?
14. How is "caseload management" defined?
15. What are some considerations for managing client caseloads?

REFERENCES

Benjamin, A. *The helping interview* (2nd ed.). Boston: Houghton Mifflin Co., 1974.
Biestek, F. P. *The casework relationship*. Chicago: Loyola University Press, 1957.

Charles, C. M. *Individualizing instruction*. St. Louis: The C. V. Mosby Co., 1976.

Johnson, D. W. *Reaching out: Interpersonal effectiveness and self-actualization*. Englewood Cliffs, N.J.: Prentice-Hall, Inc., 1972.

McGowan, J. F., & Porter, T. L. *An introduction to the vocational rehabilitation process*. Washington, D.C.: Superintendent of Documents, Government Printing Office, 1967.

Miller, L. A., & Obermann, C. E. *Initial interview* (Studies in Continuing Education for Rehabilitation Counselors, Unit 2-001). Menomonie, Wis.: Materials Development Center, University of Wisconsin–Stout, 1968.

Multi-Resource Centers, Inc. *Vocational diagnostic interviewing: Reference manual*. Minneapolis: Multi-Resource Centers, Inc., 1972.

Nylen, D., Mitchell, J. R., & Stout, A. *Handbook of staff development and human relations training: Materials developed for use in Africa* (Rev. standard ed.). Washington, D.C.: National Training Laboratories, Institute for Applied Behavioral Science, associated with the National Education Association and the European Institute for Trans-National Studies in Group and Organizational Development, Copenhagen, Denmark, undated.

Richardson, S. A., Dohrenwend, B. S., & Klein, D. *Interviewing: its forms and functions*. New York: Basic Books, Inc., 1965.

Schulman, E. D. *Intervention in human services*. St. Louis: The C. V. Mosby Co., 1974.

Third Institute on Rehabilitation Services. *Training guide in caseload management for vocational rehabilitation staff*. Washington, D.C.: Superintendent of Documents, Government Printing Office, 1965.

University of Michigan Survey Research Center. *Interviewer's manual*. Ann Arbor: The University of Michigan, 1969.

ADDITIONAL READINGS

First Institute on Rehabilitation Services. *Case recording in rehabilitation*. Washington, D.C.: Superintendent of Documents, Government Printing Office, 1963.

Garrett, A. *Interviewing: its principles and methods* (2nd ed. revised by E. P. Zaki & M. M. Mangold). New York: Family Service Association of America, 1972.

Hollis, F. *Casework: a psychosocial therapy* (2nd ed.). New York: Random House, 1972.

MEDIA RESOURCES

Visual

1. "Vocational Diagnostic Interviewing" (reference manual with exercises, videotape). Produced by Multi-Resource Centers, Inc., 1900 Chicago Ave., South, Minneapolis, Minn. 55404.

   A 2-day training package that offers a systematic approach for the inexperienced interviewer to vocational assessment, problem identification, and employability planning.

2. "Step by Step: an Instructional Program in Basic Interviewing Skills" (instructional package supplemented with videotape vignettes). Developed by the Human Resource Center, Graduate School of Social Work, University of Texas at Arlington, Arlington, Texas 76019.

   An instructional package for presenting some common skills used in an interview situation including attending, questioning, reflecting, facilitating, and interpreting. Instructional presentations are supplemented with videotape vignettes in which the skills are demonstrated.

3. "The Interviewing Skills" (filmstrips, audiotapes, and leader's guide). Developed by Addison Wesley Publishing Co., Inc., Reading, Mass. 01867.

   Five filmstrips and audiotapes on (a) General Principles of Interviewing, (b) The Employment Interview, (c) The Counseling Interview, (d) The Disciplining Interview, and (e) The Appraisal Interview. The package is primarily intended for supervisors.

4. "Initial Interview" (16 mm film, 22 minutes). Available from RT-16 University of Oregon, Rehabilitation Research and Training Center in Mental Retardation, Eugene, Ore. 97403.

   A dramatization of an intake interview between a public assistance caseworker and an applicant. The film is intended to serve as a stimulus for discussion rather than as an exemplary interview.

Audio
1. "Ten Commandments of Meaningful Communication." (Reel tape, 3¾ speed, 23 minutes). Available from McGraw-Hill Book Co., College Division, P.O. Box 402, Hightstown, N.J. 08520.
   Examines various elements of the communication process.
2. "Collecting Information from the Client" (audiotape cassette and transcript, 32 minutes). Available from Materials Development Center, University of Wisconsin–Stout, Menomonie, Wis. 54751.
   Discusses sources of information and their usefulness.
3. "Initial Interview" (audiotape cassette and transcript, 41 minutes). Available from Materials Development Center, University of Wisconsin–Stout, Menomonie, Wis. 54751.
   Intended for the rehabilitation counselor. Includes initial interview objectives, attitudes, expectancies, techniques for interaction, and expected results.

7

Vocational evaluation techniques

OVERVIEW AND OBJECTIVES

The primary goals of vocational evaluation in the public rehabilitation program are to (1) determine applicant eligibility for services, (2) identify a program of services for the client, and (3) assist the client with information and self-understanding so he may realistically make vocational decisions.

The purpose of this chapter is to briefly describe some vocational evaluation–related techniques utilized in the rehabilitation process. The chapter objective is to familiarize the reader with commonly used psychological tests, work samples and situational assessment approaches for conducting vocational rehabilitation client evaluation.

COMPREHENSIVE EVALUATION

In 1972, the Tenth Institute on Rehabilitation Services developed the following definition for vocational evaluation: "vocational (work) evaluation is a comprehensive process that systematically utilizes work, real or simulated, as the focal point for assessment and vocational exploration, the purpose of which is to assist individuals in vocational development. Vocational (work) evaluation incorporates medical, psychological, social, vocational, educational, cultural, and economic data in the attainment of the goals of the evaluation process." Though this definition emphasizes the utilization of "work" in vocational evaluation, it also reinforces the need for a comprehensive evaluation philosophy. Accurate assessments in vocational evaluation are facilitated by observing patterns among the information available.

Types of evaluation

The types of evaluation were introduced in Chapter 3. However, a brief review here will help emphasize the comprehensive nature of rehabilitation evaluation and provide a context for the description of specific techniques which emphasize vocationally-related evaluation.

Medical evaluation information can help identify major and secondary disabilities, functional limitations of the disability, and the general health status of the client. The medical evaluation will consist of (at least) a general medical examination; but it may also include special medical examinations, advice of a medical consultant, and evaluation in a comprehensive medical center.

Psychological evaluations help determine the client's present level of intellectual functioning, perceptions of self and his behavior in relation to the disability, and adjustment to the disability. The psychological evaluation can help a client make vocational plans by facilitating an understanding of personal strengths and weaknesses. Such information is usually obtained through interviews, observations of behavior, standardized tests, a review of previous information about the client, and sometimes a clinical evaluation by a psychiatrist.

Sociocultural evaluations involve identifying personal and impersonal factors in the individual's social functioning and cultural background. Included may be special relationships to himself, his family, and the community. Information about the social functioning of the client is usually obtained through client interviews, client observation, and outside sources.

Vocational evaluation information focuses on the client's work skills and attitudes. Such information is usually obtained by taking a vocational history of the client, applying some standardized tests (particularly those related to job interest and job aptitude), and utilizing samples of work and work situations for assessment of vocational potential. One of the best measures of future vocational behavior is past work experience and performance.

Educational evaluation consists of a determination of the client's level of education, learning capacity, attitudes toward learning, and special areas of interest or achievement. Most educational information can be obtained from school records. However, this is sometimes supplemented with the administration of achievement and aptitude tests.

Preliminary and thorough diagnostic studies

In Chapter 3 it was stated that an evaluation of rehabilitation potential is necessary to determine eligibility for applicants to the public rehabilitation program. The federal regulations for the 1973 Rehabilitation Act require a preliminary diagnostic study indicating that the applicant has a substantial handicap to employment and that either rehabilitation services can be expected to help him become employable or an extended evaluation of rehabilitation potential is necessary to make such determination. The information obtained from the applicant in an interview can be supplemented by routine aptitude tests and medical examinations.

Once an applicant has been determined eligible for rehabilitation services, a thorough diagnostic study is undertaken. A primary purpose of the thorough study is to determine the nature of the services needed by the individual. The thorough diagnostic study includes an evaluation of the individual's personality and intelligence level, his educational achievement and work experience, his personal, vocational, and social adjustment, any employment opportunities, and such additional other information as might be helpful in determining which services will be beneficial. Information from the thorough diagnostic study should culminate in a program of services for the client.

Perhaps the most important consideration in the conduct of an evaluation of a client is to know for what purpose and objectives the evaluation information is collected. At the preliminary diagnostic or screening stage, only general information is needed. However, during the thorough diagnostic or comprehensive evaluation stage, specific evaluation objectives should be determined. If this information is purchased from another agency, specific questions must be asked to facilitate obtaining answers to these questions. The primary purpose of the evaluation is to facilitate making decisions and plans about one's life and vocation.

PSYCHOLOGICAL TESTS

Psychological tests are usually paper-and-pencil tools of a relatively abstract nature that are, most often, intended to measure cognitive or affective traits. The following are some of the more commonly used tests in rehabilitation. Commercial tests are usually classified into three levels of complexity as suggested by the American Psychological Association (1953):

Level a. Tests which can be administered, scored, and interpreted by non-psychologists with the aid of a manual

Level b. Tests which require some technical knowledge of testing and suitable psychological training

Level c. Tests which require a qualified psychologist with substantial knowledge of testing and psychology and supervised training in the administration, scoring, and interpretation of the test

In the ensuing discussion the complexity level of the tests is shown in parentheses.

Intelligence and aptitude scales

Wechsler Adult Intelligence Scale (WAIS) (level c). The *WAIS* is the most commonly utilized measure of intelligence in rehabilitation. It is a measure of verbal and performance intelligence quotient (IQ) scales. Administering it requires considerable training.

The verbal IQ consists of six subtests: information, comprehension, similarities, arithmetic, digit span, and vocabulary. The performance IQ consists of five subtests: picture completion, block design, picture arrangement, object assembly, and digit symbol. In addition to the verbal and performance IQ scores, the *WAIS* yields a full-scale IQ. These three scores represent the primary information from the *WAIS*. However, the pattern of *WAIS* subscales can also provide meaningful indicators.

General Aptitude Test Battery *(GATB)* (level b). The *GATB* was developed

FIG. 7-1

David Wechsler, Ph.D. (Columbia University, 1925). Dr. Wechsler is best known for his outstanding contributions to the measurement of intelligence. (From Elias, M. F., Elias, P. K., & Elias, J. W. *Basic processes in adult developmental psychology.* St. Louis: The C. V. Mosby Co., 1977.)

by the United States Employment Service. It is intended to assess "vocationally significant aptitudes" which are useful in vocational counseling, job selection, and job placement. The *GATB* has been validated for over 450 different occupations, primarily in the unskilled and semiskilled areas. It requires a fifth-grade reading ability and about 2½ hours to take, and it can be administered to groups. Nine aptitudes are measured by twelve subtests. Eight of these subtests are paper-and-pencil tests whereas the remaining four utilize apparatus boards. Two of the apparatus tests use a 48-hole peg board, and two tests use a 50-hole rivet board. The nine aptitudes measured by the *GATB* are general learning ability, verbal, numerical, spatial perception, form perception, clerical perception, motor coordination, finger dexterity, and manual dexterity.

The aptitude scores are presented in the form of standard scores, with a mean of 100 and a standard deviation of 20. These nine standard scores are then combined in a variety of patterns called occupational aptitude patterns (OAP) that can be compared to requirements for specific job areas.

Other intelligence and general aptitude measures. Four other intelligence and aptitude tests will be discussed:

The United States Employment Service also designed a nonreading version of the *General Aptitude Test Battery* entitled *Non-Reading Aptitude Test Battery* (*NATB*) (level b). Many of the test items are similar to or identical with those of the *GATB*, and the same nine aptitudes are measured. Exceptions are that vocabulary items are presented orally and the mental manipulation of coins is substituted for arithmetic problems in measuring numerical aptitude. The *NATB* can be administered to as many as six persons at a time and requires approximately 3 hours to complete.

The *Otis Quick-Scoring Mental Ability Tests* (level b) is another test for obtaining an IQ score. This test also can be given to groups. Minimal training is required to administer the test. The Gamma form requires a sixth-grade reading ability and consists of 80 items involving word meaning, verbal analogies, scrambled sentences, proverb interpretation, logical reasoning, number series, arithmetic reasoning, and design analogies. The *Otis* presents a quick way to obtain a rough estimate of a client's general learning ability.

The *Revised Beta Examination,* second edition (level b) is a nonverbal test of general learning ability that can be administered to large groups. The *Revised Beta* provides a nonverbal estimate of intelligence with a single IQ score. There are six subtests: maze completion, number picture substitution, two tests involving finding the wrong drawing in a series of illustrations, form perceptions, and identifying sameness of objects. The entire test takes about 30 minutes.

The *Peabody Picture Vocabulary Test (PPVT)* (level b) is an untimed test to measure verbal intelligence through the use of word definitions. The test requires less than 15 minutes to give, and the results can be converted to an IQ scale, percentile, and mental age. The client points out one of four illustrations which best fits a stimulus word given orally by the examiner. Minimal training is required to administer or interpret the *PPVT.*

Personality inventories

Minnesota Multiphasic Personality Inventory (MMPI) (level c). The *MMPI* is intended to assess major personality characteristics related to personal and social adjustment. It requires a sixth-grade reading level and necessitates responding either true or false to 555 statements about personal characteristics, personality traits, feelings, habits, etc. There are ten subscales: hypochondriasis, depression, hysteria, psychopathic deviate, masculinity-femininity, paranoia, psychasthenia, schizophrenia, hypomania, and social introversion. There are also three validation scales. The inventory is given individually and usually requires less than 1½ hours. Raw scores are converted to standard scores by means of norm tables. Interpretation of the inventory requires graduate school training.

Sixteen Personality Factors Questionnaire (16PF) (level c). The *16PF* is intended to give information about an individual on sixteen bipolar primary personality factors and six secondary factors.

The primary factors are reserved-outgoing, less intelligent–more intelligent, affected by feelings–emotionally stable, humble-assertive, sober–happy-go-lucky, expedient-conscientious, shy-venturesome, tough–tender-minded, trusting-suspicious, practical-imaginative, forthright-shrewd, self-assured–apprehensive, conservative-experimental, group dependent–self-sufficient, undisciplined self-conflicting–controlled, and relaxed-tense. The six secondary factors are adjusted-anxious, introverted-extroverted, tender-minded emotionally–alert poised, subdued-independent, natural-discreet, and coolly realistic–prodigal subjective.

The questionnaire contains 187 multiple-choice items with three alternatives. It can be administered to groups and requires about 1 hour.

Edwards Personal Preference Schedule (EPPS) (level c). The *EPPS* provides a quick measure of 15 personality variables: achievement, deference, order, exhibition, autonomy, affiliation, intraception, succorance, dominance, abasement, nurturance, change, endurance, heterosexuality, and aggression. The schedule can be given to groups and requires less than 1 hour to complete. Since it was developed for college students and adults, it requires a fairly high reading level. The schedule contains 225 items, each having two short statements. The client selects the statement that best describes him.

Vineland Social Maturity Scale, Revised (level c). The *Vineland Social Maturity Scale, Revised,* is an individual social ability scale which has been used predominately with the mentally retarded. It is completed by an observer of the client. The items consist of a series of behavioral observations represented by five categories: self-help (general eating, dressing), locomotion, occupation, communication, and self-direction and socialization.

Tennessee Self-Concept Scale (level c). The *Tennessee Self-Concept Scale* is intended to be utilized as a description of self-concept. The counseling form consists of a total score that reflects overall level of self-esteem and three subscores that provide an internal frame of reference. These include (1) identity or "what I am" items, in which the individual describes himself in terms of his own perceptions, (2) self-satisfaction or "how I feel about or perceive myself," and (3) behavior or "what I do." The scale also provides five other scores—including a reflection of the individual's physical self, moral ethical self, personal self, family self, and social self. There are 100 descriptive statements to which the client responds on a five-point scale ranging from completely false to completely true. A high score on the instrument suggests a normal healthy openness. A low score usually indicates that the person answered in a defensive manner. The scale also includes a self-criticism score, a variability score, and a distribution (of responses) score. Norms are available. The scale may be administered to groups.

California Test of Personality (CTP) (level c). The *CTP* measures six personal adjustment factors: self-reliance, sense of personal freedom, feeling of belonging, withdrawing tendencies, nervous symptoms, and social adjustment. The social adjustment factors include social standards, social skills, antisocial tendencies, family relations, occupational relations, and community relations. Scores for each of these are converted to percentile ranks and standard scores.

The test consists of 180 questions that can be answered either yes or no and requires about 45 minutes to complete. It can be given to groups.

Achievement tests

Wide Range Achievement Test (WRAT) (level b). The *WRAT* is a quickly administered academic achievement test which measures oral reading, spelling, and arithmetic computation. It is primarily an individually administered test. However, some sections can be given to small groups. The examiner adjusts the testing range to the achievement level of the individual (from kindergarten through college).

Adult Basic Learning Examination (ABLE) (level a). The *ABLE* is intended to assess educational achievement of adults as low as the primary grade level. It provides six grade-equivalent scores: vocabulary, reading, spelling, arithmetic computation, arithmetic problem solving, and arithmetic total. It is a paper-and-pencil test that can be administered to groups. There are three levels of the test: level 1 is content for grades 1 to 4; level 2 is for grades 5 through 8; and level 3 is for grades 9 through 12. The test utilizes a multiple-choice response format and items which require writing a word or an answer to an arithmetic problem. A positive feature of this test is its utilization of adult subject matter. There are two forms for each level of the test. Levels 1 and 2 material usually require 2¼ hours for testing. Level 3 requires about 3 hours. The *ABLE* was specifically intended for adults having very little formal education.

Peabody Individual Achievement Test (PIAT) (level b). The *PIAT* is a wide-range measure of educational achievement that is individually administered in 30 to 40 minutes. Six scores are provided: mathematics, reading recognition, reading comprehension, spelling, general information, and a total score. Items of the *PIAT* are presented orally, and the client points to the correct answer among four alternative illustrations, numbers, or words. The results are converted to grade scores, percentile ranks, age scores, and standard scores. They can also be plotted on a profile sheet.

Gray Oral Reading Test (level b). The *Gray Oral Reading Test* can be used to identify reading grade level ability and oral reading difficulties. The test is administered individually and the client reads short passages aloud. Each successive passage is more difficult than the preceding. The reading time, types of errors, and responses to four comprehensive questions are recorded for each passage. The client reads until he makes seven or more errors on two successive passages. There are a total of thirteen passages ranging in difficulty from grade 1 through adult.

Vocational measures—interest surveys

Minnesota Importance Questionnaire (MIQ) (level b). The *Minnesota Importance Questionnaire* consists of 190 paired-comparison statements that measure twenty vocational needs. These needs are ability utilization, achievement, activity, advancement, authority, company policies and practices, compensation, co-workers, creativity, independence, moral values, recognition, responsibility, security, social service, social status, supervision–human relations, supervision-technical areas, variety, and working conditions. The 20 need dimensions are represented by a statement (e.g., "I could be busy all the time") and each statement is paired with all other statements. The respondent must choose the statement of the pair which represents the more important characteristic of the client's ideal job. Scoring the *MIQ* yields a measure of the degree of importance to the client for each of the twenty vocational needs. Completion of the self-administered *MIQ* takes 45 to 60 minutes and requires about a fifth-grade reading ability. However, it can also be administered orally. To determine how respondents compare with persons in various jobs, the *MIQ* can be compared with profiles of occupational reinforcer patterns for each of 148 occupations.

Kuder Occupational Interest Survey (level b). The *Kuder Occupational Interest Survey* is intended for persons with better than a seventh-grade reading ability. It is a paper-and-pencil instrument which can be administered to groups in approximately 40 minutes. There are 106 scales for men and 84 scales for women. Each survey item contains three short statements of different activities. The client chooses the one activity among the three he likes most and the one he likes least. The survey covers a broad range of jobs and can be used to determine both occupational and educational interests.

Strong-Campbell Interest Inventory (level b). The *Strong-Campbell Interest Inventory* is a 1974 revision of the *Strong Vocational Interest Blank,* which was developed in 1927. The original version had separate forms for men and women. It contained basic interest scales, occupational scales, and nonoccupational scales. The revision merged the earlier male and female forms into a single booklet with norms to eliminate sex bias from the occupational scales. The inventory provides scores for general occupational themes, basic interests, and occupational scales. The scores are used as an index of similarity between a person's interests and the interests of successful men and women in a variety of occupations. The inventory can be administered to groups. It has been most useful for identifying vocational goals that require a college education.

Other interest surveys. Three other interest measures will be discussed:

The *Wide Range Interest-Opinion Test (WRIOT)* (level b) is a test consisting of 150 sets of three pictures. The client is asked to identify which picture he likes most and which least in each set. Thus no reading is required on the part of the client. The results are given in standard T scores (normally distributed, usually with a mean of 50 and a standard deviation of 10) for each of 18 job cluster and interest areas. Examples are art, drama, sales, management, social service, mechanics, risk, ambition, sedentariness, and interest spread. Because it is a nonverbal survey, it is particularly useful for persons with limited reading ability or for use with the mentally retarded.

An interest survey especially designed for the mentally retarded is the *Voca-*

tional Interest and Sophistication Assessment survey *(VISA)* (level b). Like the *WRIOT*, the *VISA* is a pictorial survey which is administered individually. There are two forms, one for males and another for females. The male form yields interest and knowledge scores in seven areas—including garage, laundry, food service, maintenance, farm and town, materials handling, and industry. The female form provides scores in four areas—business and clerical, housekeeping, services and laundry, and sewing. A feature of the *VISA* is that it focuses on job situations that are within the potential of many mentally retarded clients.

Another interest survey which is useful for assisting in the identification of a wide range of occupational interests is the *Ohio Vocational Interest Survey (OVIS)* (level b). This is a paper-and-pencil survey which can be administered to groups within 60 to 90 minutes. It contains two parts, one asking for information about interests, educational status, and future career plans and one containing 280 items with brief descriptions of activities. Each of the 280 items requires the client to respond on a 5-point scale ranging from "likes very much" to "dislikes very much." The *OVIS* has 24 interest scales. The final scores for each of these scales are presented in percentiles and stanines (scales of 1 to 9) and can be related to *Dictionary of Occupational Titles* data (see Chapter 9 for a description of *DOT*). The *OVIS* is useful with clients having limited reading ability.

Vocational measures—manual dexterity tests

Crawford Small Parts Dexterity Test (level a). The primary purpose of the *Crawford Small Parts Dexterity Test* is to measure fine eye-hand coordination. The test consists of a board which contains 42 holes and three bins for pins, collars, and screws. The first part of the test requires the client to use a tweezers to pick up a pin and place it in a hole on the board. The client then fits a collar over the pin. The first portion of the test consists of 36 pins and collars. In the second part the client uses a small screwdriver to put 30 screws in a plate. The time required to do these two parts of the test represents the scoring. Scores are compared with norms represented, primarily, by factory workers. The test is individually administered and takes about 15 minutes to complete.

Purdue Pegboard (level a). The *Purdue Pegboard* is also a manual dexterity test. It measures gross movement of the hands, fingers, and arms and fingertip dexterity. No reading is required. The pegboard has 25 holes and four cups containing pins, washers, and collars. Clients are given 30 seconds to put the pins in the holes. The first administration involves the right hand only; the second, the left hand; and the third, both hands singly or together. A fourth administration involves assembling, within 1 minute, the pins, washers, and collars using both hands. The results are compared with norms for industrial workers and college students. The test can be given to as many as 10 persons at one time in less than 15 minutes.

Bennett Hand-Tool Dexterity Test (level a). This test measures proficiency in the use of common mechanic's tools. The test consists of moving 12 nuts, bolts, and washers of three different sizes on a hardwood frame using three wrenches and a screwdriver. Scoring is done by clocking the time in minutes and seconds needed for completion of the task. These times are then compared with norms for eight different groups which are primarily industrial. Administration takes less than 20 minutes, and no reading is required.

Other manual dexterity tests. Three other tests measuring manual dexterity will be discussed:

The *O'Connor Finger Dexterity* and *O'Connor Tweezer Dexterity Tests* (level a) are intended to assess motor coordination and finger and manual dexterity. Both tests use plates with 100 holes arranged in 10 rows. The finger dexterity test requires the client to insert three small metal pins into each of the holes. The tweezer dexterity test involves using a metal tweezer to pick up the pins one at a time and insert a single pin into each of 100 holes. Scoring is based on the time it takes to complete each task.

Another dexterity test is the *Stromberg Dexterity Test* (level a). This test is intended to measure speed and accuracy of arm and hand movement. It involves inserting 54 red, blue, and yellow disks in correspondingly colored sections of a board. The client receives four trials. The third and fourth trials are timed to obtain a score which is compared to various norms.

Other vocational measures

McCarron-Dial Work Evaluation System. The *McCarron-Dial Work Evaluation System* is a battery of tests which attempt to measure general vocational competencies and specific task productivity. It attempts to assess five factors: verbal-cognitive, sensory, fine and gross motor coordination, social-emotional, and integration-coping. The verbal-cognitive factor is assessed by the use of the *Wechsler Adult Intelligence Scale* or the *Stanford-Binet Intelligence Scale* and the *Peabody Picture Vocabulary Test*. The sensory factor is measured with the *Bender Visual-Motor Gestalt Test* and the *Haptic Visual Discrimination Test*. Motor ability is measured by the *McCarron Assessment of Neuro-muscular Development,* which involves five tasks for assessing fine motor skills and five tasks for assessing gross motor ability. The social-emotional factor is evaluated by the *Observational Emotional Inventory,* designed for use in sheltered workshops. The integration-coping factor is measured by the *Behavioral Rating Scale* developed by Dial. The criterion of general vocational competency is measured in terms of performance by the *San Francisco Vocational Competency Scale,* and productivity is measured by the *Fishing Tackle Assembly.* The tests are administered individually.

Multidimensional Objective Vocational Evaluation (MOVE). The *MOVE* was developed at Goodwill Industries of Chicago. It consists of 28 pure factor tests which take approximately 8 hours, including standardized psychological and dexterity tests and new measures developed at the Goodwill Industries of Chicago. They are intended to measure an individual's unilateral and bilateral motor skills, perceptual skills, perceptual motor coordination skills, intelligence, achievement, and physical strength. After the client is tested, the test scores and other information—including the physical limitations of the client, the work conditions to be avoided, the limitations of possible training time, and judgments regarding the client's ability to relate to people—are analyzed with a computer program. The program relates this information to jobs contained in the *Dictionary of Occupational Titles*. The program printout provides a list of *DOT* jobs for which the person has an interest and which he is capable of performing. In addition, the printout provides a list of client characteristics, test scores, functions the client is capable of performing as well as the appropriate Worker Trait Groups for those functions, and the page numbers for the Worker Trait Groups in the 1965 *Dictionary of Occupational Titles,* Volume II.

SRA Clerical Aptitudes (level b). The Science Research Associates instrument is intended to provide measures of general aptitudes necessary for clerical work. It can be administered to groups and provides three scores: office vocabulary, office arithmetic, and office checking. The vocabulary subtest contains 48 pairs of words identified as either the same or opposite. The arithmetic subtest involves problems with multiple-choice answers. Five minutes are allowed for the vocabulary subtest, 15 minutes for the arithmetic, and 5 minutes for checking. The three scores are presented in percentiles on a profile sheet. The tests do require a high level of reading ability.

Minnesota Clerical Test (level a). This test is one of clerical speed and accuracy. It has two parts: number checking and name checking. Each has 200 items. The client compares two numbers or two names to determine whether they are identical. The number correct is converted to a percentile for comparing with norms of groups. The tests require about 15 minutes. The *Minnesota Clerical Test* is a respected instrument which has been used for more than 30 years; thus the norms are quite dated.

Revised Minnesota Paper Form Board Test (level a). This test is probably the best known among the paper-and-pencil tests of spatial ability. It consists of 64 two-dimensional diagrams cut into separate parts. The client determines how the pieces fit together into a complete figure and chooses the drawing from among five which correctly shows such an arrangement. The test can be administered in 20 minutes and produces a single score given in percentiles to reflect the client's ability to visualize and manipulate objects in space.

Bennett Mechanical Comprehension Test (level a). This test is intended to measure ability to perceive and understand the relationships of physical forces and mechanical elements in practical situations. It provides information on the client's ability to learn the principles of operation by making a visual comparison between two pictures and answering a question about them—for example,

"Which would be the better shears for cutting metal?" The test consists of 68 items dealing with mechanical principles and general physical concepts. It is a test administered to groups with a 30-minute time limit. A mechanical comprehension score is reflected in percentile form for comparison with various norm groups.

MacQuarrie Test for Mechanical Ability (level a). This test undertakes to measure several aspects of mechanical aptitude, including speed and accuracy of eye-hand coordination and spatial ability. It consists of seven subtests: tracing, tapping, dotting, copying, location, blocks, and pursuit. There are norms for each subtest in addition to norms for the total score.

WORK SAMPLES

A task force of the Vocational Evaluation Project conducted by the Vocational Evaluation and Work Adjustment Association (1975) defined the work sample as "a well defined work activity involving tasks, materials, and tools which are identical or similar to those in an actual job or cluster of jobs." The primary purpose of a work sample is to assess a client's vocational aptitudes, worker characteristics, and vocational interests. The samples can range from very simple to very complex operations and can be designed to measure a single characteristic relevant to one or many jobs or the reproduction of an entire job.

There are a number of advantages of work samples, among which would be the following:

1. Their close approximation to real work
2. The concrete nature of most tasks
3. The minimal academic requirements required for attempting most tasks
4. The direct performance feedback to the client
5. The opportunity to explore various jobs and job tasks by the client

There are also a number of disadvantages of work samples, such as the following:

1. The need to continuously reconstruct and standardize work samples to keep pace with technological changes
2. The subjectivity involved in evaluation of personal characteristics
3. The fact that predictive validity of a work sample to community jobs is rarely established

Work sample approaches

TOWER system. The *TOWER* system (acronym for Testing, Orientation, and Work Evaluation in Rehabilitation) was developed by the ICD Rehabilitation and Research Center in New York City (formerly the Institute for the Crippled and Disabled). The system got its start in a guidance test class conducted by the Institute in 1937, and it became known as the *TOWER* system in 1957.

The system addresses 14 occupational areas including clerical, drafting, draw-

FIG. 7-2
Work samples offer a prevocational evaluation technique for exploring vocational potential.
(From Rusk, H. A. *Rehabilitation medicine.* St. Louis: The C. V. Mosby Co., 1977.)

ing, electronics assembly, jewelry manufacturing, leather goods, lettering, machine shop, mail clerk, optical mechanics, pantograph engraving, sewing machine operating, welding, and workshop assembly. Each of these 14 occupational areas includes a number of tasks. In all, there are more than 110 different tasks in the *TOWER* system. For each of the tasks, qualitative and quantitative criteria have been developed in accordance with industrial standards. The sequence of tasks is from simple to complex. Clients are given an opportunity to practice using the tools of a particular occupational area prior to the task evaluation. The occupational areas and tasks selected are related to the client's interests, level of functioning, assets, and limitations. The client is not required to go through the entire sequence of job tasks; rather a number of jobs representing various phases of an occupational area are tried. If the client performs poorly on one of the simpler tasks, the tests in this area are discontinued. Usually each task in a sequence for an occupation involves every tool from preceding tasks in that area. Evaluation consists of assessing the client's work and personal characteristics and performance. The evaluation involves ratings by the evaluator in terms of time and errors. Performance is rated on five levels ranging from superior to inferior. An emphasis is placed on the quality of finished products. A thorough evaluation utilizing the *TOWER* system requires approximately three weeks.

The ICD Rehabilitation and Research Center developed 13 *Micro-TOWER* work samples for use in group evaluation. One evaluator can give the same work sample to a group of individuals. The *Micro-TOWER* measures vocational aptitudes in the areas of motor, spatial, clerical perception, verbal, and numerical skills. Structured activities stimulate group discussion and examination of vocational goals and interests. Each work sample utilizes a cassette tape for presenting instructions to the group, and a large photobook with illustrations relating the work sample to actual occupations. Testing for a group takes 3 to 5 days. Client performance is compared with general and specific subgroup norms.

Philadelphia JEVS Work Sample Battery. The *Philadelphia Jewish Employment and Vocational Service Work Sample Battery* was developed beginning in the late 1950s. In 1967 the Department of Labor supported JEVS's research and development of the work sample units.

The battery consists of 28 work samples directly related to 10 worker trait groups in the 1965 *Dictionary of Occupational Titles*. These worker trait groups are handling; sorting, inspecting, measuring, and related work; tending; manipulating; routing, checking, and recording; classifying, filing, and related work; inspecting and stock checking; craftmanship and related work; costuming, tailoring, and dressmaking; and drafting and related work. The work samples are arranged in order of increasing complexity. The client's occupational potential and capabilities are estimated on the basis of his performance on the total battery. Thus the entire battery is given to each client and takes approximately 2 weeks. Examples of activities are soldering tin, lettering signs, assembling sections of pipe, disassembling and reassembling a doorlock, a telephone, and a step ladder, computing postage and payrolls, making a blouse or a vest, filing, and proofreading.

Though the complete system includes hardware to evaluate 15 clients simultaneously, each work sample is administered to clients individually. Instructions are given verbally to clients and include a demonstration. Work samples are scored on the basis of time and quality. The battery also allows for evaluation of interests and work behavior. Clients are rated on a 3-point scale for each work sample, with the highest score reflecting competitive employment potential. The evaluation is then related to the *Dictionary of Occupational Titles* for identifying areas of potential training and/or job placement.

A modification of the *Philadelphia JEVS Work Sample Battery* has been developed at the agency specifically for use with the mentally retarded. It is entitled *Vocational Information and Evaluation Work Samples (VIEWS)* and consists of 16 tasks. A major modification in the *VIEWS* approach is the emphasis on training the client to do the task prior to evaluation. Each *VIEWS* work sample involves an orientation-demonstration-training sequence with considerable positive reinforcement. Evaluation begins after a predetermined level of competence is achieved. Five to 8 days are required for completion of the 16 *VIEWS* tasks. Examples of tasks are sorting, cutting, counting, collating, assembling, weighing, tying, measuring, using hand tools, and tending a drill press. Evaluators assess work skills, tolerance for sustained activity, independence, and vocational interests.

Singer Vocational Evaluation System. The *Singer Vocational Evaluation System* is a series of work sample stations which are intended to be used for career exploration and vocational evaluation.

Presently there are 19 work stations in the *System:* basic tools; bench assembly; drafting; electrical wiring; plumbing and pipe fitting; carpentry and woodworking; refrigeration, heating, and air conditioning; soldering and welding; office and sales clerk; needle trades; masonry; sheetmetal working; cooking and baking; small engine service; medical service; cosmetology; data calculation and recording; soil testing; and photography laboratory technology. Each work station is self-contained and includes all the tools appropriate to that work station's functions. A feature of the *Singer System* is that it includes an audiovisual presentation of instructions for performing the tasks required in the work station. Each work station is equipped with a filmstrip projector, instructional filmstrips, syncronized audiocassette, and headphones. All instructions are given from a cassette, and the pace is controlled by the client. The audiovisual presentation introduces the client to the tools of that work station and provides instructions on how to use them. It also describes actual jobs related to the activities the client will carry out at that work station. It then instructs the client, step by step, in implementing the work station task.

The client is evaluated for time and errors; results are compared with norms provided in the evaluator manual. Observational checklists are also used. In addition, the client is asked to self-evaluate his performance and interest in the occupational area based upon the audiovisual description and experience with the work sample. Evaluators are provided with a list of *Dictionary of Occupational Titles* code numbers and job titles and the related industries for each of the work samples. A positive feature of the *Singer System* is that—besides helping to determine vocational aptitudes, interests, and tolerances for vocational training or job placement—it provides a career exploration dimension.

Valpar Component Work Sample Series. The *Valpar Component Work Sample Series* was marketed in 1973 after eight years of developmental effort. The *Valpar Series* is intended to be part of a comprehensive rehabilitation service delivery approach.

Presently, there are 16 samples in the *Series:* small tools (mechanical), size discrimination, numerical sorting, upper extremity range of motion, clerical comprehension and aptitude, independent problem solving, multilevel sorting, simulated assembly, whole body range of motion, trilevel measurement, eye-hand-foot coordination, soldering and inspection (electronic), money handling, integrated peer performance, electrical circuitry and print reading, and drafting. The *Valpar Series* is keyed to the worker traits data in the 1965 *Dictionary of Occupational Titles.* The manual for each work sample identifies specific occupations and related classifications in a variety of job families related to the work sample. The *Series* attempts to measure universal characteristics of human work potential. In addition, observations of client work behavior are made by the evaluator.

Each sample provides normative information—including time, error, and performance norms. The norms are represented by data collected from clients who have taken the *Valpar Component Work Sample Series* in rehabilitation facilities in Arizona and California.

Talent Assessment Program. The *Talent Assessment Program* battery of 10 measures is intended to be a functional assessment of work in industrial, technical, and service areas. It is particularly intended to measure the capabilities of persons planning to enter service occupations or low-level trade training. The developer, Wilton E. Nighswonger, recommends that it be used in combination with psychological, academic, and medical examination information to give a total picture of the individual.

The 10 tests in the *Talent Assessment Program* battery are structural and mechanical visualization, discrimination by size and shape (sorting), discrimination by color (sorting), discrimination by touch (sorting), dexterity (handling small materials), dexterity (handling large materials), fine dexterity (using small tools), dexterity (using large tools), circuital visualization (visualizing an electrical flow diagram), and retention of structural and mechanical detail. The entire battery takes about 2 hours. All directions are given verbally to the client, and no reading is required. All the tests involve manipulation and are considered "action" tests. Evaluation of the client is based on the total time it takes to do each test and the number of errors made. The information is converted into percentiles for comparing with norms developed on seven different people classifications. A profile is developed for the 10 test areas.

Generally the client's occupational potential in a given test area is classified as follows:

Less than 25th percentile   Low level service and trade occupations

25th to 50th percentile	Unskilled occupations
51st to 75th percentile	Semiskilled occupations
Above 75th percentile	Skilled occupations

The individual tests are representative of occupational clusters and are related to specific job titles in the *Dictionary of Occupational Titles* and described in the *Occupational Outlook Handbook*.

Wide Range Employment Sample Test (WREST). The *WREST* was developed by Joseph F. Jastak and marketed by Guidance Associates of Delaware, Inc. It is a battery of 10 work samples for evaluation of dexterity and perceptual ability. The 10 samples include single and double folding; pasting, labeling, and stuffing; stapling; bottle packaging; rice measuring; screw assembly; tag stringing; swatch pasting; collating; and color and shade matching and pattern making. The battery can be administered to a client in 1½ hours. Scoring is done in terms of time and errors. Results are compared with industrial norms based on 300 workshop clients and 100 employed workers. The total score for the 10 work samples provides information relative to the efficiency of the client in technical type work. The *WREST* battery does not attempt to relate results to specific jobs or occupations. However, it can be an indicator of learning potential.

Comprehensive Occupational Assessment and Training System (COATS). *COATS* is a development by Prep, Inc., of Trenton, New Jersey. This system is made up of four major components—job-matching system, employability attitudes system, work samples system, and living skills system. Each of the components contains three program levels: (1) assessment and analysis, (2) prescription and instruction, and (3) evaluation and placement. Thus *COATS* is intended to be more than a vocational evaluation system and more than a work sample approach.

The assessment approaches for the four components utilize audiotape and filmstrip cartridges for instruction. In the job-matching system 15 audiovisual cartridges present photographs and drawings of skill activities to the client in each of 16 skill categories. The clients report their experience, preference, or capability for doing the skill activities. Six audiovisual cartridges are utilized in the employability attitudes system for solving problem situations in job seeking and on the job. Alternative solutions by the client reflect different attitudes. The work samples system uses the audiovisual cartridges to give instructions for performing the work sample. The cartridge stops for each task to be performed by the client. Work samples include drafting, clerical-office, metal construction, sales, wood construction, food preparation, medical services, travel services, barbering-cosmetology, and small engine. The evaluator rates client proficiency and notes the client's efficiency, relationship to authority, and work behaviors. The client indicates his "before" and "after" expectations and interest in each work sample. In addition, clients rate the difficulty and performance quality of each task. In the living skills system six audiovisual cartridges are utilized. The cartridges contain samples of competencies for real-life situations. The client responds to 250 incidents which require cognitive skills. Normative data are included for each component in the instructor guides (Pisauro, 1976).

SITUATIONAL ASSESSMENT

Situational assessment involves observing client behavior. It is probably the most widely used approach to vocational evaluation in rehabilitation. Pruitt (1977) defines situational assessment as "a systematic procedure for observing, recording and interpreting work behavior." Situational assessment can be conducted in nearly any work situation, real or simulated. Two environments in which it is frequently conducted are sheltered workshops and job sites.

Sheltered workshops generally use either subcontract or prime production work for developing work habits and work attitudes. An advantage of the sheltered workshop for evaluation is the capability to manipulate the work environment, thus providing a variety of conditions for assessment. The disadvantages are that the sheltered workshop is dependent on subcontract work which is not always readily available and usually is of the bench assembly variety, working with others who are handicapped, and personnel who may be too permissive.

Job sites were described in Chapter 5 as a vocational adjustment tool in rehabilitation. However, they can also be used for conducting situational assessment. Job sites may be within a rehabilitation facility or with community employers. In the community they have the advantage of assessing client functioning at real jobs. Because of this, they may have more realistic standards for testing capabilities and limitations, strengths and weaknesses, job interests, and behavioral dynamics between the client, the supervisor, and co-workers. Job-site evaluation is generally utilized as a final evaluation technique before job placement.

Behavior analysis

In behavior analysis a detailed analysis of the job is made to determine the behaviors expected of a satisfactory worker in a particular job setting. Examples of behaviors studied are attending to task, self-initiated work-related interaction with the supervisor, social interaction initiated with co-workers, idle time, and scheduled and unscheduled rest breaks. It is important that expectancies for the percent of time spent in such activities be established for satisfactory workers and helpful if behaviors are stated in behavioral terms. Both behavioral expectancies and behavioral evaluations of clients can be determined by taking time estimates of workers with a stopwatch. These time estimates can be obtained by observing the worker for brief intervals at various times during the day.

In addition, behavior analysis can include information related to production. Expected production rate and acceptable scrap rates can be determined and the workers' actual rate compared with these expectancies. Substitute behaviors can also be observed. For example, a more detailed analysis of a client's idle behavior might reveal that he spends considerable time waiting for materials and waiting for the supervisor to initiate a contact.

An advantage of the behavior analysis approach is that it permits the evaluator to identify behaviors which can occur in many job settings, thus permitting prescriptions for work adjustment programming. A disadvantage is the amount of time behavior analysis takes. Considerable time is necessary for identifying behavior expectancies in a particular job setting, collecting information about a client, and comparing behavioral performance with the expectancies (Dunn, 1973a).

Assessment instruments

Situational assessment, of necessity, is dependent on observers. Dunn (1973b) offers some guidelines for making observations during evaluation: (1) describe behaviors in observable terms; (2) describe the situation in which the behavior occurred; (3) describe what happened rather than what did not happen; (4) describe a frequency, rate, or duration whenever possible; (5) begin with an action verb; (6) use a terse, direct style; and (7) record observations immediately.

Four aids to observation will now be described.

Observation and Client Evaluation in Workshops. The combination guide and manual entitled *Observation and Client Evaluation in Workshops* was developed by the Research Utilization Laboratory of the Jewish Vocational Service in Chicago. It is a systematic approach to observing and describing work behaviors in 12 areas by sheltered workshop floor supervisors. The better the client is able to perform in each of these 12 areas, the more likely he should be to maintain a job in competitive employment. The 12 areas are degree of anxiety or comfort with floor supervisors, ability to profit from instruction or criticism, quality of work, acceptance of work role, productivity, ability to socialize with co-workers, ability to cooperate on work tasks, appropriateness of personal relations with floor supervisors, response to pleasantness or unpleasantness of tasks, communication with floor supervisors, ability to organize work, and self-presentation.

Each of the 12 areas is defined. For example, the definition for area 1, degree of anxiety or comfort with floor supervisors, is as follows: "the degree to which the client is able to prevent his work from suffering because of anxiety occasioned by contact with, or even the physical presence of, floor supervisors. The less that supervisory presence is itself the occasion for discomfort or anxiety, the more promising is the client's vocational future" (Soloff, Goldston, & Pollack, 1972).

Cues for observation are provided for each of the 12 areas. Examples for area 1 are "becomes less well-organized in supervisor's presence," "fails to request help at all," and "improved performance when shown how." The cues that are provided in the manual are for illustration only. Users of the instrument are encouraged to be alert to other cues possibly reflecting behavior in the 12 areas. The manual also cross-references each of the 12 areas with others which may be behaviorally related.

The manual is accompanied by a staffing preparation form that permits supervisors to rate each of the 12 areas of behavior on a 5-point scale from positive to negative. For example, positive behavior for area 1 might be "client is quite comfortable and not anxious with supervision"; on the negative side of the scale, the "client is basically uncomfortable and anxious with supervision." The principal value of these ratings is to serve as a basis for supervisor discussion of client functioning in the sheltered workshop.

MDC Behavior Identification Format. The *MDC Behavior Identification Format* is a measurement tool for observing, identifying, and recording work and work-related behaviors developed by the Materials Development Center (1974) at the University of Wisconsin–Stout. It can be used as a basis for developing a treatment program for assisting the individual to acquire the needed behavior for employability.

The *Format* contains 22 behavior categories. Each category is defined in detail in the manual and includes examples and sample descriptions. The 22 behavior categories are as follows: hygiene, grooming, and dress; irritating habits; odd or inappropriate behaviors; communication skills as related to work needs; attendance; punctuality; ability to cope with work problems (frustration tolerance); personal complaints; vitality of work energy; stamina or 8-hour work capacity; steadiness or consistency of work; distractability; conformity to shop rules and safety practices; reactions to change in work assignment; reactions to unpleasantness or monotonous tasks; social skills in relations with co-workers; amount of supervision required after initial instruction period; recognition-acceptance of supervisory authority; amount of tension aroused by close supervision; requests for assistance from supervisors; reactions to criticism and pressure of supervisors; and work method and organization of tools and materials.

The user of the *MCD Behavior Identification Format* relates to the category definitions, examples, and sample descriptions as a guide for writing behavioral descriptions of the client's behavior. Problem behaviors can then be rated at various time intervals in terms of three major rating classifications: A, acceptable; B, selective placement; C, change needed. Each of these major classifications is subdivided into more precise ratings as follows:

> A Acceptable
>   A-1 Strength
>   A-2 No problems
> B Selective placement
>   B-1 Problem placement
>   B-2 Change to upgrade
> C Change needed
>   C-1 Change possible
>   C-2 Change doubtful

Following is an example taken from the manual for utilizing the *MDC Behavior Identification Format:*

Category	Behaviors	Date	Rating
6. Punctuality	Comes 5-15 min late to	6-7-73	C-1
	work every day	6-15-73	A-2
	Also returns from breaks	6-22-73	A-1
	2-3 min late		

The ratings suggest that the client had a problem in punctuality which needed change (C-1); it improved to no problem (A-2), then to an actual strength (A-1). The strengths of the *MDC Behavior Identification Format* are its individualized approach and its specificity regarding behaviors.

Work Adjustment Rating Form (WARF). The *WARF* is a rating scale constructed primarily for use by rehabilitation facilities staff to assess work adjustment strengths and limitations. It can be used to develop adjustment training plans and assess progress toward job readiness.

The *WARF* contains eight subscales each having five items, making a total of 40 items. The subscales are amount of supervision required, realism of job goals, teamwork, acceptance of rules/authority, work tolerance, perseverance in work, extent trainee seeks assistance, and importance attached to job training. Each of the subscales is represented by items describing five different levels of performance from low to high. The following five items are an example of the subscale "teamwork": (1) Trainee is unable to work effectively with any others. (2) Trainee can work with only one or two others whom he particularly likes. (3) Trainee can usually work with a few others without conflict. (4) Trainee works effectively in small groups (2 or 3 persons). (5) Trainee is a good team worker in any group situation.

The items are rated by checking "yes" or "no" to each and they are scaled so a positive response to an item at any level also gives a positive response to all items below that level. To minimize rater bias, the items are scrambled and the scale level of each is not known. However, it is still advisable to obtain more than one rater for each client to effect control for rater bias. The *WARF* can be completed in 3 to 7 minutes depending on the rater. Scoring, if a key template is constructed, takes approximately 5 minutes. The range of total scores on the *WARF* is 0 to 40. A profile of client strengths and limitations can be obtained by inspection of *WARF* subscale scores. A scoring form with identification of scrambled *WARF* items is included with the scale (Bitter, 1970; Bitter & Bolanovich, 1970).

Goal Attainment Scaling. Goal Attainment Scaling is a procedure developed at the Hennepin County Mental Health Service in Minneapolis, Minnesota, for identifying behaviorally defined goals and outcomes for clients on a simple scale ranging from most unfavorable outcome to best anticipated outcome.

The procedure has the following characteristics: the client's objectives are devised for or by the client; there is a system for assigning weights among these objectives; expected outcomes are identified for each objective; there is a quantifiable follow-up system for these outcomes; and a score can be obtained which summarizes outcomes across all objectives. A positive feature of this procedure is that individual goals are established and the client is compared with himself in terms of degree of success. Each goal area is weighted as to its importance in the overall service process. The weighting system allows the counselor and/or client to arbitrarily assign a level of importance to each area. One- or two-digit numbers may be used. The higher the number, the more important is the goal.

If no weights are assigned, it is assumed that all goal areas identified are of equal importance. After the identification and weighting of each goal area, behavioral descriptions of outcomes are developed on five levels and scaled from the most unfavorable outcome likely (assigned a −2 value) to the best anticipated outcome (assigned a +2 value). An expected outcome treatment for each goal area is also stated (assigned a score of 0) and is located at the middle of the scale (Kiresuk & Sherman, 1968; Kiresuk, 1973). A sample goal attainment scale is as follows:

Scale attainment levels	Scale 1: Employment (weight = 3)
Most unfavorable service outcome likely (−2)	Client unemployed and is not seeking employment
Less than expected success with service (−1)	Client finds employment but remains on the job less than 60 days
Expected level of service outcome (0)	Client is employed and has held a job for more than 60 days
More than expected success with service (+1)	Client has been employed more than 60 days and indicates satisfaction with the job
Best anticipated success with service (+2)	Client has been employed more than 90 days; is satisfied with the job; has received a raise

Similarly, scales are developed for other client goal areas and relative weights are assigned to each. The procedure for converting what are qualitative dimensions to quantitative scores is computationally simple. However, tables are also available which convert the combination of weights and levels to standard scores. A study by Goodyear and Bitter (1974) found that goal attainment scaling is a valid, reliable, and realistic method for measuring rehabilitation service effectiveness.

SUMMARY

Client evaluation in rehabilitation necessitates a comprehensive approach incorporating medical, psychological, sociocultural, vocational, and educational information. Vocational rehabilitation is a goal-oriented program. Thus the purpose of a thorough evaluation is to determine the services needed by disabled individuals so that they may make decisions about their life and vocation.

Commonly used psychological tests, work samples, and situational assessment approaches utilized in vocational rehabilitation are briefly described in this chapter. Some tests necessitate individual administration whereas others can be given to groups. The various techniques call for different degrees of training and skill for valid implementation. Though the measures described are certainly not exhaustive of those that are available to rehabilitation professionals, they are representative of vocational evaluation practice in rehabilitation.

SELF-EVALUATION QUESTIONS

1. What are the components of a comprehensive client evaluation?
2. What is the difference in purpose between the preliminary and thorough diagnostic studies?
3. Which is the most commonly utilized measure of intelligence in rehabilitation?
4. For what type of occupations has the *GATB* been primarily validated?
5. What are the differences between the *GATB* and *NATB*?
6. What are three relatively short measures of intelligence?
7. What personality inventories can be administered in groups?
8. What achievement test was specifically developed for adults with little formal education?
9. What are two interest surveys which require no reading?
10. How are the *Crawford Small Parts Dexterity Test, Purdue Pegboard,* and *O'Connor Dexterity Tests* similar?
11. Why do you think the *McCarron-Dial Work Evaluation System* is called a "system"?
12. What is a disadvantage of the *Minnesota Clerical Tests*?
13. What is a work sample?
14. What are the advantages and disadvantages to the use of work samples?
15. What are the differences between the *TOWER* and *Micro-TOWER* work sample systems?
16. What is the major difference between *VIEWS* and the *Philadelphia JEVS Work Sample Battery*?
17. What is a feature of the *Singer Vocational Evaluation System* and the *Comprehensive Occupational Assessment and Training System (COATS)* not found in other work sample approaches?
18. Who is represented in the norms for the *Valpar Component Work Sample Series*?
19. For what type of occupations and training is the *Talent Assessment Program* particularly intended?
20. What is situational assessment?
21. What is behavior analysis?
22. What are an advantage and the disadvantages of the sheltered workshop for conducting situational assessment?
23. When is job-site evaluation generally used?
24. What type of rehabilitation worker is the intended user of the assessment instrument entitled *Observation and Client Evaluation in Workshops*?
25. What is required of the user of the *MDC Behavior Identification Format*?
26. What are the primary uses of the *Work Adjustment Rating Form*?
27. What are the characteristics of Goal Attainment Scaling?

REFERENCES

American Psychological Association. *Ethical standards of psychologists.* Washington, D.C.: APA, 1953.

Bitter, J. A. Bias effect on validity and reliability of a rating scale. *Measurement and Evaluation in Guidance,* 1970, 3(2), 70-75.

Bitter, J. A., & Bolanovich, D. J. WARF: a scale for measuring job-readiness behaviors. *American Journal of Mental Deficiency,* 1970, 74(5), 616-621.

Dunn, D. J. *Situational assessment: models for the future.* Menomonie, Wis.: Research and Training Center, University of Wisconsin–Stout, 1973a.

Dunn, D. J. Recording observations. *Consumer Brief* (Research & Training Center, University of Wisconsin–Stout, Menomonie, Wis.) 1973b, 1(1), 1-3.

Goodyear, D. L., & Bitter, J. A. Goal attainment scaling as a program evaluation measure in rehabilitation. *Journal of Applied Rehabilitation Counseling,* 1974, 5(1), 19-26.

Kiresuk, T. J. Goal attainment scaling at a county mental health center. *Evaluation,* 1973, 1, 12-18.

Kiresuk, T. J., & Sherman, R. E. Goal attainment scaling: a general method for evaluating comprehensive community mental health programs. *Community Mental Health Journal,* 1968, 4(6), 443-453.

Materials Development Center. *MDC behavior identification format.* Menomonie, Wis.: Materials Development Center, University of Wisconsin–Stout, 1974.

Pisauro, M. L. Comprehensive Occupational Assessment and Training System. *Vocational Evaluation and Work Adjustment Bulletin,* 1976, 9(3), 39-45.

Pruitt, W. A. *Vocational (work) evaluation.* Menomonie, Wis.: Walt Pruitt Associates, Publishers, 1977.

Soloff, A., Goldston, L. J., & Pollack, R. A. *Observation and client evaluation in workshops: a guide and a manual.* Menomonie, Wis.: Materials Development Center, University of Wisconsin–Stout, 1972.

Tenth Institute on Rehabilitation Services. *Vocational evaluation and work adjustment services in vocational rehabilitation.* Washington, D.C.: Rehabilitation Services Administration, Department of Health, Education, and Welfare, 1972.

Vocational Evaluation and Work Adjustment Association. The tools of vocational evaluation. *Vocational Evaluation and Work Adjustment Bulletin,* 1975, 8(Special ed.), 49-64.

ADDITIONAL READINGS

American Psychological Association. *Standards for educational and psychological tests.* Washington, D.C.: APA, 1974.

Andrew, J. D., & Dickerson, L. R. (Eds.). *Vocational evaluation: a resource manual.* Menomonie, Wis.: Research and Training Center, University of Wisconsin–Stout, 1974.

Backer, T. *Methods of assessing the disadvantaged in manpower programs: a review and analysis.* Los Angeles, Calif.: Human Interaction Research Institute, 1972.

Bolton, B. (Ed.). *Handbook on measurement and evaluation in rehabilitation.* Baltimore, Md.: University Park Press, 1976.

Botterbusch, K. F. *Tests and measurements for vocational evaluators.* Menomonie, Wis.: Materials Development Center, University of Wisconsin–Stout, 1973.

Botterbusch, K. F. *A comparison of seven vocational evaluation systems.* Menomonie, Wis.: Materials Development Center, University of Wisconsin–Stout, 1976.

Botterbusch, K. F. *The use of psychological tests with individuals who are severely disabled.* Menomonie, Wis.: Materials Development Center, University of Wisconsin–Stout, 1976.

Buros, O. K. (Ed.). *Seventh mental measurements yearbook.* Highland Park, N.J.: The Gryphon Press, 1972.

Buros, O. K. (Ed.). *Tests in print II.* Highland Park, N.J.: The Gryphon Press, 1974.

Buros, O. K. (Ed.). *Personality tests and reviews II.* Highland Park, N.J.: The Gryphon Press, 1975.

Buros, O. K. (Ed.). *Intelligence tests and reviews.* Highland Park, N.J.: The Gryphon Press, 1975.

Buros, O. K. (Ed.). *Vocational tests and reviews.* Highland Park, N.J.: The Gryphon Press, 1975.

Buros, O. K. (Ed.). *Reading tests and reviews II.* Highland Park, N.J.: The Gryphon Press, 1975.

Comrey, A. L., Backer, T. E., & Glaser, E. M. *A sourcebook for mental health measures.* Los Angeles: Human Interaction Research Institute, 1973.
Department of Labor. *Dictionary of occupational titles.* Vol. I. Definition of titles (3rd ed.). Washington, D.C.: Superintendent of Documents, Government Printing Office, 1965.
Department of Labor. *Dictionary of occupational titles.* Vol. II. Occupational titles (3rd ed.). Washington, D.C.: Superintendent of Documents, Government Printing Office, 1965.
Department of Labor. *Supplement Two to the Dictionary of occupational titles: selected characteristics of occupations by worker traits and physical strength* (3rd ed.). Washington, D.C.: Superintendent of Documents, Government Printing Office, 1968.
Department of Labor. *Occupational outlook handbook, 1974 edition.* Washington, D.C.: Superintendent of Documents, Government Printing Office, 1973.
Department of Labor. *Dictionary of occupational titles* (4th ed.). Washington, D.C.: Superintendent of Documents, Government Printing Office, 1977.
Esser, T. J. *Effective report writing in vocational evaluation and work adjustment programs.* Menomonie, Wis.: Materials Development Center, University of Wisconsin–Stout, 1974.
Esser, T. J. (Ed.). *Client rating instruments for use in vocational rehabilitation agencies.* Menomonie, Wis.: Materials Development Center, University of Wisconsin–Stout, 1975.
Fry, R. R. (Ed.). *Work evaluation and adjustment: an annotated bibliography,* 1947-1973. Menomonie, Wis.: Materials Development Center, University of Wisconsin–Stout, 1974.
Fry, R. R. (Ed.). *Work evaluation and adjustment: an annotated bibliography, 1974 supplement.* Menonomie, Wis.: Materials Development Center, University of Wisconsin–Stout, 1975.
Fry, R. R. (Ed.). *Work evaluation and adjustment: an annotated bibliography, 1975 supplement.* Menomonie, Wis.: Materials Development Center, University of Wisconsin–Stout, 1976.
Materials Development Center. *Suggested publications for developing an agency library on work evaluation and work adjustment* (5th ed.). Menomonie, Wis.: Materials Development Center, University of Wisconsin–Stout, 1977.
Materials Development Center. *Work sample manual format.* Menomonie, Wis.: Materials Development Center, University of Wisconsin–Stout, 1977.
Research Utilization Laboratory. *Goal attainment scaling in rehabilitation* (RUL No. 5). Chicago: Jewish Vocational Service, 1976.
Sankovsky, R. *Evaluating rehabilitation potential of the severely handicapped: vocationally related components.* Institute, W. Va.: West Virginia Research and Training Center, 1975.
Sankovsky, R., Arthur, G., & Mann, J. (Eds.). *Vocational evaluation and work adjustment: a book of readings.* Auburn, Ala.: Alabama Rehabilitation Media Service, Auburn University, 1969.
Timmerman, W. J., & Doctor, A. C. *Special applications of work evaluation techniques for prediction of employability of the trainable mentally retarded.* Menomonie, Wis.: Materials Development Center, University of Wisconsin–Stout, 1974.
Vocational Evaluation and Work Adjustment Association. Vocational evaluation project final report. *Vocational Evaluation and Work Adjustment Bulletin,* 1975, 8(Special eds. 1, 2, 3).
Walls, R. T., Werner, T. J., & Bacon, A. *Behavior checklists.* Institute, W. Va.: Research and Training Center, 1976.

MEDIA RESOURCES

Visual
1. "Assessment" (16 mm film, 26 minutes). Available from Materials Development Center, University of Wisconsin–Stout, Menomonie, Wis. 54751.
   Describes and explains the advantages and problems in psychological testing, work samples, situational assessment, job analysis, and job tryouts.
2. "The TOWER Evaluators" (16 mm film, 21 minutes). Available from Materials Development Center, University of Wisconsin–Stout, Menomonie, Wis. 54751.
   Describes the TOWER system and portrays three evaluators learning to use the system at the ICD Rehabilitation and Research Center in New York City.
3. "Orientation to Work Evaluation Batteries Series" (slides with audiotape cassettes).
   a. Thomasat (37 slides)

b. Philadelphia JEVS Work Sample Battery (114 slides)
c. Singer Vocational Evaluation System (116 slides)
d. TOWER System (57 slides)
e. Wide Range Employment Sample Test (45 slides)
f. Orientation to Dexterity Tests (86 slides)
g. McCarron-Dial Work Evaluation System (72 slides)
h. Vocational Information and Evaluation Work Samples (VIEWS) (65 slides)
Available from Materials Development Center, University of Wisconsin–Stout, Menomonie, Wis. 54751.
   Each presentation describes the purposes, organization, and hardware of the evaluation tool. The JEVS, Singer and TOWER presentations contain a second audiotape cassette that addresses specific questions about the approach. Answers are given by five vocational evaluators familiar with the approaches.

4. "Evaluating the Retarded Client" (16 mm film). Available from Audiovisual Center, Film Rental Services, University of Kansas, 746 Massachusetts, Lawrence, Kan. 66044.
   Emphasizes a comprehensive approach to work evaluation involving various professionals including physicians, psychologists, and vocational evaluators by the rehabilitation counselor. The film also stresses the importance of continuous evaluation.

5. "Client Testing Orientation" (slides with audiotape cassettes). Produced by West Virginia Research and Training Center, Institute, W. Va. 25112.
   Intended for showing to clients. Provides an overview of psychological tests and their purpose.

6. "Administration of Projective Tests" (16 mm film, 19 minutes). Available from Pennsylvania State University, Audio-Visual Services, University Park, Pa. 16802.
   Demonstrates the administration of a variety of projective tests, excluding the Rorschach.

7. "Interpreting Test Scores Realistically" (16 mm film, 18 minutes). Available from Educational Testing Service, Cooperative Test Division, 20 Nassau St., Princeton, N.J. 08540.
   Discusses scores as estimates of ability, the value of percentile bands and norm tables.

8. "Standardized Test: Educational Tool" (16 mm film, 22 minutes). Available from University of Michigan, Audio-Visual Education Center, 416 Fourth St., Ann Arbor, Mich. 48103.
   A basic film that describes the use of testing.

9. "Work Assessment" (16 mm, 30 minutes). Available from International Society for Rehabilitation of the Disabled, Film Library, 219 East 44th St., New York, N.Y. 10017.
   Filmed in Denmark, the film describes the testing and practical work assessment of the physically disabled.

10. "Introducing You to Vocational Evaluation" (slides or filmstrip with audiotape cassette). Available from Materials Development Center, University of Wisconsin–Stout, Menomonie, Wis. 54751.
   A general introduction for clients to vocational evaluation services. Four questions are addressed: (a) What is vocational evaluation? (b) Why be evaluated? (c) What happens during evaluation? (d) What will the client get from evaluation?

Audio
1. "Job Evaluation Through the TOWER Work Sample Approach" (audiotape cassette, 41 minutes). Available from Materials Development Center, University of Wisconsin–Stout, Menomonie, Wis. 54751.
   Bernard Rosenberg of the ICD Rehabilitation and Research Center in New York City, and one of the developers of TOWER, discusses TOWER and its use at the Center.

2. "A Medical View of Vocational Evaluation" (audiotape cassette, 37 minutes). Available from Materials Development Center, University of Wisconsin–Stout, Menomonie, Wis. 54751.
   Edward Gordon presents some important medical considerations in the vocational evaluation process.

3. "Vocational Evaluation in an American Urban City" (audiotape cassette, 32 minutes). Available from Materials Development Center, University of Wisconsin–Stout, Menomonie, Wis. 54751.
   Vernon Vinson discusses vocational evaluation in urban areas.

4. "Principles of Vocational Assessment" (audiotape cassette, 36 minutes). Available from Materials

Development Center, University of Wisconsin–Stout, Menomonie, Wis. 54751.

William Gellman presents some principles and considerations for vocational assessment.

5. "Divergent Views in Work Sample Development" (audiotape cassette, 50 minutes). Available from Materials Development Center, University of Wisconsin–Stout, Menomonie, Wis. 54751.

A discussion panel involving Edward Hester, Chicago Goodwill Industries; Bernard Rosenberg, ICD Rehabilitation and Research Center; Harold Kuhlman, Philadelphia Jewish Employment and Vocational Service; Arnold Sax and Ernest Tillman, University of Wisconsin–Stout.

6. "Intelligence Tests" (audiotape cassette and transcript, 44 minutes). Available from Materials Development Center, University of Wisconsin–Stout, Menomonie, Wis. 54751.

Describes intelligence tests including the WAIS and the Otis Quick Scoring Mental Ability Tests.

7. "Interest Tests" (audiotape cassette and transcript, 59 minutes). Available from Materials Development Center, University of Wisconsin–Stout, Menomonie, Wis. 54751.

Describes interest tests including the Kuder Occupational Interest Survey.

8. "Scholastic and Achievement Tests" (audiotape cassette and transcript, 29 minutes). Available from Materials Development Center, University of Wisconsin–Stout, Menomonie, Wis. 54751.

Describes achievement tests suitable for use by rehabilitation counselors.

9. "Multiple Aptitude Tests" (two audiotape cassettes and transcripts. Part I—53 minutes, Part II—24 minutes). Available from Materials Development Center, University of Wisconsin–Stout, Menomonie, Wis. 54751.

Describes aptitude testing.

10. "Personality Tests" (audiotape cassette and transcript, 51 minutes). Available from Materials Development Center, University of Wisconsin–Stout, Menomonie, Wis. 54751.

Describes personality testing including a description of the MMPI.

11. "Assessing Client Work Information" (audiotape cassette and transcript, 17 minutes). Available from Materials Development Center, University of Wisconsin–Stout, Menomonie, Wis. 54751.

Describes the assessment of work information.

12. "Understanding Norms" (audiotape cassette and transcript, 53 minutes). Available from Materials Development Center, University of Wisconsin–Stout, Menomonie, Wis. 54751.

Describes normative information in evaluation for use by rehabilitation counselors.

13. "Collecting Information from the Client" (audiotape cassette, 32 minutes). Available from Materials Development Center, University of Wisconsin–Stout, Menomonie, Wis. 54751.

Describes sources for obtaining client information.

14. "Test Interpretation" (audiotape cassette, 39 minutes). Available from Materials Development Center, University of Wisconsin–Stout, Menomonie, Wis. 54751.

Provides fundamental guidance for interpreting tests.

15. "How to Select, Administer and Interpret Psychological Tests" by Joseph B. Moriarity (programmed text and nine audiotape cassettes). Produced by West Virginia Research and Training Center, Institute, W. Va. 25112.

Describes nine psychological tests and their effective use. There is an audiotape cassette for administration and scoring of each of the tests described in the programmed text.

8
Counseling approaches

OVERVIEW AND OBJECTIVES

Many rehabilitation professionals consider counseling to be the heart of the rehabilitation process. Although vocational rehabilitation is very much a goal-oriented program (emphasizing employment of the disabled), its philosophy incorporates development of the total person. The intent, ideally, is to provide a happy, responsible, and self-actualized person. Counseling therefore plays an important role in the development of the total person. However, there is no special counseling theory or technique for working with the disabled. The differences between the disabled and the nondisabled relate to their specific situations rather than to their basic personality structures. Thus the particular counseling theory or technique subscribed to by rehabilitation workers is related more to the background and style of the rehabilitation counselor and individual clients than to "a psychology of the disabled."

The objectives of this chapter are to provide the reader with a brief orientation to the helping relationship between counselor and client as well as give an overview of the basic concepts and applications for some counseling approaches useful in rehabilitation and an overview of group counseling.

THE HELPING RELATIONSHIP

Counseling is an extension of the casework relationship described in Chapter 6. As in casework, the core of the helping process is the relationship expressed through interaction between the helper and the person being helped. It is characterized by an intimate interaction in which each person is sensitive to the other. The relationship exists because one of the individuals needs information, instruction, understanding, or advice and this can be achieved through cooperative effort involving communication and interaction. The objective of an authentic helping relationship is change in the person being helped (Shertzer & Stone, 1974).

CONCEPTS AND APPLICATIONS OF COUNSELING APPROACHES

Patterson's (1969) survey of major approaches to counseling suggests a considerable diversity in philosophy, concepts, goals, and methods. He points out

FIG. 8-1

The helping relationship is characterized by personal intimate interaction and sensitivity. (From: Chinn, P. C., Winn, J., & Walters, R. H. *Two-way talking with parents of special children.* St. Louis: The C. V. Mosby Co., 1978.)

that the common element in all approaches to counseling is the *relationship between the client and the counselor*. Philosophically, counseling approaches range from those which view man as reactive to inner needs influenced by past experiences to those which look upon man as a future-oriented and personal being. Similarly counseling processes range from highly rational approaches to strongly affective approaches. The goals of counseling vary from solving problems to developing self-acceptance and self-concepts. Counseling techniques may range from introspection to manipulation of the environment (Patterson, 1969).

To be described in the following pages are some major counseling approaches, each addressed in terms of its basic concepts and its application techniques.

Psychoanalysis

Basic concepts. Psychoanalysis had its beginning with Sigmund Freud. Basic to the psychoanalytical approach is that the structure of the personality involves three systems: the id, the ego, and the superego. The id refers to the person's biological system, which seeks pleasure and avoids pain. The ego is the person's psychological system, which tends to relate to reality with logical thinking. The superego is the person's social system. It represents the ideals and values of society and strives for perfection.

A key intent in the psychoanalytical approach is to make the unconscious conscious. Unconscious motives influence behavior. By making such unconscious motives conscious, the client is in a better position to understand his own behavior and achieve healthy functioning.

Another basic concept in psychoanalysis is the role of anxiety. The ego is able to control anxiety with rational thinking. However, should the anxiety be so great as to prevent a rational approach, an individual may distort, falsify, or deny reality with ego defense mechanisms.

Examples of ego defense mechanisms are (1) *denial,* i.e., refusing to accept reality, (2) *projection,* or ascribing to others traits in oneself that seem unacceptable, (3) *fixation,* or fixing on an earlier stage in development to avoid the anxiety created by the next stage, (4) *regression* (or returning to an earlier stage in development), (5) *rationalization,* i.e., developing a probable reason for disappointment, (6) *sublimation,* using acceptable outlets for less acceptable impulses, (7) *displacement,* or reflecting feelings toward a substitute when unable to reflect such feelings to the original person or object, (8) *repression,* forgetting things which hurt, and (9) *reaction formation,* or behaving in a way that is opposite the way one would like to act or would impulsively act (Corey, 1977).

Application. Psychoanalysis emphasizes the unconscious and the developmental process of the individual. The therapy process entails making the client's unconscious conscious by focusing on childhood experiences. Such earlier experiences are analyzed and discussed in terms of their impact on the individual's personality. The therapeutic process is aided by "transference," another fundamental concept in psychoanalytical therapy. Transference refers to the client's attributing significant feelings or experiences from the past to the therapist. As a result the therapist becomes a substitute for significant others in the client's life, particularly his early life.

Corey (1977) describes five basic techniques of psychoanalytic therapy: free association, dream analysis, analysis of resistance, analysis of transference, and interpretation. *Free association* involves sharing with the therapist whatever comes to mind. It is a way to recall past experiences. Sharing, or ventilating emotions, in free association is known as catharsis. *Dream analysis* is intended to make unconscious motivations conscious. "Resistance" is a defense against anxiety; and the *analysis of resistance* is concerned with helping the client learn the reasons for resistance so he can deal with them. *Analysis of transference* allows the client to relive past experiences within the therapeutic relationship and is intended to help him through emotional conflicts. *Interpretation* involves explaining the meaning of behavior revealed by free association, dreams, resistance or transference.

Sigmund Freud was followed by what are referred to as neo-Freudians, i.e., psychoanalysts who related to Freud's concepts but felt that Freud's approach was limited and deterministic. Neo-Freudians included Carl Jung, Alfred Adler, Otto Rank, Karen Horney, Erich Fromm, Harry Stack Sullivan, and Erik Erikson. Though they all built upon the concepts established by Freud, the neo-Freudians emphasized interpersonal dimensions and deemphasized the instinctual motivation and sexual components.

Client-centered counseling

The client-centered counseling approach was developed by Carl Rogers as a reaction to the deterministic theory of psychoanalysis. It emphasizes the capability of the client for determining his own direction. The counselor serves as a facilitator.

Basic concepts. The client-centered approach views man as rational, social, and positive. It is dependent on the theory that man, under favorable conditions, will tend toward self-actualization. The primary responsibility for the therapeutic process is with the client. However, according to Rogers, positive personality change cannot occur except in a relationship. To be an effective therapist therefore, the counselor must have attitudes such as genuineness, positive regard, and empathic understanding. *Genuineness*, or congruence, means being onself, having the ability to know one's own inner experiencing and allowing one's inner experiencing to be apparent in the counseling relationship. *Positive regard* refers to acceptance of the client's individuality. *Empathic understanding* is the counselor's attempt to understand the internal frame of reference of the client by attempting to put oneself in the client's situation while at the same time remaining oneself in order to remain a helper. The client-centered approach hypothesizes that the client will experience growth as a result of the genuineness, positive regard, and empathy of the counselor.

Application. In the application of the client-centered approach, the counselor's attitudes are emphasized. If the counselor can communicate that he or she is a genuine (congruent) person, unconditionally accepts and cares about the client, and has empathic understanding of how the client feels, then it will become possible for the client to grow as a result of this personal relationship.

Specific techniques or knowledge are not emphasized in the client-centered approach. The counselor has the freedom to use whatever technique or style is comfortable for him. It is the counselor's attitude which is of the upmost importance (Corsini, 1973; Patterson, 1973; Corey, 1977).

Behavioral therapy approaches

Learning theory is the basis for behavioral approaches. The behavioral therapies have evolved primarily in two directions. One is based on respondent conditioning—in other words, eliminating the inappropriate behavior. It is characteristically applicable to specific problems, such as unrealistic fearful situations. The other direction is based on operant conditioning. The goal in operant conditioning is to shape behavior by rewarding desired behavior. This technique is considered appropriate for a range of problems from mild conduct disorders to severe psychotic behavior.

Common techniques in behavioral therapy include systematic desensitization, assertive training, flooding, and aversion therapy. Systematic desensitization will be described in the discussion of Wolpe's approach. Assertive training emphasizes that individuals have the right to be themselves and to freely express themselves so long as they hurt no one in the process. Assertive training uses role training as a principal method for developing assertiveness. Flooding is a technique which involves repeatedly presenting the client with anxiety-producing situations or stimuli. The counselor attempts to maintain the anxiety level of the client. Flooding occurs when the client is no longer anxious. Aversion techniques utilize punishment and the removal of positive reinforcement until the unwanted behavior subsides.

Respondent conditioning approaches. One respondent conditioning approach is that of Joseph Wolpe. For Wolpe the emphasis in behavior therapy is on behavioral change. This is accomplished through the application of techniques derived from learning theory, and success is measured by symptom improvement. Behavior therapy is characterized by specification of treatment goals, development of a treatment plan, and an assessment of the outcomes. Wolpe's approach consists of changing attitudes or feelings by changing behavior.

Behavioral therapists have many techniques. The primary technique for Wolpe is systematic desensitization, i.e., systematically pairing relaxation with anxiety. It is often referred to as reciprocal inhibition. In reciprocal inhibition the client is taught to relax and imagine anxiety-provoking experiences. He is asked to arrange these anxiety-provoking experiences in a hierarchy from least to most threatening. By asking the client to relax and visualize a series of situations which produce anxiety and beginning with the least threatening, the counselor attempts to weaken the relationship between the situation and the anxiety. The process is continued until the client can endure even the strongest anxiety-arousing stimuli.

Operant conditioning approaches. Operant conditioning involves rewarding desired behavior or withholding reward to extinguish undesirable behavior. B. F. Skinner is the psychologist primarily associated with operant conditioning, which currently is more popularly known as behavior modification and is more fully described in Chapter 5. Basically it is the use of positive reinforcement, extinction, punishment, modeling, and token economies to shape behavior.

The counseling approach of John Dollard and Neil Miller is based on reinforcement learning theory integrated with psychoanalysis. However, the approach of Dollard and Miller emphasizes a higher-order mental activity which makes it a more rational approach than traditional psychoanalysis. Basic concepts in reinforcement learning theory are drive, stimulus, response, and reinforcement. The theory is intended primarily for extinction of neurotic behavior. Emphasis is placed on providing the conditions for new learning by engaging in free association. The client's repressions are uncovered, and transference helps to reveal the nature of conflicting drives. These drives, experiences, and feelings are then labeled by the client and the counselor. By doing so, client and counselor identify differences between experiences. Generalizations can then be made to situations that are appropriately similar. The emphasis on discrimination of experiences and situations differentiates Dollard and Miller's "teaching" approach from the automatic conditioning of Wolpe (Patterson, 1973; Corey, 1977).

Biofeedback therapy. Mechanical measurement devices can be an aid in making apparent to individuals the biological functions of heart rate, digestion, and different kinds of brain waves. By having this information, individuals who are motivated can control the functions; that is, they can alter their heart rate or reduce mental tension voluntarily. The use of biofeedback is most effective with problems such as anxiety, migraine headaches, and high blood pressure. It can help individuals relax more by allowing them to conduct internal experiments to control these physiological events. By monitoring his state of tension, the subject can learn to relax and reduce the stress and its effect on his behavior (Ewing, 1977).

Gestalt therapy

Basic concepts. Gestalt therapy was developed by Frederick Perls. In it emphasis is placed on the here and now. Attention is on immediate behavior. A basic assumption is that people are capable of dealing with their life problems. The goal is for the client to assume responsibility for his own thoughts, feelings, and behavior. As a result, clients carry out much of their own therapy by making their own interpretations and finding their own meanings. The past is important only to significant themes in the individual's present functioning.

Also fundamental to gestalt therapy (*Gestalt,* German, means "shape" or "form") are concepts relating to the person (or organism) and the environment. The environment is everything external to the person. Though the person and the environment are unique, they are inseparable because every person is in contact and interaction with the environment. Transactions between the person and the environment are dependent, in large part, on the individual's level of awareness. Such transactions are often incomplete because of blocks to awareness, resulting in unfulfilled needs and unfinished business. Unfulfilled needs and unfinished business, even concern about the future, create anxiety.

Experiential awareness, either intellectual or psychophysical, that occurs from transactions is the key to growth. In the pursuit of awareness, the now and how are important. *Now* refers to this moment, which is the only moment with potential for experience. *How* tends to structure the experience and gives perspective. Thus, in the counseling situation, the counselor will ask what and how questions to engage the client in now awareness. "Why" questions are rarely asked since they result in rationalizations and self-deception about the past.

Application. Gestalt therapy employs many techniques for helping the client gain awareness of conflicts, inconsistencies, and unfinished business.

Games can help provide structure to the therapeutic process:

1. *Dialogue*. The client plays the role of both tendencies in a split personality and carries on a dialogue between them. For example, one dialogue is between the "top dog" and the "underdog." The top dog represents superego, the underdog passive resistance. The purpose is for the client to obtain an awareness of personal conflict.

2. *Making the rounds*. In this group exercise the client makes the rounds among other members of the group and says or does something with each person. The exercise can be structured by giving the stem of a sentence for the client to finish with each person. An example is, "I don't like you because . . ." The purpose of "making the rounds" is to offer the client an opportunity to take risks and disclose feelings.

3. *I take responsibility*. In this game the client is asked to make a statement about himself and add the phrase "and I take responsibility for it."

4. *I have a secret*. The client thinks of a very personal secret which involves guilt or shame and is asked to imagine how he feels others would react to the secret or how he would react to them if they were to share the secret. The game permits exploration of guilt and shame feelings.

5. *Playing the projection*. The client is asked to play the role of another person about whom he has particular feelings. In so doing, he may discover that his feelings toward others are, in fact, projections of characteristics he possesses.

6. *Reversals*. In this game the client is asked to play a role opposite his own behavior, e.g., to be aggressive instead of passive. It is thus hoped that the client will expose attributes he has tried to deny. By becoming aware of a denied side of himself, he may be able to integrate the denied side into his personality.

7. *Rehearsal*. The rehearsal game is usually done in groups and involves sharing a role the clients think they are expected to play in society. Rehearsals with one another help the clients become aware of how they try to meet expectations.

8. *Exaggeration*. The client is asked to exaggerate a statement or a body movement which may communicate significant meaning. Examples are repeating a statement with increased loudness and emphasis or exaggerating nervous hand movements when one is anxious. The purpose of the exercise is to become more aware of seemingly casual statements or movements by exaggerating them.

Dreams are also appropriate subject matter in gestalt therapy and represent unfinished business. The client is asked to play the part of various persons or objects in a dream. By acting out the dream, he may become more aware of feelings, resistances, and personality voids. Gestalt therapy can be practiced in either individual counselor-client situations or groups. Within the group situation, the counselor may focus on a single client at a time or clients may be asked to be spontaneous and interact with one another. In all techniques of gestalt therapy, emphasis is on the here and now awareness. The attempt is to complete one's unfinished business so as to be able to integrate such business into the personality and promote more effective functioning in the present (Kempler, 1973; Patterson, 1973; Corey, 1977).

Transactional analysis

Transactional analysis (TA), developed by Eric Berne, is an interactional approach best applied within a group setting. It is based on "transactions" that enable clients to increase awareness of themselves so they can make decisions about their behavior and the course of their lives.

Basic concepts. Berne's model of personality consists of three ego states termed parent, child, and adult. These three states are not roles an individual plays; rather they are learned from life experiences. Such experiences are recorded in the brain and played back throughout life. The parent ego state is represented by parental behavior and consists of judgmental and authoritarian attitudes containing "shoulds" and "oughts." The child ego state is manifested by immature, impulsive, and spontaneous behavior. The adult ego state is the rational, objective, and responsible part of our personality. The adult ego state processes information and makes decisions based on fact rather than on the "shoulds" of the parent ego state and the wants of the child ego state.

Structural analysis in TA is a study of one's personality and ego states. Transactions between individuals are analyzed to determine the extent to which each ego state is operating within an individual. There are parent, child, and adult in each of us.

Transactional analysis is a study of the types of transactions that occur between individuals. There are three types of transactions: complementary, crossed, and ulterior. *Complementary* transactions occur when the messages between persons are from the same ego state—for example, child to child, parent to parent, adult to adult. *Crossed* transactions occur when the messages from individuals are from different ego states—for example, parent-child, adult-parent. *Ulterior* transactions involve more than two ego states and are usually reflected in hidden messages. When individual transactions are extended to a series of social interactions, they are classifiable. According to Berne (1961, 1964) interactions can be classified into the following categories: withdrawal, ritual, pastime, games, activities, and intimacies.

The *life script* of a person is represented by a decision he makes about how to spend his life and how to respond to others. TA suggests there are four basic positions of life.

I'm not OK—you're OK
I'm not OK—you're not OK
I'm OK—you're not OK
I'm OK—you're OK

The first three positions are unconscious and based on feelings made early in life. The fourth position, I'm OK—you're OK, is a conscious decision by the person based on thought and/or action.

Stroking is a general term to imply recognition of another person. It may take many forms—physical, emotional, or verbal. Strokes can be either positive (which gives one an "OK" feeling) or negative (which communicates a "you're not OK" message).

A *racket* in transactional analysis is a collection of feelings a person saves in order to justify a life script. Thus one might develop an anger racket, a guilt racket, or a depression racket. *Game* playing is engaged in with others to advance such feelings.

Application. In transactional analysis the counselor assumes an equal status with the client. A hypothesis of TA is that the client has a right to know and understand whatever the counselor knows and understands; thus the counselor explains concepts such as structural analysis, transactional analysis, script analysis, and game analysis. In turn, the client must be willing to understand and accept a treatment contract. Such contracts are very specific. They identify client goals, what the client will do, and when the contract is fulfilled. The contract may be time limited, or there may be a series of contracts with each progressing a step at a time. TA counselors may draw upon techniques from other approaches and thus have a wide repertoire for fulfilling contracts. TA is also particularly suited for group situations. Conducting TA in groups affords opportunities for a greater number and variety of interactions between people and a greater number of models to observe.

In therapy, structural problems are analyzed. There are basically two types of problems: one is called *contamination,* and the other *exclusion.* Contamination refers to mixing one ego state with another. As an example, the functioning of the adult ego state may be contaminated by prejudice from the parent ego state or the fantasies of the child ego state. The counseling process involves a decontamination process in which the adult ego state is strengthened through awareness. The second type of problem, exclusion, occurs when one ego state blocks out another. As a result the client may relate primarily as the parent, the child, or the adult to the exclusion of one or both of the others.

Transactional analysis necessitates interaction between persons. Though counselors may use or borrow any technique for accomplishing contract objectives, some techniques are generally associated with TA. One of these, the *empty chair* technique, is a process whereby the client is made aware of ego states. He is asked to imagine that an ego state with which he has difficulty is "seated in a chair" placed in front of him. He is then asked to carry on a dialogue with the ego state in the empty chair. The purpose is to create awareness of ego states. *Role playing* is another technique for enhancing awareness of ego states—particularly well suited for group therapy sessions. A similar approach is *family modeling*. In this technique the client is asked to imagine a scene including as many significant persons in his past as possible, plus himself. He defines the situation and attempts to recreate it so his level of awareness of ego states and their meaning will be increased. *Analysis* of games, rackets, and scripts is also an important technique. Again the emphasis is on awareness and understanding of a person's games, rackets, and life script in order to heighten the client's awareness of transactions and, through understanding, enable him to make new decisions regarding current behavior and a direction in life.

Rational-emotive therapy

Albert Ellis (1973), the author of rational-emotive therapy (RET), describes it as a comprehensive approach to changing personality. RET involves the use of a variety of cognitive, emotive, and behavior therapy methods.

Basic concepts. A basic hypothesis of RET is that activating events (A) do not cause emotional consequences (C); rather C are caused by a belief system (B). The counseling process attempts to dispute (D) irrational beliefs with rational straightforward thinking until C disappear (Ellis, 1973).

RET is highly cognitive and directive. It assumes that individuals are responsible for creating their own emotional reactions. Through a teaching-learning process, irrational thinking can be challenged with rationality and the person can eliminate disturbances by learning to think rationally.

Application. Rational-emotive therapy is eclectic in its use of techniques and procedures. It attempts to teach a person that his thinking is irrational (rational therapy). It addresses the client's values in an effort to help him distinguish between truth and falsehood (emotive therapy), and it gives homework assignments which require practicing rational thinking (behavior therapy).

The principal technique used in the RET counseling session is rapid-fire directive persuasiveness. The counselor attempts to identify a few basic irrational ideas related to a client's disturbed behavior and to expose them as irrational and destroy them with logic. Homework assignments are very important for follow-through and are intended to give the client practice in attacking irrational fears. RET is usually relatively brief. It can be applied in a variety of ways, including individually, in groups, in marathon encounter groups, and in marriage and family therapy. It is applicable to people with emotional difficulty but who are in contact with reality and who also must, obviously, have the ability for logical thinking (Ellis, 1973; Patterson, 1973; Corey, 1977).

Reality therapy

Basic concepts. Reality therapy, developed by William Glasser in the 1950's, focuses on present behavior and emphasizes the client's responsibility for behavior. It is based on the premise that everyone has a need for identity. In order to develop a success identity, individuals must demonstrate responsible behavior. The client has the ability to control his own behavior and can become whatever he decides to become.

Glasser and Zunin (1973) identify eight principles of reality therapy:

1. The relationship between the counselor and client is a personal one. The counselor cares about the client.

2. Counseling focuses on present behavior rather than feelings or emotions. Behavior is what can be changed.

3. The counseling relationship focuses on the present, i.e., what the individual is doing now. The past is fixed and cannot be changed.

4. Success in reality therapy is dependent on the person's making a value judgment about his behavior and how it is contributing to his own failures.

5. The counselor assists the client in developing specific plans to change failure behavior into success behavior.

6. After choosing a better way, the client must commit himself to the choice; such commitment develops maturity.

7. There are no excuses for not following through on plans and actions.

8. Punishment is not a part of the counseling process since it reinforces a failure identity; rather the counselor encourages the client to develop self-discipline and assists the client in making a new plan rather than focusing on reasons for failure.

Application. Reality therapy is a verbal therapy—that is, it requires verbal interaction between the counselor and the client. It is not effective with persons who are unable to communicate such as autistic and severely mentally retarded children. Diagnosis is not a part of the therapy process. Diagnostic labels are viewed as counterproductive to promoting responsible and successful behavior since diagnostic judgments tend to perpetuate behavioral expectations.

Reality therapy attempts to assist the person in identifying life goals. The client sets his own goals in the therapeutic process. The counselor assists the client in reaching these goals. Contractual arrangements between the counselor and client might be made in order to set limits and to promote follow-through between counseling sessions. Such an approach helps to reinforce planning, which is essential in reality therapy. However, if a plan does not succeed, there are no excuses. Instead, a new plan is developed. Reality therapy is reported to be suitable for individuals and groups and in marital counseling. The group can be an aid in trying to implement individual client plans. More recently, reality therapy has been extended to school situations. In 1969 Glasser wrote a book entitled *Schools Without Failure* in which he proposed to eliminate failures in schools by emphasizing thinking, discipline, success identities, responsible behavior, and the involvement of parents (Glasser & Zunin, 1973; Corey, 1977).

Psychological counseling

The psychological counseling described in this chapter is that advocated by Edward S. Bordin. His book, entitled *Psychological Counseling,* was first published in 1955. A second edition appeared in 1968.

Basic concepts. Bordin's psychological counseling emphasizes rational factors in the counseling relationship. It is intended for relatively mature persons needing help with a limited problem, for example, a vocational choice. Though it is viewed primarily as a problem-solving approach, it is concerned with feelings and motivations as they are related to the specific problem situation. A heavy emphasis is placed on the use of psychological tests. In fact, tests are an integral part of the counseling process and are used as an educational-vocational counseling tool for solving client problems and for testing the reality of client interests and self-perceptions.

Applications. In addition to an emphasis on the use of psychological testing, interpretations of tests and interactions are important techniques in the application of psychological counseling. The interpretation of test results must be accurate and must afford the client a whole range of alternatives based on the outcomes. Interpretations of interactions is not encouraged during the early stages of the counselor-client relationship since the client may at this stage be quite defensive. Interpretation becomes an appropriate technique when the client is able to express feelings. Interpretation may be used for clarification of a client's thoughts or feelings, for comparison between similarities and differences in the client's behavior, and for highlighting client motivation and defenses. Because of the emphasis on cognitive factors and the use of tests for problem solving, psychological counseling is especially suited for clients who are essentially mature and minimally anxious and who have vocational problems (Patterson, 1973).

Other counseling approaches

Edmund G. Williamson. Williamson's approach is a rational problem-solving approach which attempts to be scientific by gathering objective information about the client, making a diagnosis, predicting an outcome, and planning a program of action based on the objective data. The approach is directive; that is, problem solving is with direct guidance or teaching by the counselor. The counselor presents the client with information and alternatives. Decisions are made by the client. Since the counseling process is highly dependent on the diagnosis for the client, there is considerable emphasis on making an accurate diagnosis. Because techniques utilized in the counselinig process are determined by the needs of the individual client, Williamson provides little guidance in the choice and use of counseling techniques. He views the counselor as an instrument for helping clients achieve their own goals. For him the purpose is to increase rational behavior and achieve a higher level of cognitive behavior.

The primary techniques for Williamson are in creating a learning situation for the client by asking questions, providing the client with information about himself, giving advice, and proposing alternative courses of action (McGowan & Porter, 1967; Patterson, 1973).

Robert R. Carkhuff. Carkhuff's approach to counseling represents a technology for helping, rather than a theory based on personality development. However, he draws heavily from the concepts of Carl Rogers. The basic premise of Carkhuff's approach is that interaction between individuals can have either facilitating or retarding effects. The counselor's effectiveness is independent of his or her theoretical orientation. Further, the counselor's effectiveness can be explained by a core of dimensions. The most important of these dimensions are emphatic understanding, positive regard, genuineness, and concreteness. *Emphatic understanding*, as mentioned earlier in the chapter, is an attempt by the counselor to permit himself or herself to merge in the experience of the client and communicate this understanding to the client. *Positive regard* is the respect the counselor shows toward the client. It is reflected by a deep respect for the client's worth as a person and his rights as an individual. It is perhaps best demonstrated in the counselor's effort to understand the client. *Genuineness* is reflected by the honesty the counselor has with himself and with the client in the counseling process. *Concreteness* refers to the counselor responses that are not too far removed emotionally from the client's own feelings, that are accurate, and that attend specifically to the problem areas of the client.

Carkhuff quantified his approach by developing five levels of functioning by the counselor. Level 3 represents a minimal level of facilitative functioning. Levels 1 and 2 represent retarding levels of functioning. A level-4 counselor can make things happen whereas a level-5 counselor is capable of helping others self-actualize. Basic to Carkhuff's approach is the necessity for the counselor to be functioning at a higher level than the client in terms of empathic understanding, positive regard, genuineness, and concreteness in order to be an effective helper (Carkhuff & Berenson, 1967).

For Carkhuff, helping is a cyclic process involving three phases: exploration, understanding, and constructive action. The overall goal of helping is new behavior. For new behavior to occur the client must first explore where he is in relationship to himself and the environment. The counselor can facilitate self-exploration (the first phase) by being responsive to the psychological needs of the client. The second phase in the helping process is self-understanding—understanding where the client is in relation to where he wants to be and recognizing what it is that the client is unable or unwilling to do that prevents him from reaching the desired goal. Constructive action (the third phase) is an attempt by the client to get to where he wants to be or where the counselor operationalizes his goal to be; in other words, the counselor helps develop the steps that will get the client to where he wants to be.

Certain counselor behaviors are advocated by Carkhuff for helping the client get to where he wants to be: attending, responding, initiating, and communicating. The counselor can communicate an interest in the client by attending physically and psychologically to the client and by listening. Examples of attending physically are posturing oneself to communicate a personal interest (e.g., facing the client fully and inclining forward). Attending psychologically is exemplified by maintaining eye contact, observing cues to the client's internal behaviors, and communicating interest through attentiveness. Helpful listening is achieved by being nonjudgmental about client messages, resisting distractions, waiting to respond, looking for patterns in messages, and reflecting on the content of a message.

Responsive behavior by the counselor involves responding to the feeling and meaning of the client's messages; e.g., "You feel discouraged (feeling) because job opportunities are scarce (meaning)." Feelings are about content, and meaning is achieved by providing a reason for the feeling. Responding behavior by the counselor facilitates a client's self-exploration and understanding.

To help a client move toward constructive action necessitates that the counselor initiate new directions or perceive deeper levels of presented material. Initiating behavior by the counselor is reflected in attempts to help the client put his experiences together into a pattern, personalizing the responses, and, when appropriate, initiating confrontation (such as pointing out discrepancies in the client's behavior). Initiating by the counselor is an attempt to help the client find direction. When the client finds direction, the counselor is in a position to facilitate action through full communication.

Communicating involves both responding and initiating behavior on the part of the counselor. The goal is to help the client achieve directionality. Directionality occurs in three steps: (1) defining the need, (2) identifying the goal, and (3) specifying the intermediary steps to achieving the goal.

For Carkhuff, effective helping by a counselor is dependent on the ability to develop necessary skills for attending, responding, initiating, and communicating (Carkhuff, 1973).

Some similarities and differences among counseling approaches

Patterson (1969) identifies some similarities and differences among the various theories of counseling. He points out that, with the exception of behavior therapy (which claims greater success), the rate of success for the various approaches to counseling is about the same. Approximately two thirds of all clients treated achieve some sort of success. The element most common to the various approaches to counseling is the relationship between the client and the counselor. This relationship is the heart of the counseling process and involves a genuineness between two human beings characterized by interest, concern, and understanding. Regardless of approach, the counselor-client relationship involves some degree of both rational and affective dimensions, utilizes verbal interaction as a major component, and is characterized by an expectation that change will occur in the client.

However, the counseling *process* is viewed differently among counseling approaches. Some examples follow:

1. In psychoanalysis the emphasis is on insight based on past experiences; by contrast, client-centered counseling emphasizes the experience within the counseling relationship.
2. Contracts for client activity are utilized in some approaches, e.g., transactional analysis, behavior therapy, and reality therapy.
3. Evaluation and diagnosis are used in psychoanalysis, behavior therapy, rational-emotive therapy, and transactional analysis; however, these techniques are not a part of client-centered counseling, gestalt therapy, and reality therapy.
4. Affective approaches seek more general outcome goals, whereas the behaviorally oriented approaches emphasize specificity in objectives.

Thus there are similarities and differences among counseling approaches. Regardless of orientation, however, all approaches seem to have some success with the target clientele. Most rehabilitation counselors will choose to be eclectic in their approach, drawing on various theories and techniques in developing a counseling style that is comfortable for them and appropriate for the individual client.

GROUP COUNSELING

Group counseling involves two or more persons who interact with the counselor and each other. As in individual counseling, the intent is for positive change on the part of participants. The group situation has a number of advantages. It affords an individual the opportunity to test various behaviors within a relatively comfortable situation. It provides an opportunity to observe a wider range of behaviors and reactions to those behaviors. It permits a more efficient use of counselor time. Group counseling can be particularly valuable with disabled clients. If a client is involved with a group of people who have similar disabilities, it may be helpful for gaining insights into coping with a disability. Being in a group with other disabled persons may facilitate the sharing of feelings and promote awareness of unrealistic misconceptions, particularly if the group is composed of individuals in various stages of the rehabilitation process. Persons who have worked through their problems can share their experience with more recently disabled individuals (Manley, 1973).

Generally group interaction is better when the group is relatively small. Optimal size is regarded as four to six members; but successfully functioning groups may contain as many as 12 people. Usually the larger the group, the more reliance there is on the counselor and the more the counselor has to speak to the group as a whole rather than to members as individuals.

In addition to the opportunity for a greater number and variety of interactions which can serve as examples or models for effects of behavior, the group situation also permits the use of role playing. Role playing enables clients to practice various behaviors and to share feelings spontaneously in a simulated situation. It also permits both the counselor and the clients to gain a better perspective of the client. Shertzer and Stone (1974) caution, however, that role playing should not be a hiatus from the observance of basic principles governing human behavior. They advise that the purpose of role playing be understood by all members of the group. This requires explanation and, perhaps, a short demonstration.

There are some similarities and differences between individual and group counseling. Individual and group counseling are similar in the following ways: (1) overall objectives; both approaches seek positive, forward movement on the part of clients in achieving self-direction, self-acceptance, and self-responsibility; (2) both approaches necessitate an accepting climate and a confidential relationship; (3) both approaches necessitate a constructive role by the counselor in terms of attending and responding behaviors and providing directionality. Group counseling also differs from individual counseling: (1) the client in a group has an opportunity to test others' perceptions of himself; (2) the client may give as well as receive help; (3) the counselor's role is somewhat more complex in the group because of the need to be aware of the dynamics of interactions within the group (Shertzer & Stone, 1974).

Among the counseling approaches discussed in this chapter, those which are particularly well suited for group counseling situations are client-centered counseling, behavior therapy, gestalt therapy, transactional analysis, rational-emotive therapy, and reality therapy.

SUMMARY

The purpose of counseling in the rehabilitation process is, ideally, to help the total person become a happy, responsible, and self-actualized individual. Some approaches to counseling are briefly described—limited to a few that are potentially useful in rehabilitation. Those selected are chosen because they represent a range in current rehabilitation counseling practice.

There is no one approach which is most suitable for helping disabled clients. The approach taken with a given client is apt to relate as much to the background and style of the rehabilitation counselor as to the abilities and needs of the client and the specific situation. Most rehabilitation counselors are eclectic in their approach.

The relationship between the counselor and the client, the helper and the person being helped, is the heart of the counseling process. Though all approaches involve some degree of rational and affective dimensions, some approaches emphasize one more than the other.

Certain counseling approaches are particularly suitable for groups of clients. Group counseling can be helpful for sharing experiences, testing and practicing behaviors, and permitting clients to be helpers in addition to receiving help.

SELF-EVALUATION QUESTIONS

1. What is the core of the helping process?
2. What is the objective of the helping relationship?
3. What are the three systems of the personality in the psychoanalytic approach to therapy?
4. What is a key intent of the psychoanalytic approach?
5. What are some ego-defense mechanisms identified with the psychoanalytic approach?
6. What are the basic techniques of psychoanalytic therapy?
7. Who are the neo-Freudians?
8. What role does the counselor serve in the client-centered approach to counseling?
9. What are the counselor attitudes that must be present for a therapist to be effective in the client-centered approach?
10. Theoretically what is the basis for behavioral approaches?
11. What is the difference between respondent conditioning and operant conditioning in behavioral therapy?
12. How is success measured in Wolpe's behavioral approach to therapy?
13. What is reciprocal inhibition?
14. What is the more popular current term for "operant conditioning"?
15. What is a difference between the behavioral approach of John Dollard/Neil Miller and psychoanalysis? Between the Dollard/Miller approach and Wolpe's approach?
16. What is the role of biofeedback in behavior therapy approaches?
17. What is the goal of gestalt therapy?
18. What is the relationship between the person and the environment in gestalt therapy?
19. What is the role of "experiential awareness" in the gestalt approach?
20. What are some games for providing experiential structure to the therapeutic process in the gestalt approach?
21. What are the three ego states identified in the transactional analysis (TA) approach?
22. What is "structural analysis" in Berne's approach to counseling?
23. What are the types of transactions in TA?
24. What is a "life script" in TA? What are the four basic life positions?
25. What is the relationship of the counselor to the client in TA?
26. What techniques are particularly associated with TA?
27. What is the basic hypothesis of rational-emotive therapy (RET)?
28. What is the principal technique used by the RET therapist?
29. What are some principles of reality therapy?
30. What are the techniques of Bordin's psychological counseling?
31. What is Williamson's primary counseling technique?
32. What is a basic premise of Carkhuff's technology for helping?
33. What are the core dimensions of Carkhuff's approach?
34. What are the three phases of the helping process for Carkhuff?
35. What counselor behaviors are advocated by Carkhuff for helping the client get where he wants to be?
36. What is the element most common to various approaches to counseling?

37. What do psychoanalysis, behavior therapy, rational-emotive therapy, and transactional analysis have in common?
38. What are the advantages to group counseling over individual counseling?
39. How can group counseling be helpful with disabled clients?
40. What is an optimal size for group counseling?
41. What are the ways that group counseling and individual counseling are similar and the ways they are different?
42. What counseling approaches are particularly well suited for group counseling?

REFERENCES

Berne, E. *Transactional analysis in psychotherapy*. New York: Grove Press, Inc., 1961.

Berne, E. *Games people play*. New York: Grove Press, Inc., 1964.

Bordin, E. S. *Psychological counseling* (2nd ed.). New York: Appleton-Century-Crofts, 1968.

Carkhuff, R. R. *The art of helping*. Amherst, Mass.: Human Resource Development Press, 1973.

Carkhuff, R. R., & Berenson, B. G. *Beyond counseling and therapy*. New York: Holt, Rinehart & Winston, Inc., 1967.

Corey, G. *Theory and practice of counseling and psychotherapy*. Monterey, Calif.: Brooks/Cole Publishing Co., 1977.

Corsini, R. (Ed.) *Current psychotherapies*. Itasca, Ill.: F. E. Peacock Publishers, Inc., 1973.

Ellis, A. Rational-emotive therapy. In R. Corsini (Ed.), *Current psychotherapies*. Itasca, Ill.: F. E. Peacock Publishers, Inc., 1973.

Ewing, D. B. Twenty approaches to individual change. *Personnel and Guidance Journal*, 1977, *55*(6), 331-338.

Glasser, W., & Zunin, L. M. Reality therapy. In R. Corsini (Ed.), *Current psychotherapies*. Itasca, Ill.: F. E. Peacock Publishers, Inc., 1973.

Kempler, W. Gestalt therapy. In R. Corsini (Ed.), *Current psychotherapies*. Itasca, Ill.: F. E. Peacock Publishers, Inc., 1973.

Manley, S. A definitive approach to group counseling. *Journal of Rehabilitation*, 1973, *39*(1), 38-40.

McGowan, J. F., & Porter, T. L. *An introduction to the vocational rehabilitation process*. Washington, D.C.: Superintendent of Documents, Government Printing Office, 1967.

Patterson, C. H. Theories of counseling. In D. Malikin & H. Rusalem (Eds.), *Vocational rehabilitation of the disabled: an overview*. New York: New York University Press, 1969.

Patterson, C. H. *Theories of counseling and psychotherapy*. New York: Harper & Row, Publishers, Inc., 1973.

Shertzer, B., & Stone, S. C. *Fundamentals of counseling* (2nd ed.). Boston: Houghton Mifflin Co., 1974.

ADDITIONAL READINGS

American Personnel and Guidance Association. Counseling the severely disabled. *Rehabilitation Counseling Bulletin* (Special issue), 1975, *18*(4).

American Personnel and Guidance Association. Counseling the culturally different. *Personnel and Guidance Journal* (Special issue), 1977, *55*(7).

Davis, J. W. Constructive action in the art of helping. *Personnel and Guidance Journal*. 1975, *54*(3), 156-159.

Dyer, W. W., & Vriend, J. *Counseling techniques that work: application to individual and group counseling*. Washington, D.C.: American Personnel and Guidance Association, 1975.

Glasser, W. *The identity society*. New York: Harper & Row, Publishers, Inc., 1972.

Hatcher, C., & Himelstein, P. (Eds.). *The handbook of gestalt therapy*. New York: Jason Aronson, Inc., 1976.

Muthard, J. E., & Salomone, P. R. The roles and functions of the rehabilitation counselor. *Rehabilitation Counseling Bulletin* (Special issue), 1969, *13*(1).

Sussman, M. B., Haug, M. R., Hagan, F. E., Kitson, G. C. & Williams, G. K. Rehabilitation counseling in transition: some findings. *Journal of Rehabilitation*, 1975, *41*(3), 27-33, 40.

MEDIA RESOURCES

Visual

1. "Sessions in Gestalt Therapy with Fritz Perls" (16 mm film). Available from Mediasyn Corporation, P.O. Box 486, Del Mar, Calif. 92014.
2. "HRD Videotape Series": (a) Helping Model Module, (b) Attending Module, (c) Responding Module, (d) Personalizing Module, (e) Initiating Module. Available from Human Resource Development Press, Box 863, Dept. M21, Amherst, Mass. 01002.
   Describes Robert R. Carkhuff's approach to counseling and the four phases of effective helping.
3. "Albert Ellis: Rational-Emotive Psychotherapy" (16 mm film, 30 minutes). Available from APGA Film Department, 1607 New Hampshire Ave., N.W., Washington, D.C. 20009.
   Discussion by Ellis of the origin, philosophical bases, hypotheses, and therapeutic process for rational-emotive therapy.
4. "Albert Ellis: Rational-Emotive Psychotherapy Applied to Groups" (16 mm film, 30 minutes). Available from APGA Film Department, 1607 New Hampshire Ave., N.W., Washington, D.C. 20009.
   Definitions by Ellis of the role of the leader and the use of exercise in RET applied to groups.
5. "Concepts in Transactional Analysis" (16 mm film). Available from APGA Film Department, 1607 New Hampshire Ave., N.W., Washington, D.C. 20009.
   a. "Therapy in a Group Setting with Morris and Natalie Haimowitz: Mary" (25 minutes). *Focuses on script analysis.*
   b. "Therapy in a Group Setting with Morris and Natalie Haimowitz: Bruce" (25 minutes). *Focuses on parent-child-adult ego states.*
   c. "Therapy in a Group Setting with Morris and Natalie Haimowitz: Charlotte" (25 minutes). *Emphasizes the four TA life positions and the constructs of "rackets," "saving stamps," and "rubber bands."*
   d. "Stroke Seeking Behavior: Therapeutic Traps and Pitfalls" (30 minutes). *Excerpts from group sessions illustrate stroke-seeking behaviors by clients which divert the therapeutic process.*
   e. "Building a Nurturing Parent Therapy in a Group Setting with Morris and Natalie Haimowitz: Patsy" (18 minutes). *Explores how to help a client help himself.*
6. "Behavioral Counseling: a Multi-Film Package" (16 mm film). Available from APGA Film Department, 1607 New Hampshire Ave., N.W., Washington, D.C. 20009.
   a. "Identifying the Problem" (21 minutes). *Demonstrates the identification of a problem in behavioral terms.*
   b. "Formulating the Counseling Goal" (19 minutes). *Demonstrates how to narrow a variety of counseling goals down to a specific behavioral goal.*
   c. "Observing and Recording Behavior" (17 minutes).
   d. "Counseling Techniques: Reinforcement Procedures" (13 minutes). *Demonstrates the use of verbal and nonverbal reinforcement techniques.*
   e. "Counseling Techniques: Social Modeling" (15 minutes). *The counselor models behavior for the client to learn by observation.*
   f. "Counseling Techniques: Assertive Training" (14 minutes).
   g. "Counseling Techniques: Desensitization" (Part 1, 25 minutes; Part 2, 16 minutes). *A demonstration of desensitization with a client having a fear of snakes.*
   h. "Counseling Techniques: Self-as-a-Model" (12 minutes). *Demonstrates an approach used at the University of California–Santa Barbara.*
7. "Client-Centered Counseling" (16 mm film, 35 minutes). Available from APGA Film Department, 1607 New Hampshire Ave., N.W., Washington, D.C. 20009.
   Discussion by C. H. Patterson of the assumptions underlying client-centered counseling, the goals of counseling, determining when self-actualization is achieved, the three levels of goals, client freedom, and the future of client-centered therapy.
8. "Carl R. Rogers on Empathy" (16 mm film; Part I, 25 minutes; Part II, 25 minutes). Available from APGA Film Department, 1607 New Hampshire Ave., N.W., Washington, D.C. 20009.
   In Part I, Rogers defines empathy and the three decades of research on empathy. In Part II, he discusses the effects of emphatic responses.

9. "Carl Rogers on Facilitating a Group" (16 mm film, 30 minutes). Available from APGA Film Department, 1607 New Hampshire Ave., N.W., Washington, D.C., 20009.

   Discussions by Rogers of the role of the group leader and the levels on which a group should operate.

10. "Carl Rogers Conducts an Encounter Group" (16 mm film, 70 minutes; 2 reels). Available from APGA Film Department, 1607 New Hampshire Ave., N.W., Washington, D.C., 20009.

    Narration by Rogers of the various phases of group process during a group session in which he is facilitator.

11. "B. F. Skinner on Counseling" (16 mm film, 25 minutes). Available from APGA Film Department, 1607 New Hampshire Ave., N.W., Washington, D.C. 20009.

    Discusses how behavior is changed, the role of the counselor, the relationship between the counselor and the client, and the personal responsibility in behavior change.

12. "Behavior Therapy or Client-Centered Therapy: a Debate (John D. Krumboltz and C. H. Patterson)" (16 mm film, 35 minutes). Available from APGA Film Department 1607 New Hampshire Ave., N.W. Washington, D.C., 20009.

    A discussion of similarities and differences in methods and approaches between behavior therapy and client-centered therapy. Krumboltz and Patterson debate the role and function of the counselor.

13. "Three Approaches to Psychotherapy" (three 16 mm films, 50 minutes each). Available from Psychological Films, Inc., 1215 East Chapman Ave., Orange, Calif. 92669.

    Three films with Carl Rogers, Frederick Perls, and Albert Ellis demonstrating their approach to counseling the same client, Gloria. Each film has a postdiscussion relating what the therapist was trying to accomplish in the counseling session.

Audio

1. "Gestalt Tapes: Exercises and Experiments" (12 audiotape cassettes, 30 minutes each). Available from Gestalt Tapes, Box 19559b, Philadelphia, Pa., 19124.

   Minilectures and 93 gestalt exercises and experiments emphasizing how gestalt approaches can be used to promote awareness, responsibility, and effective living.

2. "Strategies for Novice Counselors" (audiotape cassette, 75 minutes). Available from APGA Publications Sales, 1607 New Hampshire Ave., N.W., Washington, D.C. 20009.

3. "Cross-Cultural Counseling" (audiotape cassette, 60 minutes). Available from APGA Publications Sales, 1607 New Hampshire Ave., N.W., Washington, D.C. 20009.

4. "Counseling Strategies: a Developmental Model" (audiotape cassette, 26 minutes). Available from Materials Development Center, University of Wisconsin–Stout, Menomonie, Wis. 54751.

   Describes the rehabilitation counselor as a manager of counseling strategies.

9

Job placement techniques

OVERVIEW AND OBJECTIVES

This chapter is intended to provide the reader with information and considerations that are important to job placement of the disabled. The chapter is divided into five major sections: (1) background, (2) five typical roles of the counselor in the placement process, (3) occupational information, with an emphasis on an orientation to the *Dictionary of Occupational Titles*, (4) some job placement approaches, and (5) postemployment services to clients.

Objectives of this chapter are to emphasize the importance of careful job placement of clients as the culmination of the vocational rehabilitation process, to acquaint the reader with some alternatives for counselors in approaching the job placement responsibility, to familiarize the reader with basic occupational information and techniques for achieving vocational objectives for clients, and to describe the purpose and scope of postemployment services for rehabilitated clients.

BACKGROUND

Rehabilitation is a goal-oriented program culminating in gainful activity. Legislation which authorizes the public program in rehabilitation requires that the scope of services include placement in suitable employment and the post-employment services necessary to help disabled persons maintain their employment (Department of Health, Education, and Welfare, 1974).

Job placement is a part of the total rehabilitation process and culminates in gainful activity. Examples of gainful activity are jobs in the competitive employment market, self-employment, unpaid family worker, and homemaker (Department of Health, Education, and Welfare, 1976). In Chapter 3 it was stated that the Individualized Written Rehabilitation Program (plan) requires a long-range employment goal. Thus consideration must be given to job placement at the beginning of the rehabilitation process. Though this employment goal can change during the rehabilitation process as a result of services and evaluation of progress toward the goal, job placement must receive continuous consideration throughout the provision of rehabilitation services. Services related to job placement include (1) continuous assessment of the appropriateness of an employment goal and the services needed for reaching that goal, (2) provision of information related to employment, such as job duties and rates of pay, (3) individual and/or group counseling in the techniques for seeking and retaining employment, (4) employer contact and on-site job analysis, and (5) assistance to employers. In the last category would be suggestions for modifying jobs to accommodate the disabled; help in eliminating architectural, procedural, and attitudinal barriers to employment for the disabled; suggestions for the development and conduct of affirmative action programs (which require that employers recruit, employ, and advance qualified handicapped workers); consultation to employers and clients for job adjustment following employment; and collaboration with various employment agencies involved in providing manpower assistance.

The goal of rehabilitation services is to have both the client and the employer satisfied, in other words, the occupation consistent with the client's abilities and the client having the necessary skills to perform the work satisfactorily. The public rehabilitation program defines suitable employment as "that which has been maintained for at least sixty days" (Department of Health, Education, and Welfare, 1974). Sixty days is considered the minimum; many clients may require a much longer period before it can be determined whether or not the employment outcome represents a suitable and satisfactory placement.

ROLE OF THE COUNSELOR

Kelso (1974) identifies a continuum of five rehabilitation counselor role orientations to job placement:

Arranger—Agent—Instructor—Guide—Therapist

The *arranger*-oriented counselor considers the placement function to be an opportunity to refer the client to others who can put him in contact with suitable employment. This placement activity consists of coordinating, conferring, and cooperating with other agencies or persons (for example, the United States Employment Service, an agency placement specialist, rehabilitation facilities, trade, business, or technical schools with knowledge of employment opportunities).

The *agent*-oriented counselor considers the placement function to be a job of selling the client to prospective employers. Like the arranger, the agent-oriented counselor focuses on factors external to the client. By taking information regarding the client related to needs, assets, and liabilities, the agent-oriented counselor feels prepared to contact potential employers on behalf of the client. In the agent role the counselor may seek job openings for clients, inform potential employers of the capabilities of the disabled, and study the various job requirements and employment needs of employers in the community. Solicitation may take the form of mail advertisements, telephone calls, and personal visits.

The *instructor*-oriented counselor attempts to teach the client behaviors that will help him obtain employment. The intent is to give the client the skills necessary to find his own employment opportunities. This process begins with an analysis of the client's present job-seeking skills and behavior; then follows the preparation of the client to complete job application forms and to learn to respond to difficult questions both written and oral regarding the client's work history or disabling conditions. Topics which might be covered include why people work, how to fill out employment applications, how to seek à job, personal cleanliness and grooming, what employers look for, typical personnel policies of employers, and job etiquette. Through adequate preparation, the client becomes responsible for locating his own employment. Such an approach to job placement by the rehabilitation counselor requires the client to be able to learn and develop job-search skills and behaviors. Thus, this approach may be unsuited for clients with low verbal ability.

The *guide*-oriented or guidance-oriented counselor views himself as an information resource to the client. This role involves providing information and advice to the client (such as methods to improve the client's job-seeking skills, the advantages and disadvantages of various occupations, and occupational information regarding community job conditions). In this approach the client is responsible for the decision making about seeking and obtaining suitable employment.

The *therapist* is internally oriented; in other words, he or she views the placement function as assisting the client to better understand himself. The therapeutic counselor reasons that with understanding the client will be better able to match his capabilities and limitations to the opportunities in the employment market. Through such an approach, it is hoped that the client will develop increased independence, responsibility, and confidence for making vocational choices.

OCCUPATIONAL INFORMATION

There are many informational resources for use in the job placement of disabled persons: community survey information, recruitment literature, various career exploration materials, want ad surveys, government documents, occupational information, descriptive literature produced by business and industry, and the yellow pages of the local telephone directory. One of the best sources for occupational information, however, is the *Dictionary of Occupational Titles* (*DOT*) produced by the United States Department of Labor.

DOT identifies more than 20,000 occupations in the United States. It was first published in 1939. A second edition appeared in 1949, a third in 1965, and a fourth in 1977. The fourth edition contains numerical and alphabetical listings and definitions.

Nine occupational categories are identified in the *DOT*:

0.
1. } Professional, technical, and managerial

2. Clerical and sales	6. Machine trade
3. Service	7. Bench work
4. Farming, fishery, and forestry	8. Structural work
5. Processing	9. Miscellaneous

The digits 0 to 9 identify general occupational categories. These nine categories are divided into 83 divisions and are identified in the *DOT* coding system by a second digit. For example, a two-digit code of 20 would be interpreted as follows: the 2 refers to the general occupational category (i.e., clerical and sales); the 0 refers to an occupational division within the general clerical or sales occupations category (stenography, typing, filing, and related occupations).

Similarly the 83 occupational divisions are divided into more than 600 occupational groups and identified by a third digit. For example, a three-digit code of 207 would refer to the occupational group entitled "duplicating machine operators." Thus the first three digits refer to an occupational group arrangement that includes the occupational category, occupational division, and occupational group.

A decimal point separates the first three digits from a second set of three digits. The second set refers to worker function arrangements. These are reflected, sequentially, as a relationship to data, people, and things. Worker functions are organized in a hierarchy: the lower the number, the greater the complexity of the function. Worker functions (in the fourth edition) are listed below.

Data	People	Things
0 Synthesizing	0 Mentoring	0 Setting up
1 Coordinating	1 Negotiating	1 Precision working
2 Analyzing	2 Instructing	2 Operating-controlling
3 Compiling	3 Supervising	3 Driving-operating
4 Computing	4 Diverting	4 Manipulating
5 Copying	5 Persuading	5 Tending
6 Comparing	6 Speaking-signaling	6 Feeding-offbearing
	7 Serving	7 Handling
	8 Receiving instruction	

Thus a worker function arrangement of .672 involves the following:

Data	People	Things
6, Comparing	7, Serving	2, Operating-controlling

A third set of three-digit codes is also included in the system. Codes in the seventh, eighth, and ninth positions are referred to as suffix codes. The suffix codes offer further specification of an occupation by identifying job titles. The three-digit suffix codes are in increments of four, with the first job title assigned 010; the second job title, 014; the third, 018; etc.

In the third edition of the *DOT*, significant worker trait components were included with the job definitions:

I. Training time (general educational development, specific vocational preparation)
II. Aptitudes
III. Interests
IV. Temperaments
V. Physical demands
VI. Working conditions

The fourth edition of the *DOT* has expanded this material and placed it in a separate volume. In the third edition, worker trait components were provided as a profile of qualifications for 22 broad areas of work within which all occupations would fall. The fourth edition identifies only 11 career areas replacing the 22 broad work areas of the third edition.

The 11 career areas in the fourth edition of the *DOT* are intended to reflect interest factors of individuals that can be obtained through an interest inventory. An advantage of this change from the third to the fourth edition is an individual's interest scores can be related to worker trait groups which reflect job characteristics (Isaacson, 1977).

Some advantages of the *DOT* for job placement are (1) it classifies and describes occupations in the United States; (2) it identifies occupational and worker characteristics; (3) the general qualifications needed for various occupational areas are identified; and (4) it permits a job analysis to be conducted (Georgia Division of Vocational Rehabilitation, 1974; Isaacson, 1977; Andrew & Dickerson, undated).

Job analysis

Job analysis is an excellent, but involved, method for assessing job requirements. The Department of Labor (1972) has developed a structured procedure for obtaining and recording job analysis data. The procedure involves a systematic study of the worker in a job in terms of the *work performed* and *worker traits*.

The most important aspect of work performed is worker functions. An analysis of worker functions involves determining what the worker does in relation to data, people, and things. The combination of worker functions in these three areas reflects the complexity of the job-worker situation. In addition to worker functions, the work performed is assessed in terms of methodology, the machine, tools, equipment, and work aids that are used, and the materials, products, subject matter, or services which result.

Worker traits are also identified in job analysis. Components studied include (1) training or education required for a particular job situation, (2) aptitudes necessary for learning the job, (3) personal traits or temperament required of the worker by the job situation, e.g., "adaptability to performing repetitive work," (4) interest in the job, and (5) physical or environmental demands on the worker, e.g., cold, heat, noise, or humidity.

There are two basic procedures for conducting a job analysis study. The first is to examine the technology of the job and the characteristics of the particular industry. Such study involves reading books, periodicals, or other literature related to the job; examining any catalogs, flow charts, organizational charts, and process descriptions the employer might have; and consulting technical literature related to the job description and job processes which are developed by trade associations or unions of professional groups as well as pamphlets and other materials prepared by governmental departments related to the job area. Once the job analyst has a solid informational background regarding the job, the second step is to observe workers performing their jobs and interview those workers, supervisors, and others. The Department of Labor has developed very detailed forms for structuring the job analysis and recording data.

Job analysis for job placement is valuable as a source of information about a job and the requirements made upon the worker for comparing clients with job expectations. Such analysis can be applied to community and sheltered jobs.

Wage and hour law and regulations

The Fair Labor Standards Act obligates employers to pay a minimum hourly wage if the employee is engaged in interstate commerce or in the production of goods for interstate commerce. To facilitate the employment or training of a disabled rehabilitation client, regulations were established by the Secretary of Labor for exemptions from the minimum wage law. These federal regulations (Title 29; Part 524, January, 1971, and Part 525, March, 1971) make provisions for some certificates of minimum wage exemption for disabled workers. Under these regulations, state rehabilitation agencies have the authority to issue 90-day certificates permitting employers to pay clients less than the minimum wage rate according to their productivity but not less than 50% of the current minimum wage.

If a client is so severely disabled that his productivity is less than 50% of normal, a regional office of the Department of Labor's Wage and Hour Division may, upon adequate documentation, issue a certificate below the 50% level but not less than 25% of the minimum wage. The wage identified in a temporary certificate must reflect the client's productivity and be consistent with wages paid nondisabled workers in the community for essentially the same quality and quantity of work. Thus a client's sub-minimum wage rate might be set above the 50% statutory minimum wage. The wage rate must also be adjusted to reflect changes in client productivity. It is possible to apply for a continuing certificate which can be issued for a period of up to one year at a time, if necessary and documented. Such an application would be made during the 90-day temporary certificate period.

Similarly, special certificates for payment of subminimum wages can be made to sheltered workshops and sheltered workshop clients. Certificates are available for regular sheltered workshop programs which permit the workshop to pay as little as 50% of the current minimum wage. However, as with the certificate for disabled in competitive employment, the workshop must pay the client according to his productivity unless this amount is less than the shop's certificate rate. Clients in sheltered workshops must also be paid a wage commensurate with the prevailing wage rates in the community for the same or similar types of work. Again, if the individual produces at less than the 50% rate, a special rate of not less than 25% the minimum wage may be requested from the regional office of the Department of Labor's Wage and Hour Division.

Three program categories, i.e., evaluation, training, and work activity center programs, may apply for certificates in which no minimum wage guarantee is required.

1. In the case of evaluation and training programs, a written curriculum and progress reports for each client must be maintained on a regular basis. However, if goods are produced while in evaluation or training the client must be paid wages commensurate with his productivity.

2. A work activity center program must be physically separate and must have activities which are primarily therapeutic in nature for severely disabled clients with an inconsequential productive capacity. Currently, to be eligible for a work activity center certificate the average productivity of all clients in the work activity center must not exceed $850.00 a year or, if wages are determined by piece rate, an average of $600.00 per client.

Affirmative action

Title V of the Rehabilitation Act of 1973 requires employers not to discriminate against individuals on the basis of a physical or mental handicap if the individual is qualified to do the job and reasonable accommodations are possible on the part of the employer. The law applies to state rehabilitation agencies and facilities, departments and agencies of the executive branch of the federal government (Section 501), contractors and subcontractors of the federal government who hold annual contracts of $2500.00 or more (Section 503), and all recipients of federal funding under any program or grant (Section 504).

"Reasonable accommodations" is a key phrase in the definition. It refers to the elimination of barriers to the disabled without causing an undue hardship on the employer. For example, it would apply if the disabled person is capable of getting to the worksite. The employer would then be obliged to create ramps, reserve special parking, rearrange furniture, or remove obstructions in walkways. It could also mean some modifications in the worksite. Depending on the person's disability, it could mean altering a workbench or desk, replacing hand controls with foot controls, or purchasing reaching and grasping tools to facilitate the accomplishment of a job. Some job restructuring may be reasonable and as simple as rearranging the job tasks. One of the most important considerations in the modification of the worksite is to ensure accessibility to the restroom. The rest-room doors and at least one commode stall must be wide enough to accommodate a wheelchair. The sink, soap, and towels must also be within reach.

Affirmative action can be a positive job-promotion device. Akabas (1976) found that industrial representatives lacked information in a number of areas: disabling conditions and their impact, the rehabilitation process, the nature and use of assistive devices, the nature of architectural barriers and remedies, job restructuring techniques, and sources of assistance. Rehabilitation personnel are in a position to help employers implement affirmative action programs. Such assistance can take the form of help in developing an affirmative action plan, training on affirmative action, recruiting eligible applicants, and providing work-site and job modification consultation.

Worker's compensation

Worker's compensation refers to the insurance coverage employers must have if employees should be injured on the job. Each state has its own requirements and regulations for worker's compensation coverage. This coverage may be obtained from many insurance carriers. The insurance premium rates are based on the number and cost of past employee accidents for an employer and occupational classifications. An erroneous notion is that hiring the disabled will increase these premium rates. Most states also have second injury clauses in their worker's compensation insurance policies. Such clauses limit the liability of an employer to the specific injury incurred on the job and exclude liability for prior disabilities.

Organized labor

Organized labor is a major force in the work world. Though employers hire workers, organized labor unions and their membership have a tremendous influence on working conditions and practices. Rehabilitation workers with responsibility for job placement would be well advised to become informed about the organization and functioning of labor unions.

Central to the structure of organized labor are the international unions. Independent international unions represent various industries. Each international union is made up of regional organizations, which, in turn, are made up of local unions. Most international unions belong to a federation of independent internationals, called the American Federation of Labor–Congress of Industrial Organizations (AFL-CIO). The purpose of the federated structure is to influence policy and legislation at national, state, and local levels. International unions provide technical assistance to their local unions and represent their membership within the federated structure for influencing policy, legislation, and negotiated contracts with management. Local unions, on the other hand, provide for employer-union contract enforcement and assistance to union members in non–work-related areas (e.g., personal concerns and recreation).

The local unions usually have three levels of organization. At the highest level is an elected representative of the union membership. His title might be president or secretary-treasurer. His responsibility is to interact with the international union office and serve as spokesperson for the local union membership with management. This elected representative may or may not be paid for his responsibility. At the second level, most unions have a business agent. The business agent is usually paid by the union. The responsibilities of the business agent include recruitment of personnel, introducing new employees to the job, involvement in contract enforcement, and handling grievances. At the third level is the shop steward. The shop steward may be either elected or appointed. The key responsibility of the shop steward is maintenance of the employee on the job—which may involve activities ranging from personal counseling to formally handling grievances of the workers he represents (Moriarty & Akabas, undated).

JOB PLACEMENT APPROACHES

As was emphasized in Chapter 1, rehabilitation in the United States is a goal-oriented program. Thus job placement is considered an integral part of the entire rehabilitation process, beginning with the identification of a vocational goal with a client. Consideration for an employment outcome then continues—including vocational evaluation, the delivery of service (e.g., counseling, restoration, and training), and the search for employment opportunities.

There are many approaches to the placement of disabled persons, and each placement counselor will develop his own style for achieving success. Some examples of placement approaches include identification of available jobs by reading newspaper want ads; contacting the U.S. Employment Service; writing, calling and personally visiting employers; preparing clients to seek jobs on their own; and developing cooperative efforts with employers such as trial placements, job analysis, and job development.

To successfully place rehabilitation clients requires specific knowledge in a number of areas. The placement person must be knowledgeable about the local labor market, labor unions, worker's compensation, wage and hour regulations, and, of course, an in-depth knowledge of the client (Newman, 1973).

Job-seeking skills training

Teaching job-seeking skills to clients puts the rehabilitation worker in the role of an instructor. The client is taught how to look independently for work. A widely used approach for this purpose is the job-seeking skills (JSS) instructional program developed by Multi-Resource Centers, Inc., of Minneapolis. The JSS program is intended to teach clients to prepare employment applications, develop resumés, and handle an employment interview. Clients are taught how to explain their skills, answer problem questions, and dress for an interview. In addition, they are given instructions on developing job leads. The instructional program involves considerable practice in developing applications and in role-playing job interviews. It contains prepared audiovisual aids for facilitating learning, including demonstration videotapes for interview behavior, a programmed videotape for reinforcing JSS principles, slides, and transparencies. Practice is given in handling various questions and comments. Examples are open-ended questions, like "Tell me something about yourself," and explaining skills, previous firings, the lack of work experience, poor references, mental illness, a prison record, or receiving welfare benefits (Minneapolis Rehabilitation Center, Inc., 1971a).

McClure (1972) found that placement through improvement of the client's job-seeking skills, as exemplified in the JSS program, was an effective and efficient approach to job placement and resulted in a higher proportion of placements when compared with the "traditional approach to placement of vocational rehabilitation clients" (presumably the placement agent role described earlier in the chapter).

Job development

Job development refers to the development of job sources that may lead to a job or job interview where an opportunity did not previously exist. Various approaches can be used. Potential job opportunities can be sought through former clients, former employers, the state employment service, Chambers of Commerce, service clubs, and labor unions. Multi-Resource Centers, Inc., in Minneapolis, has also developed a job development instructional program for rehabilitation workers. It is intended to complement the JSS package for clients. Job development by rehabilitation workers occurs after clients have job-seeking skills. Content areas include how to establish contact with employers, creating and developing an interest in the client, describing applicants' qualifications, handling objections, and obtaining an interview (Minneapolis Rehabilitation Center, 1971b).

Another approach has been described by Ugland (1977) for helping clients organize employer contacts. Ugland refers to the process as "job seeker's aids." The aids include industry lists, industry maps, a job seeker's guide, and a feedback system. The aids represent a systematic procedure for processing available information to facilitate the job search. The local industry lists were compiled from information solicited from business associations, Chambers of Commerce, directories, the Yellow Pages of the telephone directory, etc. Numbered pins are used to locate each company on a street map with public transportation routes superimposed. The "job seeker's guide" consists of reference cards which program a day's job search. Each card includes an itinerary for contacting employers in a particular industry in as few days as possible. The back of the card has an outline for recording the results of each employer contact. Such feedback information can be useful for further guidance to the client and as a record of hiring patterns.

Ugland has found that the foregoing approach resulted in increases in the employer contact rate (by 150%), applications taken (by 200%), and located job openings (by 300%).

A job-finding club approach to obtaining employment has been studied by Azrin, Flores, and Kaplan (1977). The club involves mutual assistance and sharing of job leads among members. Efforts of the clients include searching want ads, role playing, telephoning, constructing resumés, contacting friends, relatives, and former employers, and helping with transportation. Clients participating in the program were compared with clients who did not. The program appeared to be effective; within two months 90% of the club members and only 55% of the non–club members obtained full-time employment. In addition, the jobs were obtained sooner for club members (average, 2 weeks) than for non–club members (average, 8 weeks); the average starting salary was about 33% higher.

The Michigan state rehabilitation agency developed a selective job placement system involving job and skill banks. The system involved pooling job-development efforts among rehabilitation personnel. Each rehabilitation counselor was responsible for developing a relationship with at least one large employer (100 or more employees). As job openings occurred, qualified client applicants were solicited by a "job central staff" for an interview with them before referral to the employer. Clients screened and rejected by job central staff were returned to the counselor. Clients referred and rejected by the employer became part of a job central skill bank. The system was supported by job-seeking skills clinics for clients, job placement training for staff, and employer services such as worker's compensation assistance and affirmative action consultation (Molinaro, 1977).

An interesting approach has been developed by the Job Development Laboratory at George Washington University. It involves job analysis and the matching of job tasks to the client's capabilities and aptitudes. It is referred to as a job laboratory approach and involves a job analysis as just described, a site analysis (which includes a determination of environmental barriers), an assessment of the client's physical and mental functioning as related to various job tasks, and the development of engineering aids for adapting the work environment to the client's capabilities. Examples of engineering aids are substituting a tape recorder for hand-written notes for someone with a neuromuscular disability and designing a mail sorter at the appropriate height and angle for someone with limited shoulder extension.

The Job Development Laboratory maintains that such adaptations can create many jobs within the capabilities of the disabled. Examples of jobs in which the program staff have placed severely physically disabled persons include computer programming, keypunching, optical character recognition coding and typing, microfilming utilizing various cameras, microfilm image inspecting, microthin jacket filling, microthin jacket titling, insurance claim adjustment, abstracting, statistical analysis, customer claim adjustments, updating computer files, inventory analysis, remote proofreading, mail clerk, information receptionist, accounts maintenance, and clerk typist (Mallik & Sablowsky, 1975).

In St. Louis the Jewish Employment and Vocational Service has conducted a job development program for persons 60 years of age and older. Its intent is to supplement the older person's income and help that person remain active. Entitled Project EARN, the agency has established community job development centers in each of four counties. In addition to the four centers, seven satellite offices have been established. One of the purposes of the program is to prevent deterioration in many older persons by dealing with the basic problem of an inadequate income. A hypothesis of the project is that, if income can be improved, older persons can continue to manage their own affairs and lead dignified and useful lives. Thus the project aims to help each applicant find a suitable job in accordance with his interests and abilities and, if appropriate, to refer such applicants to other community resources for different problems. The project utilizes older persons to help other older persons. In addition to hiring older adults as personnel in the centers, the program staff recruit applicants for personal services of other older persons—for example, handyman services and day companions. The procedures for developing jobs include using the media, personal appearances before service and senior groups, and phone calls to both applicants and employers. The project has been very successful. Most of the placements are in regular part-time jobs and temporary jobs. Placements have been with families, schools, retail businesses (including supermarkets, specialty shops, and variety stores), and service businesses (laundromats, cafeterias, parking lots, and security guards) and in manufacturing and professional and business offices (Kaufer, 1975).

Home-based employment is another resource for job development. An interesting project entitled Home-Based Employment to Accomplish Rehabilitation (HEAR) was conducted by the Rehabilitation Center at University Hospital in San Diego (McGraw, Convery, & Minteer, 1977). The project was intended for persons with arthritis, spinal cord injury, and stroke. They were served on an outreach basis and either were convalescing from recent hospitalization or had been in a homebound status for several months. Interviews were conducted with the patients during their hospitalization or, if on an outpatient basis, during weekly clinics. In addition, some referrals were received by physicians in the community. During the initial interview, a vocational skills profile was obtained for the individual outlining both vocational experience and current interests. Occupational therapists assessed current physical ability and vocational skills. The occupational therapists were also a resource during the program for obtaining or developing special adaptive devices for home-based workers. Training was provided for the subcontract tasks done in the home. Nine different kinds of subcontract work were reported: envelope stuffing, color code painting, taping microfilm reader inserts, packaging, assembly, logic board stripping, electrical switch reworking, electrical harness work, and header component soldering.

Some of the reasons provided for the success of the project were that contact was made during hospitalization and gave patients a productive activity to look forward to, that an excellent quality control system for subcontract work was established to involve workers in the examination of their own work, that the program served as a productive interim activity for persons seeking eligibility for vocational rehabilitation services, and that many community job opportunities became available in the same firms which provided subcontract work for home-bound employment.

A variation of home-based employment is a home-craft program described by Towne (1972). Home craft, in contrast to industrial-type work, is intended to motivate a client to learn a craft activity which is suitable to his interests, disability, and home situation. In the program described by Towne, the state rehabilitation agency provided arts-and-crafts teachers, instructional materials, and equipment. Craft products were then sold through a number of stores and organizations. Proceeds from the sales were returned to the clients.

Job tryout

Job tryouts can serve the purpose of vocational evaluation, job preparation, and trial employment. In a program described by Allen and Shinnick (1973), job tryouts were effective and economical for placing clients with a potential employer so they could learn about the job in a natural work setting. Some of the advantages of the job tryout approach to placement, according to Allen and Shinnick, are that it allows for extended training under actual job conditions, it permits job failure without the rejection experienced in being fired, it permits the employer to be reasonably sure the client will be a useful asset to his business, and the employer has minimal investment in the client prior to employment.

Another job-tryout approach is the work crew. Hansen (1969) described a work-crew approach conducted in the San Juan Unified School District of Sacramento, California. The approach involved a small crew of workers for conducting various community jobs, under supervision, on a contract basis. Examples of jobs were lawn work, ditch cleaning, weed pulling, trash removal, gardening, and cleaning up recreational areas.

Projects With Industry

The Projects With Industry (PWI) program represents an attempt by the Rehabilitation Services Administration of the Department of Health, Education, and Welfare to open new job opportunities for the disabled by involving profit-making corporations in the rehabilitation service delivery process. The program started with the 1968 amendments to the Vocational Rehabilitation Act. Organizations receiving grants for the PWI program are usually rehabilitation facilities. The facilities, in turn, enter into a contract with profit-making corporations. The relationship between the rehabilitation facility and the profit-making corporations varies. Some provide vocational training; however, the emphasis is on job placement. The success ratio of the PWI program has been very high, with approximately 75% of persons served in the program becoming placed in the competitive labor market. The range in size and type of corporation involved in the PWI program is considerable. Among the largest and best known corporations which have been involved are Sears Roebuck, IBM, Metropolitan Life, INA (Insurance Company of North America), and Bankers Trust of New York.

POSTEMPLOYMENT SERVICES

Though postemployment follow-through has always been a part of the rehabilitation program, the Rehabilitation Act of 1973 put a new emphasis on helping rehabilitated clients maintain employment. The concept of postemployment services has been broadened over past practice to include now any rehabilitation service or combination of services necessary to help the rehabilitated client maintain successful employment. There are, however, restrictions on what is appropriate. The service or services provided during the postemployment phase must be related to the original rehabilitation plan. If a comprehensive rehabilitation effort is necessary, a client's case should be reopened and a new evaluation made for determination of eligibility. This requires a new Individualized Written Rehabilitation Program for the client. Postemployment services are not intended to mean provision of the entire rehabilitation process; rather, only those services needed to sustain the rehabilitation benefits the client received prior to job placement are provided. Under the public program any rehabilitation service may be furnished if needed for maintenance of the employment situation, so long as the service is not for an acute condition. Problems related to the prior condition are not precluded. Postemployment service may even be provided to help an individual obtain a better (i.e., more suitable) job.

There is no time limit for the provision of postemployment services to clients. The decision to terminate postemployment services is generally made by the rehabilitation counselor based on the client's ability to function independently in a relatively secure employment situation.

Considerable judgment is required by the rehabilitation counselor in providing postemployment services. Judgments are needed for identifying acute conditions, upgrading a client's employment situation, and determining when comprehensive and complex services are needed and when services are necessary for maintenance of employment.

In summary, postemployment services (1) are provided to clients who are successfully rehabilitated, (2) are provided to maintain employment, (3) may include any rehabilitation service, (4) must relate to the original handicapping conditions for which a rehabilitation plan was developed, and (5) must not involve comprehensive or complex services that would necessitate a new rehabilitation plan.

SUMMARY

Job placement is a consideration throughout the rehabilitation process and represents the culmination of that process. Five rehabilitation counselor role orientations to job placement are described in this chapter—including arranger, agent, instructor, guide, and therapist. The effectiveness of each orientation is an individual consideration dependent upon the counselor and client.

One of the best sources for occupational information is the *Dictionary of Occupational Titles (DOT)*. The recent fourth edition describes more than 20,000 occupations in the United States and classifies them with nine-digit codes. In addition to describing occupations, the *DOT* identifies worker characteristics and required qualifications. Job analysis, though quite involved, is also an excellent source of occupational information.

To facilitate the employment or training of disabled rehabilitation clients, special exemptions for low productivity can be made for the minimum wage requirements. In addition, the Rehabilitation Act of 1973 requires that employers not discriminate against disabled persons. Wage exemptions and affirmative action by employers can be positive job promotion opportunities for rehabilitation counselors.

A number of job placement approaches are described in this chapter: (1) job-seeking skills training for clients, (2) job development, including job-seeker's aids, job-seeking clubs, centralized job and skill banks, engineered aids and/or adaptive devices, community job development centers, and home-based employment, (3) job tryouts, and (4) Projects With Industry.

The provision of postemployment services is an important concept in the rehabilitation process. The 1973 Rehabilitation Act placed an increased emphasis on maintaining clients in employment. As a result any rehabilitation service related to the original handicapping condition and rehabilitation plan may be provided to clients to maintain them in employment.

Thus "job placement" is a part of the total rehabilitation process and begins with the first interview between counselor and client. It is a consideration during preliminary and thorough diagnostic studies, in developing and amending Individualized Written Rehabilitation Programs, in the provision of rehabilitation services, and in the actual search for suitable and satisfactory employment.

SELF-EVALUATION QUESTIONS
1. What are examples of "gainful activity"?
2. At what point must job placement become a consideration in the rehabilitation process?

3. How is "suitable employment" defined in the public rehabilitation program?
4. How do the five rehabilitation counselor role orientations to job placement (i.e., arranger, agent, instructor, guide, therapist) differ?
5. What are the primary information resources that may be useful in the job placement of disabled individuals?
6. What does each of the nine digits represent in the *Dictionary of Occupational Titles (DOT)* coding system?
7. What are the advantages to using the *DOT* for job placement?
8. What are the two basic procedures for conducting a job analysis study?
9. What is the minimum rate an employer with a certificate of minimum wage exemption can pay a disabled client?
10. What are some considerations in determining the wage identified in a temporary certificate of minimum wage exemption?
11. What are the program categories for which no minimum wage guarantee is required?
12. Which employers are required to have an affirmative action policy under Title V of the Rehabilitation Act of 1973?
13. What are some examples for providing "reasonable accommodations" for the disabled by employers?
14. What are ways in which rehabilitation personnel can assist employers in implementing affirmative action programs?
15. What is worker's compensation?
16. How is the worker's compensation insurance premium rate determined for an employer?
17. What are the usual responsibilities of the business agent in a local labor union?
18. What are the intents of the job-seeking skills program developed by Multi-Resource Centers, Inc.?
19. What is job development?
20. What is included in the job seeker's aids approach to job placement?
21. What is a job-finding club?
22. What activities are involved in the job laboratory approach utilized at George Washington University?
23. What are some of the reasons given for the success of the home-based employment program conducted at University Hospital, San Diego?
24. What are the advantages of the job-tryout approach to placement?
25. What is the primary purpose of the Projects With Industry (PWI) program?
26. What is the intent of postemployment services?
27. What are the restrictions for providing postemployment services?
28. What judgments are required by rehabilitation counselors in providing postemployment services?

REFERENCES

Akabas, S. H. Affirmative action: a tool for linking rehabilitation and the business community. *Journal of Rehabilitation,* 1976, 42(3), 20-23, 42.

Allen, C. M., & Shinnick, M. D. Placement through a job tryout approach to vocational evaluation. *Vocational Evaluation and Work Adjustment Bulletin,* 1973, 6(4), 29-33.

Andrew, J. D., & Dickerson, L. R. (Eds.). *Vocational evaluation: a resource manual* (Supplement 1). Menomonie, Wis.: Research and Training Center, University of Wisconsin–Stout, undated.

Azrin, N. H., Flores, T., & Kaplan, S. J. Job-finding club: a group-assisted program for obtaining employment. *Rehabilitation Counseling Bulletin,* 1977, 21(2), 130-149.

Department of Health, Education, and Welfare. Rehabilitation program and activities. *Federal Register,* 39(103: Part II), May 28, 1974 (Section 104.39).

Department of Health, Education, and Welfare. Placement. *Program Regulation Guide,* RSA-PRG-76-39, August 20, 1976. (Rehabilitation Services Manual, Transmittal no. 51, Part 1500, Chapter 41)

Georgia Division of Vocational Rehabilitation. *Training manual: dictionary of occupational titles.* Menomonie, Wis.: Materials Development Center, University of Wisconsin–Stout, 1974.

Hansen, C. E. The work crew approach to job placement for the severely retarded. *Journal of Rehabilitation,* 1969, *35*(3), 26-27.

Isaacson, L. E. *Career information in counseling and teaching* (3rd ed.). Boston: Allyn & Bacon, Inc., 1977.

Kaufer, H. Personal communication, 1975.

Kelso, R. R. Five counselor placement orientations. Paper presented to the Great Plains Region National Rehabilitation Association Conference, Salt Lake City, 1974.

Mallik, K., & Sablowsky, R. Model for placement—job laboratory approach. *Journal of Rehabilitation,* 1975, *41*(6), 14-20, 41.

McClure, D. T. Placement through improvement of clients' job seeking skills. *Journal of Applied Rehabilitation Counseling,* 1972, *3*(2), 188-196.

McGraw, M. J., Convery, F. R., & Minteer, M. A. Home-based employment programs: effects and guidelines for program development. *Journal of Rehabilitation,* 1977, *43*(3), 33-35.

Minneapolis Rehabilitation Center, Inc. *Job seeking skills: instructing applicants,* Minneapolis: MRC, Inc., 1971a.

Minneapolis Rehabilitation Center, Inc. *Job development: reference manual.* Minneapolis: MRC, Inc., 1971b.

Molinaro, D. A placement system develops and settles: the Michigan model. *Rehabilitation Counseling Bulletin,* 1977, *21*(2), 121-129.

Moriarity, J. B., & Akabas, S. H. *Some considerations for affirmative action.* Institute, W. Va.: West Virginia Research and Training Center, undated.

Newman, R. D. Personal polarity and placement problems—reflexive rehabilitation vs. unexamined closure. *Journal of Rehabilitation,* 1973, *39*(6), 20-25.

Towne, A. Homecraft: source of home employment. *Rehabilitation Record,* 1972, *13*(5), 1-5.

Ugland, R. P. Job-seeker's aids: a systematic approach for organizing employer contracts. *Rehabilitation Counseling Bulletin,* 1977, *21*(2), 107-115.

ADDITIONAL READINGS

American Rehabilitation Counseling Association. Placement in the rehabilitation process. *Rehabilitation Counseling Bulletin,* 1977, *21*(2), whole issue.

Bowman, J. T., & Graves, W. H. *Placement services and techniques.* Champaign, Ill.: Stipes Publishing Co., 1976.

Conley, R., & Noble, J., Jr. Worker's compensation reform: challenge for the 80's. *American Rehabilitation,* 1978, *3*(3), 19-26.

Davis, J. E. Projects with industry in the computer age. *American Corrective Therapy Journal,* 1974, *28*(5), 151-155.

Department of Labor. *Supplement Two to the Dictionary of occupational titles: selected characteristics of occupations by worker traits and physical strength* (3rd ed.). Washington, D.C.: Superintendent of Documents, Government Printing Office, 1968.

Department of Labor. *Handbook for analyzing jobs.* Washington, D.C.: DOL Manpower Administration, 1972.

Department of Labor. *Occupational outlook handbook, 1974 edition.* Washington, D.C.: Superintendent of Documents, Government Printing Office, 1973.

Department of Labor. *Dictionary of occupational titles* (4th ed.). Washington, D.C.: Superintendent of Documents, Government Printing Office, 1977.

Donaho, M. W., & Meyer, J. L. *How to get the job you want: a guide to resumes, interviews and job hunting strategy.* Englewood Cliffs, N.J.: Prentice-Hall, Inc., 1976.

Dunn, D. J. *Placement services in the vocational rehabilitation program.* Menomonie, Wis.: Research and Training Center, University of Wisconsin–Stout, 1974.

Echols, F. H. Rehabilitation counselor's responsibility for placement. *The Journal of Applied Rehabilitation Counseling,* 1972, *3*(2), 72-75.

Fourth Institute on Rehabilitation Issues. *The rehabilitation of the severely handicapped home-bound*. Hot Springs, Ark.: Arkansas Rehabilitation Research and Training Center, University of Arkansas, 1977.

Galvin, D. E. Job placement: an unseemly occupation? *Journal of Applied Rehabilitation Counseling*. 1976, 7(4), 198-207.

Newman, L. Instant placement: a new model for providing rehabilitation services within a community mental health program. *Community Mental Health Journal*, 1970, 6(5), 401-410.

Sweet, D. H. *The job hunter's manual*. Reading, Mass.: Addison-Wesley Publishing Co., 1975.

MEDIA RESOURCES

Visual

1. "A Little Harder" (16 mm film, 17 minutes). Available from Skye Pictures, Inc., 2225 Floyde Ave., Richmond, Va. 23220.

    Depicts developmentally disabled persons as successful workers. Some advantages of hiring the disabled are discussed by employers.

2. "Placement and Follow-up of Severely Disabled Persons: a Training Program for Vocational Counselors" (slides, audiotapes, and handbooks). Developed by Arbec, Inc., 3909-G.N.I.H. 35, Austin, Texas 78722.

    A training program in job placement consisting of ten units. Topics included:

    Unit I—"Brainstorming." *Uses an analogy involving the identification of 30 uses of a brick and 30 job possibilities for a client.*

    Unit II—"Placement." *Emphasizes the identification of placement activities throughout the rehabilitation process.*

    Unit III—"Occupational Resource Development." *Gives an overview of job analysis, labor market analysis, job market surveying, and developing community contacts.*

    Unit IV—"Selling." *Describes six steps to low-key selling.*

    Unit V—"Client's Rights." *Indicates the legal rights of rehabilitation clients.*

    Unit VI—"Job Expectations." *Illustrates a model for relating to client job expectations.*

    Unit VII—"Creative Problem-Solving." *Explores various solutions to a specific problem.*

    Unit VIII—"Time Management." *Describes typical time wasters and emphasizes setting objectives and priorities.*

    Unit IX—"Client Readiness." *Helps counselors identify client employment skills and deficiencies and resources for correcting deficiencies.*

    Unit X—"Follow-up." *Addresses critical incidents in client work adjustment.*

3. "Employer Services" and "Common Ground" (two ¾" videotape cassettes). Available from Region V Center for Continuing Education, Multi-Resource Centers, Inc., 1900 Chicago Ave., Minneapolis, Minn. 55405.

    Videotape entitled "Employer Services" discusses ways rehabilitation personnel can assist employers (e.g., affirmative action assistance, employee programming). Videotape entitled "Common Ground" discusses affirmative action requirements, a definition of handicapped, and reasonable accommodations for the disabled.

4. "Introduction to Job Analysis" (66 slides with 30-minute audiotape). Developed by Materials Development Center, University of Wisconsin–Stout, Menomonie, Wis. 54751.

    Describes the Department of Labor's approach to job analysis.

5. "Employment of the Physically Handicapped" (filmstrip with audiotape and worksheets). Available from Multi-Media Office, Mt. San Jacinto College, 21400 Highway 79, San Jacinto, Calif. 92382.

    Presents 11 case studies that depict employment opportunities for the physically disabled.

6. "Good People" (16 mm film, 30 minutes). Available from K. G. Brown, Public Relations & Advertising, Hughes Aircraft Co., Bldg. 100, Mail Station A-531, P.O. Box 90515, Los Angeles, Calif. 90009.

    Depicts successfully employed disabled persons.

7. "The Job" (16 mm film, 12 minutes). Available from Community Education Department, ICD Rehabilitation & Research Center, 340 East 24th St., New York, N.Y. 10010.

    Traces the rehabilitation process culminating in employment.

8. "Balance Sheet" (16 mm film, 28 minutes). Available from Continental Studios, 100 North Gordon St., Elk Grove Village, Ill. 60007.

     Presents a systematic approach to answering employer questions about hiring the disabled.

9. "Functional Job Analysis" (filmstrip with 22-minute audiotape and posters). Available from Bob Jones, 13813 Willoughby, Upper Marlboro, Md. 20870.

     Presents an introduction to the Dictionary of Occupational Titles *and a functional analysis for matching client skills and jobs.*

10. "Working from a Wheelchair" (½" videotape). Available from Texas Institute for Rehabilitation and Research, Texas Medical Center, P.O. Box 20095, Houston, Texas 77025.

     Illustrates real-life situations for four disabled individuals in a wheelchair in their job situations. An interview is held with each.

11. "Understanding the Guidelines for the Rehabilitation Act of 1973 on Post-Employment Services" (slides and tape with study guide, 20 minutes). Developed by the West Virginia Research and Training Center, University of West Virginia, Institute, W. Va. 25112.

     An interpretation of the 1973 Rehabilitation Act relative to postemployment services.

12. "Job Quest Series" (slides and audiotape with instruction guide and script). Available from Materials Development Center, University of Wisconsin–Stout, Menomonie, Wis. 54751.

     Developed for use with clients. Contains three slide-tape presentations:

     a. "Job Sources" (64 slides, 16 minutes). *Identifies various community job resources.*

     b. "Writing About You: Application Forms and Resumes" (67 slides, 20 minutes). *Describes the steps involved in preparing resumés and applications.*

     c. "Interviewing for a Job" (65 slides, 19 minutes). *Emphasizes matching worker and job.*

13. "Job Survival Skills (thirteen filmstrips with audiotape, group leader instruction book, participant's workbook, and simulation materials). Available from Singer, Education Division, 3750 Monroe Ave., Rochester, N.Y. 14603.

     An instructional package related to job behavior for group use with clients. Examples of topics include job-seeking skills, personal appearance, resumés, applications, and interviews. The material is written at a sixth grade reading level and requires minimal writing skills.

14. "Vocational Rehabilitation: Come Work With Us" (16 mm film, 20 minutes). Available from West Virginia Research and Training Center, University of West Virginia, Institute, W. Va. 25112.

     Illustrates affirmative action in operation. Depicts disabled employees in a variety of employment situations.

15. "Title V: an Overview" (slides and audiotape cassettes). Available from West Virginia Research and Training Center, University of West Virginia, Institute, W. Va. 25112.

     Covers Sections 501, 502, 503, and 504 of Title V of the Rehabilitation Act of 1973. Gives counselors some "do's" and "don'ts" relative to affirmative action.

Audio

1. "Job Game" (four audiotape cassettes with a workbook and leader's guide). Available from Employment Training Corp., 300 Central Park West, New York, N.Y. 10024.

     A package that is intended to develop job-seeking skills utilizing exercises, games, and self-questionnaires. It can be self-administered. The package is divided into eight segments.

2. "A Job in Your Future" (audiotape cassette, 60 minutes). Available from Dialogue Publications, Berwyn, Ill. 60402.

     Presents job-seeking concepts (e.g., finding jobs, making appointments, completing forms, being interviewed).

3. "Placement in Vocational Rehabilitation" (audiotape cassette with script, 48 minutes). Available from Materials Development Center, University of Wisconsin–Stout, Menomonie, Wis. 54751.

4. "Job Analysis in Placement" (audiotape cassette with script, 44 minutes). Available from Materials Development Center, University of Wisconsin–Stout, Menomonie, Wis. 54751.

5. "Occupational Information" (audiotape cassette with script, 39 minutes). Available from Materials Development Center, University of Wisconsin–Stout, Menomonie, Wis. 54751.

6. "Using Occupational Information" (audiotape cassette with script, 38 minutes). Available from Materials Development Center, University of Wisconsin–Stout, Menomonie, Wis. 54751.

10

Community resources

OVERVIEW AND OBJECTIVES

This chapter offers the reader a description and examples of various resources available in rehabilitation. The chapter is divided into six sections: (1) background, (2) types of resources, (3) services integration, (4) private rehabilitation, (5) other resources available in rehabilitation, and (6) some guidelines for interagency collaboration by rehabilitation counselors.

The objective of this chapter is to acquaint the reader with the scope of resources available for rehabilitation programming.

BACKGROUND

Emphasis throughout this text has been toward a team approach to the provision of rehabilitation services. Rehabilitation encompasses educational, social, psychological, and health-related professions. Because rehabilitation is a community-based program, rehabilitation workers are part of a comprehensive team and relate to a number of agencies, services, and facilities (Jaques, 1970). Rehabilitation for an individual may necessitate the services of a single professional or may involve a combination of services and professions. Examples are physical medicine, ophthalmology, neurology, psychiatry, physical therapy, occupational therapy, orthotics and prosthetics, rehabilitation nursing, dentistry, speech-language pathology, audiological services, psychology, social work, special education, and therapeutic recreation.

The services of such professionals are sometimes found in single offices, but more often they occur in combination as part of a team approach in a hospital or rehabilitation center. Though many professions are specialized, they are concerned with the whole person. Serving rehabilitation clients requires teamwork and coordination among various professionals.

TYPES OF RESOURCES

The following represent some of the more frequently used resources in rehabilitation.

Medical consultation

State rehabilitation programs retain the services of physicians on either a full-time or a part-time basis for the purpose of consultation regarding medical aspects of rehabilitation clients. Legislation has decreed that medical consultation must be available to all state rehabilitation counselors. The medical consultant is a resource to the rehabilitation counselor for interpreting medical data, determining the medical and vocational implications of disabilities, recommending further medical diagnoses or care, and assisting with the identification of a prognosis for the client. Though the medical consultant is a resource to rehabilitation counselors for advice and recommendations, the counselor's responsibility is to determine public program eligibility for rehabilitation services.

As indicated in Chapter 1, eligibility is based on the presence of a physical or mental disability which constitutes a substantial handicap to employment but for which there is a reasonable expectation that rehabilitation services will enable the individual to engage in a gainful occupation.

Physical medicine

Physical medicine is a medical specialty involving the application of physical modalities for diagnostic and therapeutic purposes. Some physical modalities are heat and cold, ultraviolet rays, electricity, massage, exercise, stretching, and traction (Rusk, 1977). The purpose is to diagnose, prevent, or treat physical disorders.

Ophthalmology

Ophthalmology is concerned with diseases and injuries to the eye. The ophthalmologist is a medical specialist for diagnosing and treating such diseases and injuries. Ophthalmologists are qualified to determine visual loss, prescribe medication, and perform surgery.

Neurology

Neurology relates to the nervous system. The nervous system is composed of the brain, spinal cord, and nerves. These may be affected by injury, disease, or inflammation. Physicians involved in neurology are concerned with the diagnosis and treatment of nervous system disorders.

Psychiatry

Psychiatry is concerned with the diagnoses and treatment of emotional and mental disorders. Psychiatric services are provided by private practitioners and through clinics and mental health centers. Though the psychiatrist, a medical doctor, is usually involved in cases in which reactions are outside the normal range of emotional reaction, he can also be helpful with clients having an intense emotional problem or can act as a consultant to other professionals.

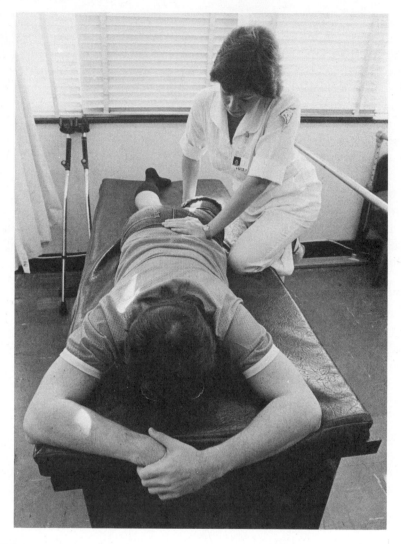

Fig. 10-1
In addition to exercise, physical therapists use massage, heat, cold, water, electricity, light, and sound to aid restoration. (From Rusk, H. A. *Rehabilitation medicine*. St. Louis: The C. V. Mosby Co., 1977.)

Physical therapy

The physical therapist is frequently a part of rehabilitation teams. Physical therapists use physical aids to treat and help restore normal body functions. They are qualified to evaluate a client's physical condition, but usually operate on the basis of a physician's prescription. The modalities used by a physical therapist include exercise, massage, heat, cold, water, electricity, ultraviolet and infrared

Fig. 10-2
Occupational therapists engage clients in purposeful activities to restore function. (From Rusk, H. A. *Rehabilitation medicine*. St. Louis: The C. V. Mosby Co., 1977.)

light, and sound. The physical therapist often works in collaboration with an occupational therapist for preparing the client to engage in activities of daily living. Physical therapists are usually found in the physical medicine department of hospitals, rehabilitation centers, and nursing homes.

Occupational therapy

Occupational therapists engage clients in purposeful activity for the purpose of restoring function. On the basis of an evaluation of the level of functioning of a client, the occupational therapist plans a program of activities for the client that may include such things as arts, crafts, homemaking, grooming, woodworking, typing, using adaptive equipment, and engaging in industrial-type work. The occupational therapist, like the physical therapist, is usually employed in a physical medicine department of a hospital, rehabilitation center, or nursing home.

Orthotics and prosthetics

Orthotics is concerned with straightening or correcting any part of the human body with devices. An orthotist is a person who designs and applies such devices (e.g., an arm or a leg brace). Prosthetics deals with the application or addition of an artificial device to the body such an artificial limb. A prosthetist is concerned with designing and fitting prostheses (artificial devices) to disabled individuals.

Rehabilitation nursing

All nurses are, in a sense, rehabilitation nurses. Nurses provide assessment, planning, and implementation of the client's restoration process (Rusk, 1977).

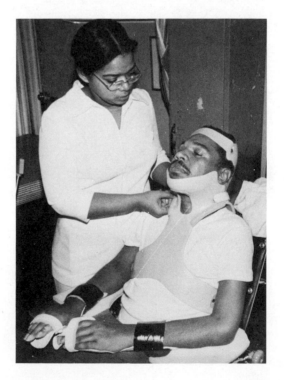

Fig. 10-3
Rehabilitation nurses provide assessment, planning, and patient care. (From Rusk, H. A. *Rehabilitation medicine*. St. Louis: The C. V. Mosby Co., 1977.)

In rehabilitation care facilities the nurse is part of a rehabilitation team of which he may often be the coordinator. In addition to having jobs in hospitals, rehabilitation centers, and nursing homes, nurses have roles in public health departments, insurance companies, labor unions, and homes.

Dentistry

The teeth and palate are very important for the articulation of many speech sounds. Thus dentists can play a decisive role in the rehabilitation process. Correction of a cleft palate or disorders of the teeth will improve speech, appearance, and/or a person's general health. Resources to rehabilitation counselors include the private dentist and, in certain localities, dental schools where outpatient treatment is provided to give advanced dental students training and practice.

Speech therapy

Speech therapy is administered by a speech-language pathologist, who is sometimes referred to as a speech therapist. The speech-language pathologist works with speech disorders including articulation, phonation, fluency, and symbolization. Speech-language pathologists provide diagnostic and treatment services. They are most commonly found in hospitals, public schools, health departments, universities, nursing homes, and private practice.

Audiological services

The audiologist works closely with the speech-language pathologist and is concerned with hearing disorders. Much of the audiologist's work is diagnosing the extent of a hearing loss and its relationship to the client's communication ability. The audiologist works with precise measurement instruments, such as an audiometer (which measures the range of hearing). Since speech-language pathologists and audiologists usually work as a team, they are often found in the same program or resource center.

Comprehensive rehabilitation centers

Comprehensive rehabilitation centers often have a medical emphasis encompassing many of the medical resources previously identified. In addition, they usually address accompanying psychological, social, educational, and vocational problems of the rehabilitation client.

One of the earliest comprehensive rehabilitation centers in the United States was the Woodrow Wilson Rehabilitation Center located at Fishersville, Virginia. The Woodrow Wilson Rehabilitation Center was established in 1947 in a temporary army hospital. The Center has an average daily enrollment of 500 clients and serves approximately 2000 clients annually with a complete rehabilitation program: medical and nursing services, physical, occupational, and speech therapy, comprehensive evaluation, counseling and recreational services, and training in a wide variety of occupational areas. Examples of occupational training are automobile servicing and repair, barbering and cosmetology, clerical accounting and data processing, stenography and typewriting, custodial and janitorial jobs, drafting, electronics assembly, electrical work, food services, furniture refinishing, health- and cosmetic-related occupations, industrial sewing, warehousing, radio and television repair, upholstering, welding, and woodworking.

The ICD Rehabilitation and Research Center in New York City is another example of the comprehensive rehabilitation center. However, in addition to being a service-oriented facility, the ICD Rehabilitation and Research Center has a strong research emphasis. The center serves all types of disabilities—with core services in medical, vocational, and social adjustment areas. The medical areas include general medicine, psychiatry, and physical and occupational therapies. Vocational services include work evaluation, work development, personal adjustment training, vocational instruction, a transitional sheltered workshop, and job placement and follow-up. Social services include psychiatric, psychological, and social evaluation and treatment activities.

Craig Hospital in Englewood, Colorado, is an example of a medically oriented rehabilitation center that emphasizes a specific disability group. Craig Hospital is an 80-bed hospital which utilizes a team approach to the treatment of patients who have suffered severe central nervous system damage (e.g., brain disorders, spinal cord injury, and stroke). In addition to the medically related services, the hospital has a family and patient service unit for personal and vocational adjustment of patients.

Another example of a medically oriented facility is the Rancho Los Amigos Hospital in Downey, California. This hospital is an 1100-bed rehabilitation center for patients with chronic disease and disability such as spinal cord injury, stroke, amputation, pulmonary disorders, and drug overdose. In addition to being an inpatient rehabilitation center, it has an outpatient service which handles more than 2000 patient visits each month. Because it is a chronic disease hospital, it has a strong medical orientation; however, it also provides vocational and social services. In addition, it conducts research and provides extensive training for rehabilitation-related professionals.

Comprehensive alcohol recovery and rehabilitation centers are increasing in number. Previously, the emphasis was on detoxification of alcoholics. Community centers now plan comprehensive programs which entail detoxification, counseling, residential treatment, and outpatient services (e.g., family counseling, marriage counseling, and crisis intervention).

Psychological and social resources

Psychological services, including diagnostic testing and counseling, for individuals, groups, and families are available from many sources: psychologists in private practice, community mental health centers, hospitals, many school systems, and some family agencies.

Most communities have a community mental health center. Depending on its size, the center may provide both inpatient and outpatient services. Every center provides counseling services. In addition, some provide child care, medication maintenance, social rehabilitation, consultation, education, and day hospital services. Treatment staff may include psychiatrists, psychologists, social workers, nurses, and other allied health specialists.

Social work services are intended to improve a person's social functioning. Emphasis in a social work relationship—whether on an individual basis, with a family, or with others in a group—is on helping disabled persons achieve social strengths. Social workers are often quite knowledgeable about community resources that can be helpful in the development and implementation of a client's rehabilitation plan. Social work services are generally found in public welfare departments, child agencies, hospitals, community mental health centers, and rehabilitation centers.

Therapeutic social clubs are an approach for facilitating social and community rehabilitation for some clients, particularly the mentally ill. A therapeutic social club is made up of persons involved in a program of activities in a social setting and uses community resources to facilitate members' social functioning. A basic principle of the social club is that peer contact helps social adaptation and community adjustment (Webb & Cox, 1976).

Independent living rehabilitation is an emerging concept in rehabilitation. Independent living centers are frequently cooperative living efforts by or for the disabled providing medical, psychological, educational, social, and vocational services. With the Rehabilitation Act Amendments of 1978, independent living has become part of the rehabilitation legislation, thus supplementing the vocational emphasis the public rehabilitation program has had since 1920.

The therapeutic recreation specialist attempts to help a disabled person achieve physical, psychological, and social goals through recreation. In addition to planned activities, the recreation therapist may serve in a consultative capacity to other lay and professional individuals for constructively utilizing the time of the disabled person. Recreational therapists are most often found in facilities such as nursing homes and hospitals.

Educational-vocational resources

Educational-vocational training programs are valuable community resources for rehabilitation programming. Opportunities for vocational preparation are available from universities, colleges, community colleges, public vocational training schools, and a wide variety of private vocational training programs.

The sheltered workshop described in Chapter 5 is one of the vocational training resources that offer a wide range of employment preparation programs for the disabled. In most workshops an emphasis is placed on adjustment to work. A principal vehicle for developing work adjustment in the disabled is the use of production work. Production work is necessary for the development of client skills and productivity; and the federal government, recognizing this, aided sheltered workshops which employ the visually disabled by passing the Wagner-O'Day Act in 1938. The Wagner-O'Day Act required federal purchases to be made from such workshops. In 1971, with the passage of the Javits-Wagner-O'Day Act, the idea was expanded to other disabling conditions. Then, in 1974, six national volunteer agencies concerned with the disabled—Association of Rehabilitation Facilities, Goodwill Industries of America, National Association of Jewish Vocational Services, National Association for Retarded Citizens, National Easter Seal Society for Crippled Children and Adults, and United Cerebral Palsy Association—created a nonprofit corporation called National Industries for the Severely Handicapped (NISH). With the help of a grant from the Rehabilitation Services Administration, NISH began to identify commodities and services that could be procured from the government on behalf of sheltered workshops (Clements, 1977).

Also important to the rehabilitation facility movement is the Commission on Accreditation of Rehabilitation Facilities (CARF). CARF was established in 1966 to provide (1) standards for facility performance, (2) a mechanism for organizational review and accountability, and (3) improved services to the disabled. Nine areas of standards are assessed in site survey reviews for facility accreditation by CARF: purposes, organization and administration, services, personnel, records and reports, fiscal management, physical facilities, community involvement and relations, and program evaluation. Facilities may seek accreditation in one or more of seven program areas depending on their service emphasis—physical restoration, social adjustment, vocational development, sheltered employment, speech pathology, audiology, and work activities. CARF is an important force in the improvement of rehabilitation facilities and services to the disabled. Many state rehabilitation agencies are now requiring that facilities be accredited in order for their rehabilitation counselors to purchase services for clients from them.

Employers are also a valuable educational and vocational resource in the rehabilitation process. Placement of a client on a job site can be for evaluation, vocational adjustment, or skill training purposes.

Placement resources

Job placement assistance can be obtained from a variety of resources. State employment agencies have offices in most major communities. Such public agencies collect labor market information, identify job openings, and provide aptitude testing and counseling services. They are also required to provide special service to handicapped applicants and veterans seeking placement assistance.

In addition to the public agencies, there are many private placement agencies that provide a similar service for a fee. Many rehabilitation facilities and vocational training schools also provide a placement service to their clients.

Voluntary community organizations

Most communities have numerous voluntary organizations which provide services to specific interest groups or as a community project:

1. Parent groups (of the disabled)—Association for Retarded Citizens
2. Peer groups—Alcoholics Anonymous, Disabled American Veterans
3. Business organizations—American Business Women's Association
4. Chambers of Commerce
5. Child care centers
6. Churches
7. Community service organizations—Jaycees, Lions Club, Rotary Club, Sertoma Club, Kiwanis Club, Optimist Club, Salvation Army
8. Counseling—Helplines
9. Education—Epilepsy Association, Family Life Education Program, League of Women Voters
10. Emergency intervention services—American Red Cross
11. Fraternal organizations—Greek Organization chapters, BPOE Elks Club, Moose Lodge
12. Fund-raising organizations—American Cancer Society
13. Health organizations—Society for the Prevention of Blindness, Muscular Dystrophy Association
14. Hobby clubs
15. Professional associations—Soroptimist Club
16. Recreational services
17. Services for senior citizens—Meals on Wheels, Homemakers Aide Service
18. Social organizations
19. Weight loss groups—TOPS Club, Weight Watchers Club, Inc.

SERVICE INTEGRATION

There has been considerable interest in recent years, particularly by funding agencies, in the integration of services and service delivery. The intent, of course, is to deliver services to persons in a more coordinated and comprehensive way. It is rationalized that existing resources can benefit more people, treat the individual as a whole person, and be more responsive to the needs of individuals and communities if services are integrated. There are various types of linkages that can be made between agencies (Department of Health, Education, and Welfare, 1972):

Administrative linkages
1. Fiscal, e.g., joint budgeting, joint funding, fund transfer, purchase of services
2. Personnel practices, e.g., consolidated personnel administration, joint use of staff, staff transfer, staff outstationing, co-location
3. Planning and programming, e.g., joint planning, joint development of operating policies, joint programming, information sharing, joint evaluation
4. Administrative support services, e.g., record keeping, grants management, central support services

Direct service linkages
1. Core services, e.g., outreach, intake, diagnosis, referral, follow-up
2. Modes of case coordination, e.g., case conference, case coordinator, case team

Thirty projects exemplifying service integration were examined by a Department of Health, Education, and Welfare study (1972). The study found that service integration had a better chance of happening when the local social and political leaders supported it, the project was a high-priority objective, the project director pursued coordination, and strong incentives were offered for service providers to cooperate. The study found that—because of the various approaches to designing service delivery systems (e.g., according to problems, functions, or geographic areas) and because there is usually very little support for a unified system from service providers—a unitary system of service delivery is difficult to create. The study did conclude that greater coordination and cooperation than now exist are possible. Cooperation can benefit clients in terms of improved accessibility of services, continuity of service, and efficiency.

The National Rehabilitation Association (NRA) also conducted a study of cooperation between rehabilitation services and other agencies. The NRA determined that interagency cooperation is dependent on satisfying an agency's internal needs, for example, autonomy, control of resources, and appropriate credit. Complementary activities can be fostered by linking objectives of agencies, sharing feedback channels, and jointly monitoring feedback (Whitten, Lamborn, Potter, & Smith, 1973).

The following are a few of the major formal programs involving an integration of services.

Social Security Disability Insurance–Supplemental Security Income (SSDI-SSI) programs

There are two programs conducted by the Social Security Administration that aid disabled people. One is entitled the Social Security Disability Insurance program (SSDI) and the other is the Supplemental Security Income program (SSI). The SSDI program is a trust fund for workers in the United States. It is an insurance program that most citizens contribute to for use in the event of disability and loss of earnings. SSDI benefits replace some of the lost earnings, dependent upon the amount of the contributions made by the individual worker.

The SSI program provides a minimum income for persons who are either disabled or aged and whose income is within certain limits.

The Social Security Administration and public rehabilitation agencies have an automatic referral system. A person may be eligible for both Social Security benefits and rehabilitation services. Special rehabilitation funds are provided by the Social Security Act to pay for rehabilitation services to SSDI and SSI beneficiaries. There are four special selection criteria for determining whether SSDI-SSI recipients may have their rehabilitation costs paid for with these special funds:

1. The person must have a physical or mental disability that is stable enough for him to return to gainful employment.
2. Without rehabilitation services, the person would probably continue to receive benefits until age 65.
3. It is realistically expected that the services will result in the individual's return to gainful employment.
4. It is reasonably expected that the person will continue in gainful employment long enough to offset the cost of rehabilitation services.

The only purpose of the four selection criteria is to assist the rehabilitation counselor in deciding whether to charge the rehabilitation services to the special fund created by the Social Security Act. It is possible for the client to receive SSDI or SSI benefits and be eligible for rehabilitation services, and yet not meet the special selection criteria for charging such services to these special Social Security funds for rehabilitation. The intent of the cooperative Social Security Administration–Rehabilitation Program is to provide the appropriate benefits to those entitled to them and at the same time maintain the trust fund for future beneficiaries (Randolph, 1977).

Comprehensive Employment and Training Act (CETA) programs

CETA is not a cooperative program with rehabilitation in the sense that SSDI-SSI is; however, it is a valuable resource for the integration of services with which rehabilitation personnel should be familiar. The Comprehensive Employment and Training Act of 1973 established a decentralized system of manpower activities as an attempt to consolidate manpower services that were previously provided by various legislation and programs.

The manpower services offered under CETA programs include assessment, orientation, counseling, classroom training, on-the-job training, work experience, job development, job placement, and support services such as transportation, health care, medical services, child care, residential support, family planning, and legal services. In addition, CETA funds can be used to remove artificial barriers to employment, restructure jobs, establish or revise merit systems, and develop and implement affirmative action plans. The CETA program, administered by the Department of Labor, is implemented through a structure of prime sponsors. Prime sponsors can be any local government with a population of 100,000 or more, combinations of local governments one of which has a population of 100,000, an entire state, or a state government to serve the balance of the state that is not included in a local prime sponsor area. Prime sponsors have the responsibility for management of a total manpower program in a geographic area. Thus all areas of a state are covered by CETA-legislated programs.

The intent is to decentralize jurisdiction from Washington, D.C., to local governments. Each prime sponsor must have a plan identifying the population to be served, the number of participants, the program services and activities, and funding for each service and activity.

Work Incentive Program (WIN)

The Work Incentive Program (WIN) is an attempt to help Social Security recipients receiving Aid to Families with Dependent Children (AFDC) become productive workers. It is another resource with which rehabilitation personnel should be acquainted—a cooperative program of the Department of Labor, through the state employment service agency and the Department of Health, Education, and Welfare. Established by the 1967 Amendments to the Social Security Act, WIN was expanded and strengthened by the 1971 Amendments (becoming known then as WIN-II). The WIN-II program emphasizes assistance in finding jobs. It provides services such as job training, counseling, medical aid, and child care. According to the 1971 Amendments, all AFDC recipients must be available for jobs and job-related services through the WIN-II program. Certain people, of course, are exempt from this requirement: children under 16, children who are in school full-time to age 21, mothers of preschool children, the disabled, and the elderly.

The intent of the WIN-II program is to give people on welfare an incentive to be hired and employers an incentive to hire. Though welfare benefits are reduced somewhat by participation, it is financially advantageous for the AFDC recipient to go to work. In addition, employers are eligible for a sizable tax credit on the wages paid to workers hired through the WIN-II program and for training and child care facilities. Employers may also be reimbursed for training costs and any loss of productivity.

Developmental Disabled Assistance and Bill of Rights Act Programs

Developmental disabilities (DD)—described on page 10 as attributable to severe chronic impairments originating before the age of 22 and continuing indefinitely—are considered to be a substantial handicap. The Developmental Disabled Assistance and Bill of Rights Act of 1975 provides appropriate treatment, services, and habilitation to such individuals. Target groups are closely related to the public rehabilitation program. Currently the legislation for the developmental disabled provides for the commingling of funds under this program with funds of other programs.

The intent is to develop comprehensive services for the developmental disabled. The program is administered through states which have the responsibility for development and implementation of programs—for example, evaluation, treatment, personal care, day care, special living arrangements, training, education, sheltered employment, recreation, counseling, legal services, follow-along, transportation, and the construction of facilities to house services for developmentally disabled persons. Currently the program is operated through a state planning council and a state agency. The state planning council must evaluate

Fig. 10-4
On-campus work assignments provide a vocational emphasis in school curricula. (From Drew, C. J., Hardman, M. L., & Bluhm, H. P. *Mental retardation: social and educational perspectives.* St. Louis: The C. V. Mosby Co., 1977.)

the state plan at least once a year and help by setting direction for the program. At least one third of the council must be made up of consumers or their representatives. The state plan is administered by one or more state agencies. Federal money can be used to plan a coordinated and integrated service delivery system. In addition, special projects may be funded directly by the federal government to improve the quality of service, coordinate available community resources, provide technical assistance relative to services and facilities, train specialized personnel, or demonstrate new and improved techniques for delivery of services. The amendments to the rehabilitation legislation for establishing a comprehensive services program for all severely handicapped people are intended to build on existing services for the developmental disabled stimulated by the DD legislation.

Special education–rehabilitation programs

The cooperative program between special education in the public schools and rehabilitation began in the late 1950's. The purposes of this cooperative program are to involve the rehabilitation agency with potentially vocationally handicapped students while they are still enrolled in school and integrate vocationally related content within the curriculum.

A typical pattern is for school personnel to increase the emphasis on vocational information and on-campus work assignments during a student's sophomore year in high school. During his junior year this vocational emphasis is expanded to include several community work experiences with employers. The last year of the student's school program provides an extended and intensive work experience with one employer. The rehabilitation counselor begins contact with the potential client during these school years and, if necessary, continues to work with the client following graduation from public school.

PRIVATE REHABILITATION

In response primarily to the need for rehabilitation services to industrially injured workers, proprietary rehabilitation agencies have recently been rapidly emerging. Worker's compensation laws in states require that employers either obtain insurance or self-insure workers against injury on the job. The purpose is to provide financial and service benefits to the industrially injured worker so the disorganization of lifestyle resulting from an injury will be reduced and the injured worker can return to gainful employment. Each state has a system for administering the worker's compensation legislation to ensure than an injured worker receives the benefits entitled to him.

An increasing emphasis is being placed on the provision of rehabilitation services. Private rehabilitation organizations and individuals are responding in increasing numbers to this emphasis on rehabilitation of the industrially injured worker. Services usually offered include vocational evaluation, counseling, retraining, on-the-job training, job development, and placement. The referrals to private rehabilitation resources come from private and state insurance carriers, self-insured employers, self-insured administrators, attorneys, hearings officers, physicians, and the state workers' compensation agency. The cost for such services is generally borne by the insurance carrier or the self-insured employer. Another insurance-related source of referrals to proprietary rehabilitation agencies results from injury cases covered by no-fault automobile insurance.

OTHER RESOURCES
Group homes

Group homes, though not a new concept in the field of rehabilitation, have become a renewed movement with the recent emphasis on deinstitutionalization. Group homes may involve transitional living arrangements for persons who have the potential for independence or may be long-term residences for persons who require such care. Generally the group home in rehabilitation has a transitional purpose and trains its residents for social adjustment and self-sufficiency. The group home is a sheltered living situation in which the person may develop independent living skills for community functioning. More and more rehabilitation facilities are establishing group homes for the purpose of promoting socialization, self-reliance, and independent living.

Group home programming reinforces the principle that rehabilitation is for the total person. Though recent growth in the group home movement has been primarily for the mentally retarded, the group living experience has been demonstrated with the mentally ill, drug addicts, and alcoholics. Group homes have also become a positive approach used in special education programs for developing disabled students' social and living skills. Usually the group home is supervised by a live-in parent or counselor. Combined with vocational preparation programs, the group home offers a continuity of service designed to address comprehensive rehabilitation needs of individuals.

Veterans Administration

The Veterans Administration (VA) provides rehabilitation, education and training, vocational counseling, and other services to help disabled veterans return to suitable employment. The VA is also responsible for providing educational opportunities to children of deceased or totally disabled veterans. In addition, a cooperative agreement between the Department of Labor and the Veterans Administration offers state employment service agency services to veterans in the areas of job counseling, employment placement, and job market information.

Family rehabilitation

Nau (1973) describes a concept of family rehabilitation which attempts to meet the needs of an entire family when disability strikes an individual member.

It is based on the premise that all members of a family are adversely affected by the disability of one member. Family rehabilitation may be residential or non-residential in approach. Services are comprehensive and may emphasize vocational education, social development, economic development, or rehabilitation.

Rural rehabilitation resources

As indicated throughout this book, rehabilitation emphasizes a planned sequence of services utilizing many rehabilitation resources. A problem in rural areas is the lack of usual resources and the distances between population centers that have such resources. However, resource and distance obstacles can be minimized in sparsely populated areas through interagency coordination and a greater utilization of client and nontraditional community resources than is generally found in urban service delivery.

Interagency coordination can be achieved through multiple-agency staffing meetings. Such meetings are helpful for client planning by developing cooperative agency plans for serving individual clients and utilizing the resources available to each agency.

Public health nurses in rural areas can be valuable information sources for rehabilitation programming. In addition to being a good source of referrals, they can provide supportive counseling, identify community resources, and provide public education. Similarly, county extension agents are helpful in identifying community resources.

Rural rehabilitation counselors must also place a greater emphasis on the utilization of client resources and resources within the client's community. Client resources include motivation, needs, and knowledge in addition to family, friends, and other resources within the client's community (such as physicians, employers, and other agencies). Employers can be valuable resources for evaluation, adjusting clients to work and specific job training and as a placement resource (Bitter, 1972).

GUIDELINES FOR INTERAGENCY COLLABORATION
BY REHABILITATION COUNSELORS

Bitter (1975) gives a number of suggestions for maximizing interagency collaboration:

Outreach and referral
1. Inform staff of other agencies about rehabilitation services.
2. Encourage a thorough personal knowledge of referrals, or potential referrals, by staff of other agencies.
3. Enlist the help of handicapped persons to serve as community representatives. Examples of assistance that the disabled can provide are (a) as an interpreter both for and to the rehabilitation office, (b) as an advocate in supporting clients, (c) as an instructor to clients on procedures, requirements, and available services, and (d) as a facilitator with transportation arrangements, moral support, and intervention.

Client planning
1. Identify specific service objectives for clients.
2. Involve the client in service planning.
3. Time services efficiently.
4. Use and promote two way communication with staff of other agencies.
5. Utilize the state agency facility specialist as a resource.

Case coordination
1. Devote time in agency offices that refer many clients to rehabilitation.
2. Use a team approach with staff of other agencies.
3. Pool mutual resources.

Community resources
1. Encourage and attend multiple-agency staffing meetings.
2. Utilize resources within the clients environment and community.
3. Complement the role of direct service providers with resource engineering, consultation, education, and community organization.
4. Utilize volunteer aides as a community resource.

Administrative coordination
1. Become involved in mutual staff development and training efforts.
2. Encourage cooperative agreements with other agencies.
3. Encourage fiscal agreements between the state agency and facilities which promote interagency collaboration.
4. Encourage the development and use of joint forms with other agencies.

SUMMARY

The rehabilitation of disabled persons requires program flexibility and a team approach to the provision of services. Community resources are abundant. Some are traditionally associated with the rehabilitation process; others are voluntary. Rehabilitation service delivery in rural areas is often more complicated due to the lack of traditional resources and the long distances between them.

Some of the more frequently used resources in rehabilitation described in this chapter are medical specialties closely related to the rehabilitation field, comprehensive rehabilitation centers, psychological and social resources, educational-vocational resources, placement resources, and voluntary community organizations.

The integration of services among programs is important for the effectiveness and efficiency of each. Five major national programs involving, or potentially involving, an integration of services with rehabilitation are briefly described: (1) Social Security Disability Insurance-Supplemental Security Income programs, (2) Comprehensive Employment and Training Act programs, (3) Work Incentive Program, (4) Developmental Disabled Assistance and Bill of Rights Act programs, and (5) cooperative special education-rehabilitation programs.

The increased emphasis on the rehabilitation of insured industrially injured workers has resulted in the proliferation of proprietary rehabilitation organizations and individuals. Private rehabilitation agencies provide many of the same services offered through the public program and their availability gives insurance carriers an option for the purchase of service.

Other concepts described as resources in this chapter are group homes, Veterans Administration, family rehabilitation, and some approaches to the use of resources in rural areas. The chapter concludes with 19 suggestions for maximizing interagency collaboration by rehabilitation counselors.

SELF-EVALUATION QUESTIONS

1. What are examples of professional service resources for rehabilitation programming?
2. In what ways is the rehabilitation medical consultant a resource to rehabilitation counselors?
3. How do physical therapy and occupational therapy differ in approach?
4. What is the difference between orthotics and prosthetics?
5. What services are usually provided by comprehensive rehabilitation centers?
6. What are the services that may be obtained from a community mental health center?
7. What is the purpose of the National Industries for the Severely Handicapped (NISH)?
8. What are the seven program areas for rehabilitation facility accreditation by the Commission on Accreditation of Rehabilitation Facilities (CARF)?
9. What are some examples of voluntary community organizations that may be potential rehabilitation resources?
10. What is the rationale for the integration of services and service delivery among agencies?
11. What are the major factors related to the success of services integration?
12. What is the difference between the Social Security Disability Insurance program and the Supplemental Security Income program?
13. What are the four criteria for determining whether SSDI-SSI recipients may have their rehabilitation costs paid by special funds provided by the Social Security Act?
14. What is a CETA prime sponsor?
15. For whom is the Work Incentive Program (WIN) intended?
16. What is the intent of the Developmental Disabled Assistance and Bill of Rights Act of 1975?
17. What is a typical curriculum pattern in cooperative special education-rehabilitation programs?
18. Where do referrals to proprietary rehabilitation agencies generally come from?
19. What is a group home?
20. What is "family rehabilitation"?
21. In what ways can a rehabilitation counselor minimize the problems resulting from a lack of the usual rehabilitation resources in rural areas?
22. How can handicapped persons help rehabilitation professionals with outreach and referral assistance?
23. What are some ways in which rehabilitation counselors can maximize interagency collaboration?

REFERENCES

Bitter, J. A. Some viable service delivery approaches in rural rehabilitation. *Rehabilitation Literature,* 1972, 33(12), 354-357.

Bitter, J. A. Guidelines for inter-agency collaboration by rehabilitation counselors. In I. P. Robinault & M. Weisinger (Eds.), *Program planning and evaluation: selected topics for vocational rehabilitation.* New York: ICD Rehabilitation and Research Center, 1975.

Clements, H. R. NISH finds its niche. *Journal of Rehabilitation,* 1977, 43(2), 16-20.

Department of Health, Education, and Welfare. *Integration of human services in H.E.W.: an evaluation of services integration projects* (Vol. I) (SRS-73-02012). Washington, D.C.: HEW, 1972.

Jaques, M. E. *Rehabilitation counseling: scope and services*. Boston: Houghton Mifflin Co., 1970.

Laurie, G. *Housing and home services for the disabled: guidelines and experiences in independent living*. Hagerstown, Md.: Harper & Row, Publishers, Inc., 1977.

Nau, L. Why not family rehabilitation? *Journal of Rehabilitation*, 1973, 39(3), 14-17, 42.

Randolph, A. H. *Keys to counselors to the VR program for SSI/SSDI recipients: a study guide*. Institute, W. Va.: Research and Training Center, 1977.

Rusk, H. A. *Rehabilitation medicine*. St. Louis: The C. V. Mosby Co., 1977.

Webb, L. J., & Cox, R. D. Social rehabilitation: a theory, program, and evaluation. *Rehabilitation Literature*, 1976, 37(6), 172-175, 191.

Whitten, E. B., Lamborn, E. M., Potter, D., & Smith, L. A. *Cooperative rehabilitation programs*. Washington, D.C.: National Rehabilitation Association, Council of State Administrators of Vocational Rehabilitation, 1973.

ADDITIONAL READINGS

Architectural and Transportation Barriers Compliance Board. *Resource guide to literature on barrier-free environments*. Washington, D.C.: Architectural and Transportation Barriers Compliance Board, 1978.

Beckman, D. D. Coordinating state and community programs. *Journal of Rehabilitation,* 1969, 35(2), 33-34.

Committee for the Handicapped/People to People Program. *Directory of organizations interested in the handicapped*. Washington, D.C.: Committee for the Handicapped/People to People Program (Suite 610, LaSalle Building, Connecticut Ave. and L. St.), 1976.

Eighth Institute on Rehabilitation Services. *Vocational rehabilitation of the disabled disadvantaged in a rural setting*. Washington, D.C.: Rehabilitation Services Administration, Department of Health, Education, and Welfare, 1970.

Gallagher, J. J. Cooperation for service. *Journal of Rehabilitation*. 1969, 35(2), 29-30.

Odell, C. E. Improving opportunities through coordination. *Journal of Rehabilitation*. 1969, 35(2), 31-32.

Roessler, R., & Mack, G. *Service integration final report: Arkansas Services Center; Jonesboro, Arkansas*. Little Rock: Arkansas Rehabilitation Research and Training Center, University of Arkansas, 1975.

Roessler, R., & Mack, G. *Strategies for inter-agency linkages: a literature review*. Little Rock: Arkansas Rehabilitation Research and Training Center, University of Arkansas, 1975.

Second Institute on Rehabilitation Issues. *Consumer involvement: Rehabilitation issues*. Little Rock: Arkansas Rehabilitation Research and Training Center, University of Arkansas, 1975.

Sieder, V. M., & Steinman, R. *The rehabilitation agency and community work: a source book for professional training*. Washington, D.C.: Rehabilitation Services Administration, Department of Health, Education, and Welfare, 1966.

Sixth Institute on Rehabilitation Services. *Principles for developing cooperative programs in vocational rehabilitation*. Washington, D.C.: Rehabilitation Services Administration, Department of Health, Education, and Welfare, 1968.

Switzer, M. E. Coordination: a problem and a promise. *Journal of Rehabilitation,* 1969, 35(2), 27-28.

MEDIA RESOURCES

Visual
1. "Rehabilitation Workshop and Other Special Facilities in Oregon" (103 slides with tape narration, 20 minutes). Developed by the Vocational Rehabilitation Division Training Center, Department of Human Resources, 505 Edgewater, N.W., Salem, Ore. 97304.
   Describes the types of rehabilitation services available in Oregon. Includes physical therapy, speech and hearing services, workshop services, etc.
2. "Bold New Approach" (16 mm film, 28 minutes). Available from International Society for Rehabilitation of the Disabled, Film Library, 219 East 44th St., New York, N.Y. 10017.
   Describes the philosophy and concepts underlying community mental health centers.

3. "What Finer Purpose" (16 mm films). Available from ICD Rehabilitation and Research Center, 340 East 24th St., New York, N.Y. 10010.

    A four-film series of the ICD Rehabilitation and Research Center.
    a. "Rehabilitation: the Science and Art" (13 minutes). *Shows how various professions work together in the rehabilitation of disabled individuals.*
    b. "The Job" (11 minutes). *Follows the rehabilitation process culminating in employment.*
    c. "The Mind" (11 minutes). *Describes the psychological side of rehabilitation.*
    d. "The Body" (10 minutes). *Describes medical rehabilitation services.*

4. "Vocational Rehabilitation in a Community Hospital" (16 mm film, 27 minutes). Available from International Society for Rehabilitation of the Disabled, Film Library, 219 East 44th St., New York, N.Y. 10017.

    Describes the advantages of a hospital-based vocational rehabilitation program. Follows actual patients through evaluation, job counseling, and job placement.

5. "Supplemental Security Income Program" (45 slides and audiotape cassette, 10 minutes). Available from RT-15 University of West Virginia Research and Training Center, Institute, W. Va. 25112.

    Describes SSI eligibility, application, referral, and the role of vocational rehabilitation.

6. "Dark Silence" (16 mm film, 10 minutes). Available from National Center for Deaf-Blind Youths and Adults, 105 Fifth Ave., New Hyde Park, N.Y. 11041.

    Describes the training and research programs of the National Center for Deaf-Blind Youths and Adults.

7. "You're It" (16 mm film). Available from Hillsborough Association for Retarded Children, Inc., P.O. Box 22125, Tampa, Fla. 33622.

    Stan Musial explains the importance of recreational activities and physical fitness for the retarded.

8. "An Overview of the Rehabilitation Center" (100 slides). Developed by the University of Minnesota Medical Rehabilitation Research and Training Center, 860 Mayo Building, Minneapolis, Minn. 55455.

    Presents a rehabilitation team approach with clients involving physicians, nurses, and physical therapy, occupational therapy, speech therapy, social service, work evaluation, and psychological testing.

9. "Changes" (16 mm film, 28 minutes). Available from Everest & Jennings, Inc., 1803 Pontius Ave., Los Angeles, Calif. 90025.

    An overview of spinal cord injury and its effects physically, psychologically, and socially as told by patients of Craig Hospital.

10. "Orientation to Rehabilitation Facility Programs" (60 slides, audiotape cassette, and script). Available from Center of Rehabilitation, Room, 3115, Jull Hall, University of Maryland, College Park, Md. 20742.

    Provides an orientation to rehabilitation facilities and includes sample introductory material taken from the Greenleigh Associates, Inc., and Department of Labor studies.

Audio
1. "Occupational Therapy in Physical Disabilities" (four-track audiotape, 77 minutes). Available from Learning Resources Facility, Audiovisual Utilization, 550 First Ave., New York, N.Y. 10016.
    The role of an occupational therapist is described.

Special rehabilitation centers

The Rehabilitation Act of 1973, with its amendments, authorizes a coordinated program of rehabilitation research and emphasizes that public program research efforts relate to the objectives and priorities of the Act. Identified in this Appendix are the following:

Rehabilitation Research and Training Centers
Rehabilitation Engineering Centers
Regional Systems of Spinal Cord Injury Rehabilitation
Regional Rehabilitation Research Institutes
The National Center for Deaf-Blind Youths and Adults

REHABILITATION RESEARCH AND TRAINING CENTERS (R&TC)

The rehabilitation R&TC were first authorized by legislation in 1961. As of 1978, there were 19 such centers: eleven specializing in medical rehabilitation, three focusing on vocational rehabilitation, three specializing in mental retardation rehabilitation, and two in deafness rehabilitation. R&TC have two major purposes: (1) to conduct research which will produce new knowledge for improved rehabilitation methodology and service delivery and (2) to conduct training programs that will promote the utilization of research findings. All R&TC are located in universities and are affiliated with a rehabilitation service delivery program for clients.

Medical rehabilitation R&TC

New York University (RT-1), New York, N.Y. 10016
University of Minnesota (RT-2), Minneapolis, Minn. 55455
University of Washington (RT-3), Seattle, Wash. 98195
Baylor University (RT-4), Houston, Texas 77030
Emory University (RT-6), Atlanta, Ga. 30322
Tufts University (RT-7), Boston, Mass. 02111
Temple University (RT-8), Philadelphia, Pa. 19141
George Washington University (RT-9), Washington, D.C. 20037
University of Colorado (RT-10), Denver, Colo. 80220
University of Alabama (RT-19), Birmingham, Ala. 35233
Northwestern University (RT-20), Chicago, Ill. 60611

Vocational rehabilitation R&TC

University of Arkansas (RT-13), Fayetteville, Ark. 72701
University of West Virginia (RT-15), Institute, W. Va. 25112
University of Wisconsin–Stout (RT-22), Menomonie, Wis. 54751

Mental retardation R&TC

University of Wisconsin (RT-11), Madison, Wis. 53706
University of Oregon (RT-16), Eugene, Ore. 97403
Texas Tech University (RT-21), Lubbock, Texas 79409

Deafness rehabilitation R&TC

New York University (RT-17), New York, N.Y. 10003
University of California, San Francisco (RT-23), San Francisco, Calif. 94143

REHABILITATION ENGINEERING CENTERS

The first Rehabilitation Engineering Centers were established in 1972. The primary purpose of the centers is to develop ways to apply advanced technology in medical, scientific, psychological, and social areas for solving rehabilitation and environmental problems of disabled persons by putting together a consortium of experts from medicine, engineering, and related sciences.

As of 1978, in addition to three international centers established in cooperation with other governments (located in Ljubljana, Yugoslavia, Poznan, Poland, and Cairo, Egypt), there were 15 Rehabilitation Engineering Centers. Each has a core area for research emphasis. The 15 Rehabilitation Engineering Centers in the United States are located in the following places:

Tufts University, Boston, Mass. 02111
Harvard–Massachusetts Institute of Technology, Cambridge, Mass. 02139
Children's Hospital Medical Center, Boston, Mass. 02115
New York University, New York, N.Y. 10016
Kruzen Research Center, Philadelphia, Pa. 19141
University of Virginia, University Station, Va. 22903
University of Tennessee, Memphis, Tenn. 38114
Northwestern University, Chicago, Ill. 60611
Case Western Reserve University, Cleveland, Ohio 44106
University of Michigan, Ann Arbor, Mich. 48109
Texas Institute for Rehabilitation and Research, Houston, Texas 77025
University of Iowa, Iowa City, Iowa 52242
Cerebral Palsy Research Foundation of Kansas, Inc., Wichita, Kan. 67218
Rancho Los Amigos Hospital, Downey, Calif. 90242
Smith-Kettlewell Institute of Visual Sciences, San Francisco, Calif. 94115

REGIONAL SYSTEMS OF SPINAL CORD INJURY REHABILITATION

The Regional Systems of Spinal Cord Injury Rehabilitation were established in 1972 in collaboration with the National Institute of Neurological and Communicative Disorders and Stroke, the Veterans Administration, the National Paraplegia Foundation, and the Rehabilitation Services Administration. The purpose of the Regional Systems is to establish the benefits and cost effectiveness of a comprehensive multidisciplinary approach to services for the spinal cord injured. The approaches of the Regional Systems encompass emergency evacuation, acute care, rehabilitation management, vocational preparation, long-term community placement and follow-through.

Regional Systems of Spinal Cord Injury Rehabilitation are located in the following places:

Boston University Medical Center, Boston, Mass. 02118

New York University, New York, N.Y. 10016

Woodrow Wilson Rehabilitation Center and the University of Virginia, Fishersville, Va. 22939

University of Alabama and Spain Rehabilitation Center, Birmingham, Ala. 35223

University of Minnesota, Minneapolis, Minn. 55455

Wesley Memorial Hospital and Rehabilitation Institute of Chicago, Chicago, Ill. 60611

Texas Institute of Rehabilitation and Research, Houston, Texas 77025

Craig Hospital, Englewood, Colo. 80110

Good Samaritan Hospital, Phoenix, Ariz. 85062

Santa Clara Valley Medical Center, San Jose, Calif. 95128

University of Washington, Seattle, Wash. 98195

REGIONAL REHABILITATION RESEARCH INSTITUTES

The Regional Rehabilitation Research Institutes (RRRI) were established as a concept in 1960 when the Rehabilitation Services Administration made a grant to the University of Minnesota. The RRRIs have three responsibilities: (1) to conduct a program of research in a core subject area, (2) to provide research consultation and technical assistance to state rehabilitation agencies, and (3) to participate in operational research at the request of public rehabilitation program offices.

In 1978 there were five Regional Rehabilitation Research Institutes located in the following places:

Columbia University, New York, N.Y. 10025
Core area: role of the unions and management in improving job opportunities for the handicapped

George Washington University, Washington, D.C. 20052
    Core area: attitudinal, legal, and leisure time barriers to the disabled
University of Michigan, Ann Arbor, Mich. 58109
    Core area: program evaluation instruments and methodologies
University of Denver, Denver, Colo. 80210
    Core area: interagency linkages
Portland State University, Portland, Ore. 97207
    Core area: job development and job placement for the severely handicapped

NATIONAL CENTER FOR DEAF-BLIND YOUTHS AND ADULTS

The National Center for Deaf-Blind Youths and Adults was authorized by legislation in 1967 and established in 1969. The Center was eventually called the Helen Keller National Center for Deaf-Blind Youths and Adults. Its purposes are to (1) develop methods for providing specialized rehabilitation services to deaf-blind individuals, (2) train professionals and other personnel to work with the deaf-blind, (3) conduct research, and (4) conduct service programs for the deaf-blind. The Helen Keller National Center for Deaf-Blind Youths and Adults is located at Sands Point, New York, and has regional offices in Sands Point, Philadelphia, Pennsylvania, Atlanta, Georgia, Chicago, Illinois, Dallas, Texas, Denver, Colorado, Glendale, California, and Seattle, Washington.

Educational institutions with federally supported rehabilitation programs (academic year 1977-1978)

REHABILITATION OF THE BLIND

University of Arkansas, Fayetteville, Ark. 72701
California State University–Los Angeles, Los Angeles, Calif. 90032
Florida State University, Tallahassee, Fla. 32306
Southern Illinois University, Carbondale, Ill. 62901
Boston College, Chestnut Hill, Mass. 02167
Western Michigan University, Kalamazoo, Mich. 49001
Hunter College of the City University of New York, New York, N.Y. 10021
Stephen F. Austin State University, Nacogdoches, Texas 75961

REGIONAL REHABILITATION CONTINUING EDUCATION PROGRAMS

University of Arkansas, Fayetteville, Ark. 72701
San Diego State University, San Diego, Calif. 92182
University of Northern Colorado, Greeley, Colo. 80639
Georgia State University, Atlanta, Ga. 30303
University of Hawaii, Honolulu, Hawaii 96323
Assumption College, Worcester, Mass. 01609
Multi-Resource Centers, Inc., Minneapolis, Minn. 55404
University of Missouri–Columbia, Columbia, Mo. 65201
State University of New York at Buffalo, Buffalo, N.Y. 14214
University of Oklahoma, Norman, Okla. 73069
University of Texas Health Science Center, Dallas, Texas 75235
University of Tennessee, Knoxville, Tenn. 37916
Virginia Department of Vocational Rehabilitation, Richmond, Va. 23230
Virginia Commonwealth University, Richmond, Va. 23284
Seattle University, Seattle, Wash. 98122

REHABILITATION COUNSELING

University of Alabama, University, Ala. 35486
Auburn University, Auburn, Ala. 36830

University of Alabama in Birmingham, Birmingham, Ala. 35294

University of Arizona, Tucson, Ariz. 85721

Arkansas State University, State University, Ark. 72467

California State University–Fresno, Fresno, Calif. 93740

California State University–Los Angeles, Los Angeles, Calif. 90032

California State University–Sacramento, Sacramento, Calif. 95819

California State University–San Diego, San Diego, Calif. 92182

California State University–San Francisco, Daly City, Calif. 94015

University of Southern California, Los Angeles, Calif. 90007

University of Northern Colorado, Greeley, Colo. 80639

University of Connecticut, Storrs, Conn. 06268

Gallaudet College (rehabilitation counseling with the deaf), Washington, D.C. 20002

George Washington University, Washington, D.C. 20052

Florida State University, Tallahassee, Fla. 32306

University of Florida, Gainesville, Fla. 32601

Georgia State University, Atlanta, Ga. 30303

University of Georgia, Athens, Ga. 30602

University of Hawaii–Manoa, Honolulu, Hawaii 96822

University of Idaho, Moscow, Idaho 83843

Illinois Institute of Technology, Chicago, Ill. 60616

Southern Illinois University–Carbondale, Carbondale, Ill. 62901

Indiana University, Indianapolis, Ind. 46205

University of Iowa, Iowa City, Iowa 52242

Emporia Kansas State College, Emporia, Kan. 66801

University of Southwestern Louisiana, Lafayette, La. 70501

University of Maine, Gorham, Maine 04038

Coppin State College, Baltimore, Md. 21216

University of Maryland, College Park, Md. 20742

Assumption College, Worcester, Mass. 01609

Boston University, Boston, Mass. 02215

Northeastern University, Boston, Mass. 02115

Springfield College, Springfield, Mass. 01109

Michigan State University, East Lansing, Mich. 48824

University of Michigan, Ann Arbor, Mich. 48104

Wayne State University, Detroit, Mich. 48202

Mankato State College, Mankato, Minn. 56001

St. Cloud State College, St. Cloud, Minn. 56301

Mississippi State University, State College, Miss. 39672

Jackson State University, Jackson, Miss. 39217

University of Missouri–Columbia, Columbia, Mo. 65201

Eastern Montana College, Billings, Mont. 59601
University of Nebraska, Lincoln, Neb. 68508
University of Nevada, Las Vegas, Nev. 89154
University of New Hampshire, Durham, N.H. 03824
Seton Hall University, South Orange, N.J. 07079
University of New Mexico, Albuquerque, N. Mex. 87131
Hofstra University, Hempstead, N.Y. 11550
Hunter College, New York, N.Y. 10021
New York University, New York, N.Y. 10003
Syracuse University, Syracuse, N.Y. 13210
State University of New York–Albany, Albany, N.Y. 12222
State University of New York–Buffalo, Buffalo, N.Y. 14214
East Carolina University, Greenville, N.C. 27834
University of North Carolina, Chapel Hill, N.C. 27514
Bowling Green State University, Bowling Green, Ohio 43403
Kent State University, Kent, Ohio 44242
University of Cincinnati, Cincinnati, Ohio 45221
Oklahoma State University, Stillwater, Okla. 74074
Oregon College of Education (rehabilitation counseling with the deaf), Monmouth, Ore. 97361
Pennsylvania State University, University Park, Pa. 16802
University of Pittsburgh, Pittsburgh, Pa. 15260
University of Scranton, Scranton, Pa. 18510
University of Puerto Rico, Rio Piedras, P.R. 00931
Rhode Island College, Providence, R.I. 02908
South Carolina State College, Orangeburg, S.C. 29117
University of South Carolina, Columbia, S.C. 29208
Memphis State University, Memphis, Tenn. 38152
University of Tennessee, Knoxville, Tenn. 37916
Texas Tech University, Lubbock, Texas 79409
University of Texas at Austin, Austin, Texas 78712
University of Texas–Southwestern Branch, Dallas, Texas 75235
University of Utah, Salt Lake City, Utah 84112
University of Vermont, Burlington, Vt. 05401
Virginia Commonwealth University, Richmond, Va. 23284
Seattle University, Seattle, Wash. 98122
University of West Virginia, Morgantown, W. Va. 26506
University of Wisconsin–Madison, Madison, Wis. 53706
University of Wisconsin–Milwaukee, Milwaukee, Wis. 53201

REHABILITATION OF THE DEAF

University of Arizona, Tucson, Ariz. 85721

California State University–Northridge, Northridge, Calif. 91324
Northern Illinois University, DeKalb, Ill. 60115
New York University, New York, N.Y. 10003
Oregon College of Education, Monmouth, Ore. 97361
University of Tennessee, Knoxville, Tenn. 37916

REHABILITATION DENTISTRY

New York University, New York, N.Y. 10010
University of North Carolina, Chapel Hill, N.C. 27514

REHABILITATION FACILITY ADMINISTRATION
Workshop administration

Auburn University, Auburn, Ala. 36830
University of San Francisco, San Francisco, Calif. 94117
University of Northern Colorado, Greeley, Colo. 80639
University of Hartford, West Hartford, Conn. 06117
University of Hawaii–Manoa, Honolulu, Hawaii 96822
DePaul University, Chicago, Ill. 60604
Southern Illinois University, Carbondale, Ill. 62901
University of Maryland, College Park, Md. 20742
Cornell University, Ithaca, N.Y. 14851
North Texas State University, Denton, Texas 76203
Seattle University, Seattle, Wash. 98122

Vocational evaluation

Auburn University, Auburn, Ala. 36830
University of Arizona, Tucson, Ariz. 85721
University of Georgia, Athens, Ga. 30602
ICD Rehabilitation & Research Center, New York, N.Y. 10010
University of Wisconsin–Stout, Menomonie, Wis. 54751

REHABILITATION NURSING

Boston University, Boston, Mass. 02215

OCCUPATIONAL THERAPY

University of Alabama, Birmingham, Ala. 35294
Loma Linda University, Loma Linda, Calif. 92354
University of Southern California, Los Angeles, Calif. 90007
Colorado State University, Ft. Collins, Colo. 80523
University of Florida, Gainesville, Fla. 32610
Medical College of Georgia, Augusta, Ga. 30902
University of Illinois, Chicago, Ill. 60680
Indiana University, Indianapolis, Ind. 46202

University of Kansas, Lawrence, Kan. 66045
Boston University, Boston, Mass. 02214
Tufts University, Boston, Mass. 02111
Western Michigan University, Kalamazoo, Mich. 49008
College of St. Catherine, St. Paul, Minn. 55105
University of Minnesota, Minneapolis, Minn. 55455
Washington University, St. Louis, Mo. 63130
Columbia University, New York, N.Y. 10032
University of North Dakota, Grand Forks, N.D. 58202
Ohio State University, Columbus, Ohio, 43210
University of Pennsylvania, Philadelphia, Pa. 19174
Texas Woman's University, Denton, Texas 76204
Virginia Commonwealth University, Richmond, Va. 23284
University of Wisconsin–Madison, Madison, Wis. 53706

PHYSICAL MEDICINE AND REHABILITATION

Good Samaritan Hospital, Phoenix, Ariz. 85062
University of Arkansas for Medical Sciences, Little Rock, Ark. 72201
University of California at Davis, Davis, Calif. 95616
University of California at Los Angeles, Los Angeles, Calif. 90024
University of California at Orange, Orange, Calif. 92668
University of California at San Francisco, San Francisco, Calif. 94143
University of Southern California, Los Angeles, Calif. 90007
Santa Clara Institute for Medical Research, San Jose, Calif. 95128
University of Colorado, Denver, Colo. 80220
Georgetown University, Washington, D.C. 20057
George Washington University, Washington, D.C. 20052
Howard University, Washington, D.C. 20060
Emory University School of Medicine, Atlanta, Ga. 30322
Chicago Medical School, Chicago, Ill. 60612
Institute of Physical Medicine and Rehabilitation, Peoria, Ill. 61603
Mount Sinai/Schwab Rehabilitation Hospital, Chicago, Ill. 60608
Rehabilitation Institute of Chicago, Chicago, Ill. 60611
University of Kansas Medical Center, Kansas City, Kan. 66103
University of Louisville, Louisville, Ky. 40202
Louisiana State University Medical Center, New Orleans, La. 70012
Tulane University, New Orleans, La. 70112
Boston University, Boston, Mass. 02215
New England Medical Center, Boston, Mass. 02111
University of Michigan, Ann Arbor, Mich. 48109
Wayne State University, Detroit, Mich. 48202
Mayo Foundation, Rochester, Minn. 55901

University of Minnesota Medical School, Minneapolis, Minn. 55455

Kirksville College of Osteopathy and Surgery, Kirksville, Mo. 63501

University of Missouri–Columbia, Columbia, Mo. 65201

Washington University, St. Louis, Mo. 63110

Albany Medical College, Albany, N.Y. 12208

Albert Einstein College of Medicine, Bronx, N.Y. 10461

State University of New York–Buffalo, Buffalo, N.Y. 14214

Columbia University, New York, N.Y. 10032

State University of New York, Downstate Medical Center, Brooklyn, N.Y. 11203

Kingsbrook Jewish Medical Center, Brooklyn, N.Y. 11203

Long Island Jewish Hillside Medical Center, New Hyde Park, N.Y. 11040

Montefiore Hospital and Medical Center, Bronx, N.Y. 10467

Mount Sinai School of Medicine, New York, N.Y. 10029

New York University Medical Center, New York, N.Y. 10016

New York Medical College, New York, N.Y. 10029

University of Rochester, Rochester, N.Y. 14642

University of Cincinnati, Cincinnati, Ohio 45267

Ohio State University, Columbus, Ohio 43212

Jefferson Medical College of Thomas Jefferson University, Philadelphia, Pa. 19107

University of Pennsylvania Hospital, Philadelphia, Pa. 19104

St. Francis General Hospital, Pittsburgh, Pa. 15201

Temple University School of Medicine, Philadelphia, Pa. 19140

University of Puerto Rico, San Juan, P.R. 00936

MeHarry Medical College, Nashville, Tenn. 37208

University of Tennessee, Memphis, Tenn. 38163

Vanderbilt University, Nashville, Tenn. 37232

Baylor University Medical Center, Dallas, Texas 75246

University of Texas at Dallas, Dallas, Texas 75235

University of Texas Medical School at San Antonio, San Antonio, Texas 78284

University of Utah, Salt Lake City, Utah 84112

University of Vermont, Burlington, Vt. 05401

Virginia Commonwealth University, Richmond, Va. 23298

University of Washington, Seattle, Wash. 98195

PHYSICAL THERAPY

University of Alabama, Birmingham, Ala. 35294

Loma Linda University, Loma Linda, Calif. 92354

University of Southern California, Downey, Calif. 90242

Stanford University, Stanford, Calif. 94305

University of Florida, Gainesville, Fla. 32610

Emory University, Atlanta, Ga. 30322
Northwestern University Medical School, Evanston, Ill. 60201
University of Iowa–Oakdale Campus, Iowa City, Iowa 52240
Boston University–Sargent College, Boston, Mass. 02215
Northeastern University, Boston-Bouve College, Boston, Mass. 02115
Simmons College, Boston, Mass. 02115
University of Michigan Medical School, Ann Arbor, Mich. 48104
Wayne State University, Detroit, Mich. 48107
University of Minnesota, Minneapolis, Minn. 55455
University of Mississippi Medical Center, Jackson, Miss. 39216
University of Missouri–Columbia, Columbia, Mo. 65201
Washington University, St. Louis, Mo. 63110
Columbia University, New York, N.Y. 10032
State University of New York, Downstate Medical Center, Brooklyn. N.Y.
   11203
Ithaca College, Ithaca, N.Y. 14850
New York University, New York, N.Y. 10016
University of North Carolina, Chapel Hill, N.C. 27514
University of North Dakota, Grand Forks, N.D. 58201
Ohio State University, Columbus, Ohio 43212
University of Pennsylvania, Philadelphia, Pa. 19174
University of Tennessee, Knoxville, Tenn. 37916
Texas Woman's University, Denton, Texas 76204
University of Texas Medical Branch, Galveston, Texas 77550
Virginia Commonwealth University, Richmond, Va. 23284

PROSTHETICS AND ORTHOTICS

University of California at Los Angeles, Los Angeles, Calif. 90024
Cerritos College, Norwalk, Calif. 90650
Northwestern University Medical School, Evanston, Ill. 60201
Delgado Junior College, New Orleans, La. 70119
New York University, New York, N.Y. 10003
New York University Medical Center, New York, N.Y. 10016

REHABILITATION PSYCHOLOGY

University of Kansas, Lawrence, Kan. 66045
Clark University, Worcester, Mass. 01610
University of Minnesota, Minneapolis, Minn. 55455
New York University Medical Center, New York, N.Y. 10016

SPEECH-LANGUAGE PATHOLOGY AND AUDIOLOGY

University of Alabama, University, Ala. 35486
University of Arizona, Tucson, Ariz. 85721

University of California at Santa Barbara, Santa Barbara, Calif. 93106
Colorado State University, Ft. Collins, Colo. 80523
University of Denver, Denver, Colo. 80210
University of Connecticut, Storrs, Conn. 06268
Catholic University of America, Washington, D.C. 20064
Gallaudet College, Washington, D.C. 20002
Florida State University, Tallahassee, Fla. 32306
University of Florida, Gainesville, Fla. 32611
Indiana University, Bloomington, Ind. 47401
Purdue University, Lafayette, Ind. 47907
University of Iowa, Iowa City, Iowa 52242
Northern Illinois University, DeKalb, Ill. 60115
Northwestern University, Evanston, Ill. 60201
Southern Illinois University, Carbondale, Ill. 62901
University of Illinois, Champaign, Ill. 61820
University of Kansas, Lawrence, Kan. 66045
Wichita State University, Wichita, Kan. 67208
Louisiana State University, Baton Rouge, La. 70803
Tulane University, New Orleans, La. 70112
Boston University, Boston, Mass. 02215
Michigan State University, East Lansing, Mich. 48824
Wayne State University, Detroit, Mich. 48201
Western Michigan University, Kalamazoo, Mich. 49001
University of Minnesota, Minneapolis, Minn. 55455
University of Missouri–Columbia, Columbia, Mo. 65201
University of Montana, Missoula, Mont. 59812
University of Nebraska, Lincoln, Neb. 68583
Adelphi University, Garden City, Long Island, N.Y. 11530
Columbia University, New York, N.Y. 10027
University of New York, Buffalo, N.Y. 10036
Hunter College, New York, N.Y. 10021
State University of New York–Buffalo, Buffalo, N.Y. 12224
Queens College of the City University of New York, Flushing, N.Y. 11367
Ohio State University, Columbus, Ohio 43212
Case Western Reserve University, Cleveland, Ohio 44106
University of Oklahoma, Oklahoma City, Okla. 73190
Phillips University, Enid, Okla. 73701
Pennsylvania State University, University Park, Pa. 16802
University of Pittsburgh, Pittsburgh, Pa. 15260
Temple University, Philadelphia, Pa. 19122
University of Puerto Rico, San Juan, P.R. 00936
South Carolina State College, Orangeburg, S.C. 29117

University of Tennessee, Knoxville, Tenn. 37916
Vanderbilt University, Nashville, Tenn. 37232
Southern Methodist University, Dallas, Texas 75275
University of Utah, Salt Lake City, Utah 84112
University of Virginia, Charlottesville, Va. 22903
West Virginia University, Morgantown, W. Va. 26506
University of Wisconsin–Madison, Madison, Wis. 53706
University of Wisconsin–Stevens Point, Stevens Point, Wis. 54481

THERAPEUTIC RECREATION

George Washington University, Washington, D.C. 20052
New York University, New York, N.Y. 10003
Pennsylvania State University, University Park, Pa. 16802

UNDERGRADUATE EDUCATION IN THE REHABILITATION SERVICES

Talladega College, Talladega, Ala. 35160
University of Arizona, Tucson, Ariz. 85721
Arkansas Polytechnic College, Russellville, Ark. 72801
California State University–Los Angeles, Los Angeles, Calif. 90032
University of Colorado, Denver, Colo. 80202
University of Connecticut, Storrs, Conn. 06268
University of South Florida, Tampa, Fla. 33620
Emporia Kansas State College, Emporia, Kan. 66801
Murray State University, Murray, Ky. 42071
Louisiana State University Medical Center, New Orleans, La. 70019
Assumption College, Worcester, Mass. 01609
University of Southern Mississippi, Hattiesburg, Miss. 39401
Central Missouri State College, Warrensburg, Mo. 64093
University of Missouri–Columbia, Columbia, Mo. 65201
Middlesex County College, Edison, N.J. 08817
New York University, New York, N.Y. 10003
Syracuse University, Syracuse, N.Y. 13210
Appalachian State College, Boone, N.C. 28608
University of North Dakota, Grand Forks, N.D. 58202
Wilberforce University, Wilberforce, Ohio 45384
East Central Oklahoma State College, Ada, Okla. 74820
Pennsylvania State University, University Park, Pa. 16802
University of South Carolina, Columbia, S.C. 29208
Memphis State University, Memphis, Tenn. 38162
Stephen F. Austin State University, Nacogdoches, Texas 79561
University of Texas at Dallas, Dallas, Texas 75235

North Texas State University, Denton, Texas 76203
Seattle University, Seattle, Wash. 98122
Marshall University, Huntington, W. Va. 25701
University of Wisconsin–Stout, Menomonie, Wis. 54791

APPENDIX C

Acronyms[*]

AAHPER American Association for Health, Physical Education, and Recreation
AAIN American Association of Industrial Nurses
AAMD American Association on Mental Deficiency
AART American Association for Rehabilitation Therapy
AAWB American Association of Workers for the Blind
ABE Adult basic education
ABLE *Adult Basic Learning Examination*
ADA American Dental Association
AFDC Aid to Families with Dependent Children
ADL Activities of daily living
AERFP Association of Educators of Rehabilitation Facility Personnel
AFB American Federation for the Blind; American Foundation for the Blind
AFL-CIO American Federation of Labor –Congress of Industrial Organizations
AHA American Hospital Association
AIA American Institute of Architects
AMA American Medical Association
ANA American Nurses Association
AOPA American Orthotic and Prosthetic Association
APA American Psychological Association
APGA American Personnel and Guidance Association
APTA American Physical Therapy Association
APTD Aid to Permanently and Totally Disabled
APWA American Public Welfare Association
ARCA American Rehabilitation Counseling Association (of APGA)
ARF Association of Rehabilitation Facilities
ARN Association of Rehabilitation Nurses
ASHA American Speech and Hearing Association
ATBCB Architectural and Transportation Barriers Compliance Board
BEH Bureau of Education of the Handicapped
CA Chronological age
CARF Commission on Accreditation of Rehabilitation Facilities
CEC Council on Exceptional Children
CETA Comprehensive Employment and Training Act
CFR *Code of Federal Regulations*

---

*Selected, in part, from Cawood, L. T. (Ed.). *WORDS: Work-oriented rehabilitation dictionary and synonyms*. Seattle: Northwest Association of Rehabilitation Industries, 1975; and from Cawood, L. (Ed.). *DORA: Directory of rehabilitation acronyms*. Seattle: Northwest Association of Rehabilitation Industries, 1977.

COATS *Comprehensive Occupational Assessment and Training System*
CORE Commission on Rehabilitation Education
CP Cerebral palsy
CRC Certified Rehabilitation Counselor
CSAVR Council of State Administrators of Vocational Rehabilitation
CTP *California Test of Personality*
DAT *Differential Aptitude Test*
DAV Disabled American Veterans
DD Developmental disability(ies)
DDU Disability Determination Unit
DHEW Department of Health, Education, and Welfare
DOL Department of Labor
DOT *Dictionary of Occupational Titles*
DVR Division of Vocational Rehabilitation
EEOC Equal Employment Opportunity Commission
EFA Epilepsy Foundation of America
EHA Education for the Handicapped Act
E&I Experimental and Innovative Training Program
EIN Employer identification number (of IRS)
EMR Educable mentally retarded
EOE Equal opportunity employer
EPPS *Edwards Personal Preference Schedule*
ES Employment Security
ESE Extended sheltered employment
ESEA Elementary and Secondary Education Act
FDA Federal Drug Administration
FICA Federal Insurance Contributions Act
FTE Full-time equivalent
FY Fiscal year
GAO General Accounting Office
GATB *General Aptitudes Test Battery*
GED General education development (high school equivalence)
GIA Goodwill Industries of America
GPO Government Printing Office
GSA General Services Administration
HEAR Home-based Employment to Accomplish Rehabilitation
HIP Hospital Improvement Program
HMO Health Maintenance Organization
HUD Housing and Urban Development (Department of)
ICF Intermediate care facility
ILR Independent living rehabilitation
IPP Individual Program Plan
IQ Intelligence quotient
IRI Institute on Rehabilitation Issues
IRS Internal Revenue Service
IWRP Individualized Written Rehabilitation Program
JCAH Joint Commission on Accreditation of Hospitals
JEVS Jewish Employment and Vocational Service
JOBS Job Opportunities in the Business Sector
JPD Job Placement Division (of NRA)

JSS Job-seeking skills
JVS Jewish Vocational Service
LEAA Law Enforcement Assistance Administration
LD Learning disabled
LPN Licensed Practical Nurse
MA Mental age
MD Muscular dystrophy
MDC Materials Development Center
MDTA Manpower Development and Training Act
MHC Mental health center
MIQ *Minnesota Importance Questionnaire*
MMPI *Minnesota Multiphasic Personality Inventory*
MOVE *Multidimensional Objective Vocational Evaluation*
MR Mentally retarded
MRC Multi-Resource Centers, Inc.
MS Multiple sclerosis
MSW Master of Social Work
NAD National Association of the Deaf
NADE National Association of Disability Examiners (of NRA)
NAID National Association of Interpreters for the Deaf
NAJVS National Association of Jewish Vocational Services
NAMH National Association for Mental Health
NARC National Association of Retarded Citizens
NARI Northwest Association of Rehabilitation Industries; National Association of Re-
    habilitation Instructors
NARS National Association of Rehabilitation Secretaries (of NRA)
NATB *Non-Reading Aptitude Test Battery*
NATTS National Association of Trade and Technical Schools
NCRE National Council on Rehabilitation Education
NCRHIP National Congress on Rehabilitation of Homebound and Institutionalized Per-
    sons (of NRA)
NECA National Employment Counselors Association
NFB National Federation of the Blind
NIB National Industries for the Blind
NIE National Institute of Education
NIH National Institutes of Health
NIMH National Institute of Mental Health
NISH National Industries for the Severely Handicapped
NRA National Rehabilitation Association
NRAA National Rehabilitation Administration Association (of NRA)
NRCA National Rehabilitation Counseling Association (of NRA)
NTID National Technical Institute for the Deaf
NTIS National Technical Information Services
NVGA National Vocational Guidance Association (of APGA)
OE Office of Education
OEO Office of Economic Opportunity
OHD Office of Human Development
OJT On-the-job training
OMB Office of Management and Budget
ORS Office of Rehabilitation Services

OSHA Occupational Safety and Health Act
OT Occupational therapy
OVIS *Ohio Vocational Interest Survey*
PA Public assistance
PAR Program administration review
PASS *Program Analysis of Service Systems*
PAT Personal adjustment training
PFP Program and finance plan
PHS Public Health Service
PIAT *Peabody Individual Achievement Test*
PL Public law
PPVT *Peabody Picture Vocabulary Test*
PT Physical therapy
PWI Projects With Industry
R&D Research and development; research and demonstration
RET Rational-emotive therapy
RFP Request for proposal
RN Registered Nurse
RRCEP Regional Rehabilitation Continuing Education Program
RRRI Regional Rehabilitation Research Institute
RSA Rehabilitation Services Administration
R&T Research and training
R&TC Research and Training Center
RUL Research Utilization Laboratory
SBA Small Business Administration
SCI Spinal cord injured
SGA Substantial gainful activity
SRA Science Research Associates
SRS Social and Rehabilitation Service
SS Social services
SSA Social Security Administration
SSDI Social security disability income
SSI Supplemental security income
TA Technical assistance; transactional analysis
TMR Trainable mentally retarded
TOWER *Testing, Orientation, and Work Evaluation in Rehabilitation*
UAF University affiliated facility
UCPA United Cerebral Palsy Association
USES United States Employment Service
USOE United States Office of Education
VA Veterans Administration
VE Vocational education
VEWAA Vocational Evaluation and Work Adjustment Association (of NRA)
VGRS Vocational Guidance and Rehabilitation Services (Cleveland)
VH Visually handicapped
VIEWS *Vocational Information and Evaluation Work Samples*
VISA *Vocational Interest and Sophistication Assessment Survey*
VNA Visiting Nurses Association
VR Vocational rehabilitation
WAC Work activity center

WAIS *Weschler Adult Intelligence Scale*
WARF *Work Adjustment Rating Form*
WAT Work adjustment training
WEC Work Experience Center
WHO World Health Organization
WIN Work Incentive Program
WISC *Weschler Intelligence Scale for Children*
WRAT *Wide-Range Achievement Test*
WREST *Wide-Range Employment Sample Test*
WRIOT *Wide-Range Interest-Opinion Test*

Name index

Subject index

Tests—cont'd
  manual dexterity, 156-157
  psychological, 150-159
  in psychological counseling, 186
Theories and practice of vocational adjustment, 114-116
Therapeutic cardiovascular diseases, 70-71
Therapeutic communities for drug abusers, 85
Therapeutic recreation, institutions teaching, 247
Therapeutic social club, 221
Therapist counselor, 197
Therapists, recreation, 221
Therapy
  aversion, 179
  behavioral, 178-180
  biofeedback, 180
  change, internal, for alcoholic person, 65
  gestalt
    application, 181-182
    basic concepts, 180-181
  occupational, 217-218
    institutions teaching, 242-243
  physical, 216-217
    institutions teaching, 244-245
    latissimus bar, 102
  rational-emotive, 184
  reality, 185-186
  speech, 219
  supportive, for alcoholic person, 65
Thorough diagnostic study for rehabilitation client, 40-43
Time out, 122
Token economy system, 122
  example of, 126
TOPS Club, 223
TOWER system of work samples, 159-161
Training, 45
  adjustment, personal, 45
  assertive, 179
  communication, for deaf and hard of hearing, 76
  compensatory skill, 45
  definition of, 10
  job-seeking skills, 203-204
  prevocational, 45
  in sheltered workshop, 119-120
  vocational, 45
  work adjustment, 116
Training program model, specialized, 120
Training programs, educational-vocational, 221-222
Transactional analysis
  application, 183-184
  basic concepts, 182-183
Transactions
  in gestalt therapy, 180
  in transactional analysis, 182
Transference
  analysis of, 177
  in psychoanalysis, 177

Transitional sheltered workshop, 118
Transplant, kidney, 96
Transportation support, 46
Treatment approaches
  for alcoholism, 64-65
  for counteralcoholic, 65
Treatment contract in transactional analysis, 183
Tremor type of cerebral palsy, 77
Tryouts, job, 207
Tumors, brain, 86-87
  rehabilitation services, 88
Tunnel vision, 68

U

Ulterior transactions in transactional analysis, 182
Unconsciousness and psychoanalysis, 177
Undergraduate education in rehabilitation services, institutions with, 247-248
Understanding
  of client, 141
  empathic, 178, 187
Unions, labor, 202-203
United Cerebral Palsy Association, 31, 222
United States rehabilitation program, philosophy of, 4
University of Alabama, Birmingham, Center for Developmental and Learning Disorders, 126-127
Uropathy, neuromuscular, 95

V

Valpar Component Work Sample Series, 163
Variable interval schedule of reinforcement, 121
Variable ratio schedule of reinforcement, 121
Variables, worker, to vocational adjustment, 114
Verbal approaches to vocational adjustment, 116
Veterans Administration, 26-27, 229, 237
Veterans Bureau, 26
Veterans Readjustment Assistance Act, 27
Veterans and Rehabilitation Divisions of Federal Board for Vocational Education, 26
VGRS (Vocational Guidance and Rehabilitation Services, Cleveland), 28, 123-124
VIEWS (Vocational Information and Evaluation Work Samples), 162
Vineland Social Maturity Scale, 82
  Revised, 153
VISA (*Vocational Interest and Sophistication Assessment*), 155-156
Visual impairments
  blindness, 68-69
  classification, 68
  congenital, 68
  tunnel vision, 68
Vocational adjustment
  approaches, 116-123
  definition, 10-11
  environmental manipulation, 116-117
  job skill factors, 114-115
  plans, 117